Fernando Pessoa

Titles in the series Critical Lives present the work of leading cultural figures of the modern period. Each book explores the life of the artist, writer, philosopher or architect in question and relates it to their major works.

In the same series

Fernando Pessoa

Bartholomew Ryan

REAKTION BOOKS

For Noa

Tudo vale a pequena
Se a alma não é pequena.

Published by Reaktion Books Ltd
Unit 32, Waterside
44–48, Wharf Road
London N1 7UX, UK

www.reaktionbooks.co.uk

First published 2024
Copyright © Bartholomew Ryan 2024

Printed and Bound in Great Britain by Bell & Bain, Glasgow

A catalogue record for this book is available from the British Library

ISBN 978 1 78914 934 0

Contents

A 'provisional visual representation of oneself' (as Fernando Pessoa wrote on the back of the photograph). Pessoa age 25, January 1914.

Prologue: To Be as Radical as Reality Itself

The strange case is that of Fernando Pessoa, who doesn't exist, strictly speaking.
Álvaro de Campos[1]

There has always been a tension between the human imagination and practical existence. Reality can be applied to both. Vladimir Lenin once said: 'one must always try to be as radical as reality itself.'[2] He was talking to a teenage poet called Valeriu Marcu in Zurich in 1917, on the eve of a revolution. But reality can be a very elusive thing, a totality of what is known and what is unknown. A poet called Álvaro de Campos, who never really existed and yet is very much real today, wrote:

> We all have two lives:
> The true one, which is the one we dreamed of in childhood,
> And that we go on dreaming, adults, in a substratum of fog;
> The false one, which is the one we live in coexistence with others,
> Which is the practical, the useful,
> The one which ends up putting us in a coffin.[3]

This poet was one of the many invented writers of Fernando Pessoa, the astonishing Portuguese poet who was born in 1888 and died in 1935.

For the philosopher Alain Badiou, the twentieth century was the century of the Real, or, as he writes, 'the passion for the real' asserted itself during 'the century of destruction'.[4] Pessoa was part of the generation that witnessed the collapse of empires, the First World War and the use of chemical warfare for the first time, the Russian Revolution and the formation of the Soviet Union, the rise of fascism in Italy and Nazi rule in Germany. Portugal saw the end of a centuries-old monarchy and the foundation of a republic, which was then replaced by the Estado Novo (New State) led by the dictator António de Oliveira Salazar. The ideas and dreams of the nineteenth century were being put into practice in the twentieth century with devastating consequences. After Marx and Engels called for revolutionary praxis instead of mere contemplation and theory in texts such as *Theses on Feuerbach* and *The Communist Manifesto*, new ideas were implemented in politics. Passion for the real – drawing on the literal meaning of *passio* as suffering – transformed the world and created and destroyed regimes, peoples and borders.

Pessoa went in a different direction. But he was not alone in exploding preconceived notions of space and time where everything is in flux, and offering new approaches to representing reality. This was happening, for example, in politics, science, music, painting and philosophy too. From Russia to Mexico, Leon Trotsky was declaring a 'permanent revolution' in his call for international revolutionary political upheaval; in Bern, Zurich, Prague and Berlin, Albert Einstein was writing revolutionary papers on the equivalence of mass and energy and the theory of special relativity in science; in Vienna, 'the Second Viennese School', which included Arnold Schoenberg, was making radical innovations in music with its experimentations in atonality and the 'emancipation of dissonance'; and in Paris, Pablo Picasso and Georges Braque co-founded Cubism, an artistic movement where perspective no longer had a single point of view and geometric shapes were used which could overtake the represented forms. In philosophy, thinkers as disparate as Edmund Husserl, Henri Bergson and Ludwig Wittgenstein, through different methods and approaches, were offering new ways of seeing and perceiving reality. Pessoa's reality and passion for the real were created from a constellation of poets with different points of views and styles of writing, which accompanied him throughout his life, creating a startling response

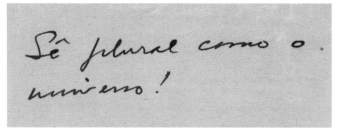
'Sê plural como o universo' written by Pessoa on a piece of paper.

to the modern world in the twentieth century. Declaring his lifelong vocation, Pessoa wrote down on a loose sheet of paper: 'Be plural like the universe!'[5]

The 'Demon of Reality' haunted Pessoa throughout his life, as it haunts his unfinished prose masterpiece, *The Book of Disquiet* (*Livro do Desassossego*).[6] For Pessoa, reality was greater than truth, greater than the everyday human existence of goals and plans and living a worthwhile life, and greater than the temporalities of the past, present and future. Reality was both the dream and the nightmare of existence that propelled Pessoa forward in his vocation as a poet of multiplicities.

Pessoa created a series of fictitious writers which he called heteronyms, among them three great poets. The first, Álvaro de Campos, the poet of a machinic future, writes: 'Always the impossible as stupid as reality'; the second, Ricardo Reis, the poet yearning to restore a lost past, writes: 'Reality is always/ More or less/ Than what we want'; and the master of them all, Alberto Caeiro, the poet of an eternal present, declares: 'But I don't want the present, I want reality./ I want the things that exist, not the time that measures them.'[7] To sum it all up, Bernardo Soares, the heteronymic author Pessoa assigned to *The Book of Disquiet*, and to whom Pessoa might have been closest in personality, reflects: 'The only problem is that of reality, as insoluble as it is alive.'[8] The questions, then, for Pessoa and his poetic–philosophical–dramatic universe and for this book, are how and why does Pessoa enter reality as a poet of his time, and what reality does he enter?

The separation between the dream and reality was dissolved by Pessoa from a young age. His first major heteronym was called Alexander Search. At the age of eighteen, Search wrote a little poem in English called 'Epigram':

'I love my dreams,' I said, a winter morn,
To the practical man, and he, in scorn,
Replied: 'I am no slave of the Ideal,
But, as all men of sense, I love the Real.'
Poor fool, mistaking all that is and seems!
I love the Real when I love my dreams.[9]

And there you have it: the Real emerges only through the dreaming. The interpenetration between the two is essential for Pessoa's vocation and vision as a poet. Almost seventy years later, the Brazilian writer Clarice Lispector would write in *Água Viva*, her mystical novel of absolute presence and absence: 'I reach the real through the dream. I invent you, reality.'[10] The poet William Butler Yeats, Pessoa's contemporary from Ireland, writes: 'In dreams begins responsibility';[11] for Pessoa we might modify this to say, 'in dreams begins reality.' Pessoa encountered the real through his literary imagination. As his heteronym Bernardo Soares wrote:

All literature is an attempt to make life real. All of us know, even when we act on what we don't know, life is absolutely unreal in its directly real form; the country, the city and our ideas are absolutely fictitious things, the offspring of our complex sensation of our own selves.[12]

In pondering reality and the Real in the writings of Pessoa, we may also think of Jacques Lacan's conception of the Real, which is one of the parts of what he calls triadic Borromean rings, or the three simple closed curves of the mind. These are the Imaginary, which is derived from perceptual and fantasized mental processes; the Symbolic, which is derived from culture and through language; and, finally, the Real, which is derived from our senses. Thus, it seems for Lacan that it is impossible to attain reality even though that is where we exist primordially. Entering the universe of Pessoa and thinking of his reality, I propose three intermingling elements: the impossible (dream), the nothing (void) and the monster (self).

In one of the most famous opening lines in poetry in the Portuguese language of the twentieth century, Álvaro de Campos writes in 'The Tobacco Shop' ('Tabacaria'):

> I am nothing.
> I will always be nothing.
> I cannot want to be something.
> But I have in me all the dreams of the world.
> [*Não sou nada.*
> *Nunca serei nada.*
> *Não posso querer ser nada.*
> *À parte isso, tenho em mim todos os sonhos de mundo.*][13]

The three aspects of reality are all to be found in these four lines. The element of nothing is present in the word *nada* at the end of the first three lines, which are all negative statements, two beginning with *Não* (no/not) and one with *Nunca* (never). In the original Portuguese, the negation is more explicit because of the language's capacity for double negatives. The monster as the revelation of the self and being is present in all four lines. The verb 'to be' appears in the first three lines: in the present tense in the first person singular (*sou*), in the future tense in the first person singular (*serei*), and in the infinitive state (*ser*), while the fourth line contains the words 'in me' (*em mim*). 'The impossible' is in the fourth sentence, in the affirmation of the dream, in having all the dreams of the world inside oneself.

The Impossible, the Nothing and the Monster

The 'impossible', the first of the three elements of Pessoa's reality, is the part of the imagination that is not only limitless but out of reach in our concrete daily lives. We can try to show it and articulate it

presença

fôlha de arte e crítica
coimbra, julho, 1933

TaBaCaRia

Não sou nada.
Nunca serei nada.
Não posso querer ser nada.
Aparte isso, tenho em mim todos os sonhos do mundo.

Janelas do meu quarto,
Do meu quarto de um dos milhões do mundo que ninguém
                   sabe quem é
(E se soubessem quem é, o que saberiam?),
Dais para o mistério de uma rua cruzada constantemente
                   por gente,
Para uma rua inacessível a todos os pensamentos,
Real, impossivelmente real, certa, desconhecidamente certa,
Com o mistério das coisas por baixo das pedras e dos sêres,
Com a morte a pôr humidade nas paredes e cabelos brancos
                 nos homens,
Com o Destino a conduzir a carroça de tudo pela estrada de
                 nada.

Estou hoje vencido, como se soubesse a verdade.
Estou hoje lúcido, como se estivesse para morrer,
E não tivesse mais irmandade com as coisas
Senão uma despedida, tornando-se esta casa e êste lado da
                 rua
A fileira de carruagens de um comboio, e uma partida api-
                 tada
De dentro da minha cabeça,
E uma sacudidela dos meus nervos e um ranger de ossos
                 na ida.

Estou hoje perplexo, como quem pensou e achou e esqueceu.
Estou hoje dividido entre a lealdade que devo
À Tabacaria do outro lado da rua, como coisa real por fora,
E a sensação de que tudo é sonho, como coisa real por dentro.

Falhei em tudo.
Como não fiz propósito nenhum, talvez tudo fôsse nada.
A aprendizagem que me deram,
Desci dela pela janela das traseiras da casa.
Fui até ao campo com grandes propósitos.
Mas lá encontrei só ervas e árvores,
E quando havia gente era igual à outra.

Saio da janela, sento-me numa cadeira. Em que hei-de
                 pensar?

Que sei eu do que serei, eu que não sei o que sou?
Ser o que penso? Mas penso ser tanta coisa!
E há tantos que pensam ser a mesma coisa que não pode
                 haver tantos!
Génio? Neste momento
Cem mil cérebros se concebem em sonho génios como eu,
E a história não marcará, quem sabe?, nem um,
Nem haverá senão estrume de tantas conquistas futuras.
Não, não creio em mim.
Em todos os manicómios há doidos malucos com tantas cer-
                 tezas!
Eu, que não tenho nenhuma certeza, sou mais certo ou
                 menos certo?
Não, nem em mim...
Em quantas mansardas e não-mansardas do mundo
Não estão nesta hora génios-para-si-mesmos sonhando?
Quantas aspirações altas e nobres e lúcidas —
Sim, verdadeiramente altas e nobres e lúcidas —,
E quem sabe se realizáveis,
Nunca verão a luz do sol real nem acharão ouvidos de gente?
O mundo é para quem nasce para o conquistar
E não para quem sonha que pode conquistá-lo, ainda que
                 tenha razão.
Tenho sonhado mais que o que Napoleão fêz.
Tenho apertado ao peito hipotético mais humanidades do
                 que Cristo,
Tenho feito filosofias em segrêdo que nenhum Kant escreveu.
Mas sou, e talvez serei sempre, o da mansarda,
Ainda que não more nela;
Serei sempre o que não nasceu para isso;
Serei sempre só o que tinha qualidades;
Serei sempre o que esperou que lhe abrissem a porta ao pé
                 de uma parede sem porta,
E cantou a cantiga do Infinito numa capoeira,
E ouviu a voz de Deus num pôço tapado.
Crer em mim? Não, nem em nada.
Derrame-me a Natureza sôbre a cabeça ardente
O seu sol, a sua chuva, o vento que me acha o cabelo,
E o resto que venha se vier, ou tiver que vir, ou não venha.
Escravos cardíacos das estrêlas,
Conquistámos todo o mundo antes de nos levantar da cama;

ano sétimo   **39**   volume segundo

First page of 'Tabacaria' (The Tobacco Shop), in *Presença* magazine, July 1933.

through language, but it will never be quite enough and we will always fall short. The author of *The Book of Disquiet* writes: 'Let us always search for the impossible, since that is our destiny, and let us search for it by way of the useless, since no path goes by any other way.'[14] The poet pursues the impossible, sometimes bringing it to life in verse, shedding light on impossible forms of existence in an attempt to get closer to attaining or glimpsing reality. Clarice Lispector evokes this challenge when she writes a remarkable sentence in another one of her novels, *The Passion According to G.H.*: 'Creating isn't imagination; it's taking the great risk of grasping reality.'[15] At the end of a text with the title 'Sentimental Education' (which Pessoa originally called 'The Shadow of Death'), in what sounds like a Hegelian expression or a trope from philosophy of classical India, the fictitious author writes the words 'Absolute Reality'.[16] This absolute or ultimate reality could be read as a totality of the known and the unknown but also simply as a process of perpetual change. The same text begins with the words: 'For those who choose to make dreams their life'.[17] The dream of reality can save us from the oppressiveness of the real, or, in Pessoa's case, give space to the impossible. Pessoa's best poems, to quote from 'The Tobacco Shop' by Álvaro de Campos, are 'a broken gateway to the Impossible'.[18] This is the dream of literature: the expansive universe of infinite stars may be impossible to grasp in its entirety, but poetic writing is an attempt to present a window to that impossibility. Pessoa's heteronymic dream was his impossible reality, and it is a reality today as we read the extraordinary poems and prose of Alberto Caeiro, Álvaro de Campos, Ricardo Reis and Bernardo Soares.

Alongside the 'impossible', there is the element of the 'nothing'. This nothingness or void is that from which we emerge, from which we construct ourselves, and to which we return. Campos describes the world as a 'dynamic void' in 'Salutation to Walt Whitman' (which, if completed, would have been one of his longest poems), and then again ten years later in an untitled poem which begins with the line, 'If you want to kill yourself, why don't you want to kill yourself?'[19] Campos is a poet of the void, not only in his perception of the ontology of the world but in how he feels about his own subjectivity, as expressed in his longest poem, 'Maritime Ode': 'There's nothing in me but a void, a desert, a nocturnal sea.'[20] What make Pessoa and his most vociferous heteronym so modern are the emptiness and loss of meaning of reality that they encounter along with their ability to go on writing, anticipating Beckett's 'I can't go on, I'll go on.'[21] Hence, in the despair of the reality of the void, Campos writes: 'I invoke my own self and find nothing.'[22] Fully realizing the challenge of being modern, separated from the poets of antiquity and Dante, Campos writes in another poem: 'The ancients invoked the Muses./ We invoke ourselves.'[23] The poets were once the vessels of the muses; now they are, as the philosopher Vilém Flusser wrote, 'the channels through which nothingness spills over language, realizing themselves in it'.[24] The poets seek to produce new realities; hence Pessoa sought to not only create new mythologies with his heteronyms but rewrite mythologies such as his own version of *Faust* in Portuguese, a hundred years after Goethe completed his masterpiece in German, with Mephistopheles at the centre as the self-describing 'spirit of perpetual negation'.[25] Throughout his adult life, Pessoa wrote verses for this long dramatic poem, leaving behind a fragmented mess with the title *Faust: Subjective Tragedy*.

The third element of reality is 'the monster' – as the self, 'I' or a self-conscious entity in being in the world. The root of the Latin word *monstrare* is to show, and this monster is something that reveals, that permits itself to be seen.[26] When T. S. Eliot writes in his poem 'Burnt Norton' that 'human kind/ Cannot bear very much reality', it implies that we might need illusion or else we could easily be overwhelmed.[27] Yet, the monster also continues to conceal in revealing different faces. It takes a poet like Pessoa to enter the abyss to wrestle with monsters, which are ourselves. Bernardo Soares in *The Book of Disquiet* writes: 'By day I am null [*nulo*], and by night I am I [*sou eu*].'[28] One is reminded of the words of 'I am that I am' that God speaks to Moses in Exodus 3:14. Moses is the only human who came face to face with God and conversed without a mediator. By night, Soares is pure being: 'I am that I am,' like

God. And yet Pessoa strays from Judaeo-Christianity and instead explores and embraces various pagan lines of plurality. Once again it is Álvaro de Campos who makes the bold statements in published print: 'For Christian self-centredness, the greatest man is the one who can most honestly say, "I am I" [*eu sou eu*]; for science, the greatest man is the one who can most sincerely say, "I am everyone else."'[29] The monster starts to become omnipresent when Pessoa pluralizes the 'I' as an inventor of selves and creator of myths. God and the creator of the self are everywhere and nowhere. Thus, God and the 'I am' or 'self' can be both the reality of being and a groundless nothing, always just beyond reach. Angelus Silesius, in the seventeenth century, described God as an ungraspable nothing that still 'is', reverberating in the silence, not dissimilar to the 'profusion of selves'[30] that we all have within us:

> God is not grasped,
> God is a resounding Nothing,
> touched not by Now nor Here;
> the more you reach out for Him,
> the more he eludes you.[31]

The Argonaut of Modernity

We come now to Pessoa's poetic thought in having to fight monsters of the mind and delve into the depths of the elusive 'I'. In a text that Pessoa wrote in the preliminary stages of *The Book of Disquiet*, he refers to the Argonauts of old, who had a saying that 'to sail is necessary; but to live is not.'[32] The Portuguese reads as '*navegar é preciso; viver não é preciso*', which maintains an ambiguity that is lost in translation as the word *preciso* means both 'necessary' and 'precise'. This motto is rendered from the Latin *Navigare necesse est; vivere non est necesse* from the first-century poet Plutarch. Pessoa attributes this phrase to Jason and the Argonauts, but according to Plutarch it was shouted out by Pompey the Great to the men on his ships, commanding them to set sail despite a violent storm at sea. This expression was taken up as a mantra for the second

Caravel, *c.* 1775, blue tile (*azulejo*) panel, Old Fountain of Paço d'Arcos, Oeiras.

coming of the Argonauts – meaning the Portuguese explorers of the fifteenth and sixteenth centuries – as an inspiration to sail despite the danger, to seek adventure and enter the unknown, the *terra incognita* beyond the great oceans. The explorers saw themselves as opening up the world but the nineteenth century witnessed the demise of the Portuguese Empire, and in a world where the ocean has supposedly been conquered, Pessoa wrote, probably in the 1930s and probably intended to be written by Bernardo Soares: 'now let's master the psychological ocean.'[33] It is worth quoting in full Pessoa's passage on the Argonauts, which distinguishes two kinds of monsters:

> Your argonauts grappled with monsters and fears. In the voyage of my thought, I also had monsters and fears to contend with. On the path to the abstract chasm that lies in the depths of things there are horrors that the world's men don't imagine and fears to endure that human experience doesn't know. The cape of the common sea beyond which all is mystery is perhaps more human than the abstract path to the world's void.[34]

The word 'Argonaut' is also used by Caeiro in the 46th poem from his collection *The Keeper of Sheep*: 'I'm the Discoverer of Nature./ I'm the Argonaut of true sensations./ I bring to the Universe a new Universe,/ Because I bring to the Universe its own self.'[35] Caeiro is giving another glimpse into what he later calls 'the science of seeing'[36] – the ability to see nature, to show the universe its own self. Caeiro is holding up a mirror to nature. In reading Pessoa and his heteronyms, the monster is what we see in the mirror. But what we see is the ever-shifting visage of reality that can always elude us and deceive us. Hamlet famously talks of this: 'To hold as twere the/ mirror up to nature: to show virtue her feature, scorn her own/ image, and the very age and body of the time his form and/ pressure' (III.2). Pessoa marked a sentence of a book he had in his personal library called *Afterthoughts* by Logan Pearsall Smith, published in 1931: 'All mirrors are magical mirrors, and we never see our faces in them.'[37] Like his contemporary James Joyce, Pessoa saw Shakespeare as the greatest writer of overflowing multitudes and inventions of the self, and the writer to be surpassed. Quoting again from the play *Hamlet*, the first two words that are spoken are: 'Who's there?' This immediately throws us into disorientation about who is present and who is absent, which taps into feelings of confusion about the identity, location, reality and unrealities of the self. In an age that is sometimes obsessed with identities, which causes not only distrust and division but a limiting and reducing of ourselves, perhaps we should think more of the self as an open reality. Pessoa was far more interested in reality than in identity,

All mirrors are magical mirrors, and we never see our faces in them.

A sentence marked by Pessoa in his personal copy of Logan Pearsall Smith, *Afterthoughts* (1931).

because it reveals and encapsulates multiple, shifting and dissolving identities. The monster is the self, which is an abyss, a nothing, from and of which one must create again and again.

The philosopher Arthur Schopenhauer writes in *The World as Will and Representation*:

> as soon as we enter into ourselves fully by directing our knowledge inwards, we lose ourselves in a bottomless void; we find ourselves like a hollow glass globe, from the emptiness of which a voice speaks. But the cause of this voice is not to befound in the globe, and since we want to comprehend ourselves, we grasp with a shudder nothing but a wavering and unstable phantom.[38]

These words precede Pessoa but could fit into one of the many passages from the forever unfinished *Book of Disquiet*, such as: 'By thinking too much, I became echo and abyss. By delving within, I made myself into many.'[39] Pessoa created a large poetic authorship constructed upon the void and gave himself the impossible task of excavating the monster that is the self. In another coincidence – one which would have appealed to Pessoa's liking for signs, symbols and synchronicities – even his name relates to this reality of having to interpret and decipher the self. The name 'Pessoa' alludes to the words 'person' – derived from 'persona', which means 'mask' – and 'personne', which can also mean 'no one' in French. And the name 'Fernando' probably derives from the Proto-Germanic *fardiz* (journey) and *nanþaz* (daring to or ready to). Thus the name 'Fernando Pessoa' could be translated as the one daring to journey in people, in masks, or in no one! *Nomen est Omen*.

Layout of the Book

In the following eight chapters, this book interweaves Pessoa's life and remarkable literary output to illuminate the reality of the impossible, the nothing and the monster. Pessoa's literature was his reality. His self-imposed exile was his life from a very early age, and the first chapter covers his early travels from Lisbon to South Africa and back to Lisbon.

The second chapter scrutinizes the roots and development of Pessoa's philosophical impulse and his interest in philosophy on his return to Lisbon as a young man. Pessoa distinguished philosophy from poetry, while creating a mode of thought in poetry as well as mirroring and conversing between the two disciplines, which helped form him as a writer.

Chapter Three shows how Pessoa helped bring literary modernism to Portugal via two editions of the avant-garde literary magazine *Orpheu*, which he published with his (flesh and bone) best friend, Mário de Sá-Carneiro.

Chapter Four explores the plurality of the subject and the creation of the concept of heteronymy, as Pessoa forges and feigns his way through a productive period with the invented poets Alberto Caeiro, Álvaro de Campos and Ricardo Reis.

Chapter Five covers Pessoa's ideas on politics and society in Portugal during the years of the republic and the beginning of the dictatorship. It explores his dream of a nation of poets, the fabled 'Fifth Empire' and the myth of Sebastianism.

Chapter Six focuses on the esoteric realm that is present in Pessoa's thought and readings, and which is interwoven into his vision for literature and life, and infused his poetry. He was a master of astrology and he read and studied a wide array of texts on magic, Kabbalah, the Rosicrucian Enlightenment and other secret societies, and formed theories for a 'new paganism' out of his early interest in pantheism. He also corresponded and met with the notorious guru of black magic Aleister Crowley.

Chapter Seven traverses the friendships, loves and non-loves during Pessoa's life. He was never going to have a conventional middle-class Portuguese life. From a very early age he was distant from others and prioritized and fetishized his imagination and literary universe over any possibility of a practical life, of the real life of appearances. He never married or had children, and he never had a sexual life per se, though there was a girlfriend called Ophelia Queiroz, who was present during two brief periods of his life. Then there is a homoerotic element that is apparent in his friendships and in many of his unpublished notes and essays on other writers who were possibly homosexual. His sexual life was transferred into what he called 'self-fecundation' – a self-fertilization or self-reproduction in the creation of heteronyms and countless, diverse writings.

Nulla dies sine line (no day without [writing] a line) was the essence of most of Pessoa's life. The suffering of not being able to finish much of what he started became part of his aesthetic and a reflection of the age of modernism. The final chapter focuses on his prose masterpiece *The Book of Disquiet* and the concept and aesthetic of ruins in Pessoa's work, which comes to encapsulate another aspect of modernity – the modern urban experience. This 'non-book', 'anti-book', 'impossible book' or 'nightbook' shows the 'king of gaps' and 'spy of nothing' wandering in lucid daydreams and tedium through the city of Lisbon writing exquisite prose. These ruinous writings, which Pessoa produced between 1913 and 1934, occurred against the backdrop of an old nation on the periphery of the European continent experiencing the slow death of its maritime empire, the fall of the monarchy, the birth and death of a new democratic republic, and the emergence of a repressive autocratic state run by a dictator. When Pessoa died at the age of 47 in 1935, he left behind a large trunk filled with thousands of unpublished papers for future generations to discover.

So begins this journey through the creative life and intensive reality of Fernando Pessoa. It is a journey of the impossible, the nothing and the monstrous self.

1

The Early Years: Lisbon, Durban and the World

The only childhood he could recall belonged to the homeland of his dream; the only adolescence he remembered was the one he'd created . . . His entire life was the life he'd dreamed – and he realized he could never have had any other life.

Second Watcher, in Fernando Pessoa, *The Mariner*[1]

Fernando António Nogueira Pessoa was born on 13 June 1888 on the fourth floor of an apartment in São Carlos Square opposite the opera house in the centre of Lisbon. For Pessoa, a destiny of greatness was already suggested by his date and place of birth: he was born in sight of the opera house on a holiday marking the death of the city's most beloved and celebrated saint under the astrological sign of Gemini in a year that contains the mystical number eight three times.

The feast day of Santo António of Padua falls on 13 June. Although not the patron saint of Lisbon, Santo António is definitely the city's favourite saint and his feast is celebrated during the first two weeks of June, with sardines, beer and wine on the streets of the old neighbourhoods of Alfama, Graça and Bica. As a future astrologer and reader of magic and alchemy, Pessoa always made links to dates and numbering. This can be seen in his decisions about the birthdays of his three great heteronymic poets and the dates of some of his poems. Pessoa became a master of mapping astrological charts, so it is fitting that he was born under the star sign of Gemini as it represents the mutable, shifting and playful chameleon. He was born in 1888. The number '8' turned on its side is the symbol of infinity, and appears three times, like the trinity, preceded by the first prime number '1'. The four numbers added together make up '25', which added together is '7', the number of God, according to the Bible. All Pessoa's calculations and searching for signs hint at the folly and purposiveness of being a poet.

Pessoa's mother, Maria Madalena Pinheiro Nogueira, was born on 30 December 1861 on the island of Terceira in the Azores archipelago in the middle of the Atlantic Ocean. When she was three years old, her family moved to Porto and then to Lisbon. She was well educated and fluent in Portuguese, French and English. She was an avid reader of literature and wrote her own poems. Pessoa's father's name was Joaquim de Seabra Pessoa, and his family was from the area around the coastal town of Tavira in the Algarve, the southeast corner of Portugal. He was born in Lisbon on 28 May 1850. As an adult, he was a civil servant at the Ministry of Justice. He was also a music lover, and was a respected music and

View of Lisbon, 1890.

Pessoa's father, Joaquim de Seabra Pessoa, around thirty years old.

theatre critic for the newspaper *Diário de Notícias* (Daily News), which still exists today.

Maria and Joaquim married on 5 September 1887 at the parish church in Santos-o-Velho in Lisbon, where Maria's family came from. She moved in with Joaquim and his mother, Dionísia, in the apartment on São Carlos Square, and very soon after she was pregnant with Fernando. Fernando was baptized at Our Lady of the Martyr Church, even though his father was not interested in the Catholic Church. Some of Joaquim's ancestors from the seventeenth and eighteenth centuries were the da Cunha family, who were Jewish

Pessoa's mother, Maria Madalena Pinheiro Nogueira, in her mid-twenties, before she was married.

and from the centre of Portugal. They were New Christians (Jews who had converted to Christianity in the wake of the Inquisition). Though not a big believer, Pessoa's mother baptized her children in the Roman Catholic faith, as was the tradition in her family. The church itself is linked to two pivotal dates in Portuguese history: it was founded in 1147, the year that Lisbon began its independence from the so-called 'Moors' (*os moros* in Portuguese), Muslim peoples who had ruled the city and most of the Iberian peninsula for the previous four hundred years, and the church was relocated and rebuilt after the devastating earthquake that hit Lisbon in 1755. On 21 January 1893 Pessoa's mother gave birth to a second son called Jorge. Six months later, on 12 July 1893, Pessoa's father died of tuberculosis at the age of 43 in the same apartment where Pessoa was born.

In November 1893 Maria moved her two sons and her mother-in-law (who was suffering from dementia and madness) from São Carlos Square to a more modest third-floor apartment on Rua de São Marçal. But tragedy struck again when, on 2 January 1894, Pessoa's baby brother also died of tuberculosis. Pessoa was five years old. In the midst of these two tragic deaths, a miracle occurred. At the end of the same month when Jorge died, Fernando's mother boarded a horse-drawn streetcar in Lisbon and sat opposite João Miguel Rosa, a ship's captain who had sailed all over the world. They struck up a conversation; there was instant mutual attraction and they fell in love. At the end of 1894, João Miguel Rosa was promoted to work briefly as a port's captain in Mozambique, which was a

Pessoa, almost three years old, and his aunt Anica sitting down. His mother is standing in the middle, with her cousins on either side of her.

part of Portugal's overseas territories at the time. He worked in Lourenço Marques, which was renamed Maputo after Mozambique gained independence in 1975, and soon after he was given the job of Portuguese consul in Durban, capital of what was then the British colony of Natal in South Africa.

On 30 December 1895 Maria Madalena married João Miguel Rosa at the Igreja de Nossa Senhora das Mercês in Lisbon. Maria's second marriage at 34 years of age seems to have been very happy from the start. However, João Miguel was in Africa for the actual wedding ceremony, so his older brother, Henrique, stood in for the groom that day. Henrique Rosa would become a positive and inspiring figure who encouraged the creative side of Pessoa's life. Henrique was curious and open-minded about politics and philosophical ideas, and he wrote and published poems in newspapers and journals in Lisbon. He was very fond of Pessoa and the feeling was reciprocated. Just before Fernando and his mother set off for a new life in Durban, Pessoa invented his first fictional friend, the Chevalier de Pas, and also wrote his first poem.

The First Heteronym: Chevalier de Pas

The Chevalier de Pas was conceived by Pessoa at five or six years old, thus beginning the activity of writing as someone else at a very young age. The name of this first invented other is revealing. First, it is in French rather than Pessoa's mother tongue of Portuguese; second, the meaning of the name itself – which can be translated as 'Knight of Not' or 'Knight of Step' – alludes to a feeling of absence as well as to the presence of an imaginary friend. Pessoa wrote in a letter at the beginning of the last year of his life, on 13 January 1935:

> I can remember what I believe was my first heteronym, or rather, my first nonexistent acquaintance – a certain Chevalier de Pas – through whom I wrote letters from him to myself when I was six years old, and whose not entirely hazy figure still has a claim on the part of my affections that borders on nostalgia.[2]

Pessoa, age seven.

Fictional reality had made a claim on Pessoa in the appearance of a nonexistent friend. Was this a case of the experience of loss, solitude and presence of death at such an early age in losing his father and brother in the space of less than a year? Or perhaps the intense presence of his grandmother Dionísia with her dementia, madness and multiple personalities? Or was it a first glimpse of Pessoa's prodigious imagination and flair for literary invention? It may be that all three played a part in the appearance and persona of the Chevalier de Pas, as well as simply being the creation of a child who liked to invent imaginary friends. From a very early age, Pessoa was already unconsciously haunted by the paradoxical presence of nothing or negation. Later, as a teenager he formed an imaginary writing club of fictional friends called 'Ultimus Joculatorum' (The Last of the Jokers), which was also called 'The Nothingness Club' and 'The Zero Club'.[3] This work and club never really developed, but it is another early example of Pessoa's lifelong reflection on 'nothing'.

South Africa

On 26 July 1895, six months before he left Lisbon, Pessoa wrote his first known poem in Portuguese. He was seven years old and he wrote the poem for his mother:

> To my dear Mother
> Here I am in Portugal
> The land where I was born.
> However much I love it,
> I love you even more.[4]

On 20 January 1896 Maria Madalena and her son Fernando sailed to Durban via Madeira for a new and different life. Later that year, Maria gave birth to a daughter, Henriqueta Madalena (known as Teca), who was followed by sons Luís Miguel (1901) and João Maria (1903). Another daughter, Madalena Henriqueta (an inversion of the first daughter's name) was born in Durban in October 1898, but died of meningitis almost three years later. Although Pessoa

View of West Street, Durban, 1890s.

rarely mentioned his childhood spent in Durban and living in South
Africa, this period nonetheless was crucial for his formation as a
person, poet and cosmopolitan Portuguese citizen. There are a few
reasons for this. It was a turbulent period in South Africa. The Boer
War, which began in 1899, shook both the establishment and the
media of the British Empire with the experience of guerrilla warfare
from the Boers and the system of brutal concentration camps
that were set up by the British Army. This was a sinister glimpse
of what would come to pass in the twentieth century with Nazi
and Japanese concentration camps and Soviet gulags. In Durban
at the time there were two young men who would later become
iconic figures of the twentieth century: a war correspondent called
Winston Churchill and a humanitarian lawyer called Mohandas
Karamchand Gandhi (he was later named 'Mahatma' by the great
Bengali poet Rabindranath Tagore). From the perspective of reading
and understanding Pessoa, it is significant that these three figures –
Pessoa, Churchill and Gandhi – were all in the city of Durban at the
same time.

Natal – which means 'Christmas', 'natal' and 'birth' in
Portuguese – was a British colony on the south coast of Africa.

It was named by Portugal's most celebrated naval explorer, Vasco da Gama, when he landed on the coastline on Christmas Day in 1497 on his way to India for the first time, so creating the first official ocean route to link Europe and Asia. Luís de Camões, Pessoa's rival for the title of the greatest Portuguese poet, based his epic poem *The Lusíads* (1572) on the maritime journey and achievements of Vasco da Gama. But the British were the first European settlers in the coastal region of Natal. Portugal and Britain boast the longest European alliance in history, and both empires had a strong presence in Africa. When Pessoa was living in Natal, Churchill was a journalist, but he later fought in the Boer War and was a proud apologist for British colonialism. He became Britain's most famous prime minister of the twentieth century, leading Britain against Nazi Germany in the Second World War. He also later won the Nobel Prize in Literature. Churchill despised Gandhi, to whom he referred as a 'malignant subversive fanatic'.[5]

Gandhi completes this colonial and cosmopolitan scenario. It was in Durban that Gandhi came to international renown for his defence of equal rights for Indian workers (as British citizens), and where he would first use the practice of non-violent resistance. Gandhi arrived in Durban in 1893 and spent 21 years in South Africa before returning to India to lead the struggle for independence. In the 1920s Pessoa would write on a piece of paper: 'Mahatma Gandhi is the only truly great figure in the world today, and this is true because, in a certain sense, he does not belong in the world and he denies it.'[6] This gives us a fascinating insight into Pessoa, who is mostly critical of world leaders.

Gandhi was a paradox for Pessoa. He was a multifaceted person of spirituality and action who changed the world, and yet he also denied the world. He combined the two realities of the outer and inner world, the practical and imaginary. Was it for this reason that Pessoa wrote such a generous sentence on Gandhi? Notice also the way Pessoa inserted the word 'truly' and 'in a certain sense', which gives a glimmer of the 'Absolute Reality' that the author of 'Sentimental Education' spoke of. For Pessoa, Gandhi has denied the relative reality and belongs elsewhere, where the impossible, nothing and monstrous self reside. Gandhi also conveyed the idea and practice of global tolerance, which Pessoa would have been sympathetic to and later express in an age of extremes.

This brings us to the question of trying to be as radical as reality. For Pessoa, India represents both the imagination and the fabled past of an ancient exotic culture and an audacious and powerful Portuguese Empire. Edward Said would probably have a few things to say about the exoticism that Pessoa applies to India. Said begins his book *Orientalism* by stating: 'The Orient was almost a European invention, and had been since antiquity a place of romance, exotic beings, haunting memories and landscapes, remarkable experiences.'[7] Pessoa's India belongs to his imagination. He would never wish to go there, as the reality of it in his mind, as expressed by his heteronyms, is far more vivid and extraordinary and mysterious. Bernardo Soares prefers what he calls an 'impossible India', writing: 'My Imagination is a city in the Orient,' and the 'Ganges also passes by the Rua dos Douradores [the street in Lisbon where Soares worked and lived]'.[8] In his first poem, 'Opiary', Álvaro de Campos asks: 'Why did I visit the India that exists,/ If there's no India but the soul I possess?'[9] In the same poem, which was written on a ship passing through the Suez Canal, Campos writes: 'I belong to that class of Portuguese/ Who, once India was discovered, were out/ Of work.'[10] In a way, Vasco da Gama landing in Kerala in India was the peak of Portuguese history for poets such as Camões and Pessoa, and so was also the beginning of the end.

A crucial aspect of Pessoa's upbringing in Durban was the education he received in a British colony with links to Portugal's 'age of discoveries'. The British schooling would be vital in forming and distinguishing Pessoa as a poet. He spoke Portuguese and French at home and English at school. It was in Durban where he first read Shakespeare, Milton, Carlyle, Dickens, Percy Shelley, Byron, Poe, Keats, Wordsworth, Tennyson and Browning. He was particularly partial to Dickens's *The Posthumous Papers of the Pickwick Club* and Carlyle's *Sartor Resartus*. Other books in English that would be pivotal for him in the future were the poetical works of Walt Whitman, who was a model for the heteronyms Alberto Caeiro and

Pessoa, age ten.

Álvaro de Campos.[11] Writing in 1917, Pessoa said: 'Only one poet, Walt Whitman, has appeared with a sensibility large enough to embrace the passive opportunities of the mind before this enlarged world.'[12] Another key book was Edward Fitzgerald's translations of the Persian poet Omar Khayyam, known as the *Rubáiyát of Omar Khayyám*. Of all Pessoa's books in his private library, he made the most notes and marks in this one. The education and culture he experienced in Durban made Pessoa initially want to be an English-language poet, and so he wrote most of his early poems in English and later tried to publish them in England, but with no success.

In March 1896 Pessoa was enrolled in St Joseph's Convent School, which was run by Roman Catholic nuns. Three years later, he entered Durban High School, and in 1901 he passed his school exams with high honours. In June 1901, the whole family set sail for Lisbon and took a one-year holiday, which included a visit to relatives near Tavira in the Algarve. In May 1902, the family visited Terceira in the Azores, and returned to Durban in June of that year. Pessoa, however, stayed with relatives in Lisbon while he prepared for the national elementary education exam. Pessoa was becoming quite accustomed to solitude, isolation, separation, long journeys

Pessoa and his family at their home in Durban, 1902.

The front page of Pessoa's Latin primer: Benjamin Hall Kennedy, *The Revised Latin Primer*, 7th edn (1898).

at sea and the deaths of family members. All these formative experiences haunted him and his powerful imagination for the rest of his life. It is notable, then, that one month before embarking on the one-year holiday to Portugal, Pessoa wrote his first poem in English, which was called 'Separated from Thee'. While in Lisbon, away from his family, he published his first poem on 18 July 1902 in a Lisbon newspaper called *O Imparcial* (The Independent).[13] Three months after his family had left, he returned on a ship alone to join them in Durban. In October 1902 he entered Commercial School, and within the month he sat the Matriculation Examination for the University of the Cape of Good Hope and won the Queen Victoria Memorial Prize for best essay in English. He was fourteen when he sat the exam and his prize was impressive given that he had only been learning English since he was seven-and-a-half years old. In February 1904 Pessoa returned to Durban High School and sat the Intermediate Examination in Arts from the University of the Cape of Good Hope. He obtained the highest score in the province of Natal.

Ocean voyages continued to resonate in Pessoa's works. The Cape of Good Hope was previously named the Cape of Storms by Bartolomeu Dias, another legendary seafarer from the fabled 'age of discoveries' who first rounded the Cape in 1487. In 1500, on his second voyage around the Cape, his ship was lost during a storm and he was drowned. Both Pessoa and Camões immortalized Bartolomeu Dias in their work. Pessoa calls Dias 'The Captain of the End [O Capitão do Fim] who rounded Terror' in *Mensagem*.[14] In *The Lusíads*, Camões would go as far as to create a mythical godlike sea-monster called Adamastor who emerges out of the storm around the Cape and causes the death of Dias. He is the only mythical figure among the Greek and Roman gods that Camões invented, and he had this to say to Vasco da Gama when he asked him the question 'who are you?':

I am that vast, secret promontory
you Portuguese call the Cape of Storms
which neither Ptolemy, Pompey or Strabo,
Pliny, nor any authors knew of.

Here Africa ends. Here its coast
Concludes in this, my vast inviolate
Plateau, extending southwards towards the Pole
And, by your daring, struck to my very soul.[15]

The name Adamastor derives from the Greek word for 'untameable'
(*adamastos*), which was a fitting description of the treacherous
waters that both Vasco da Gama and Pessoa passed through. In
August 1905, on finishing school, Pessoa once again embarked
on a ship without his family and crossed the Cape of Good Hope,
voyaging over the Atlantic Ocean to Lisbon to begin university
there. He never went back to Durban.

The Exiled Self

Exile and dislocation are something that Pessoa felt all his life,
which is ironic as, like James Joyce, Pessoa is regarded as the great
poet of a particular place. But as Joyce took a boat from Dublin
at the age of 21 never to return except for one brief visit, Pessoa
travelled the other way around. In 1905, when Pessoa was seventeen,
his ship docked in Lisbon and he would never leave Portugal again.
Lisbon was a once-regal city and capital of a maritime empire, but
in Pessoa's time the city was poor, dishevelled and marginal, though
beautiful, poetic and mysterious. Pessoa went on to spend his entire
adult life in the city, living in a myriad of different apartments –
between 1914 and 1919 alone he moved at least eight times – writing
in cafés night and day, and walking the streets whose names appear
in his works. And yet Pessoa felt this inner exile all his life, which is
emblematic of whom he became and how he interwove himself with
Portugal's maritime history and mirrored the hangover from the age
of navigation. This feeling is also, ultimately, a large part of what it
is to be modern.

    The exiled self articulates for many an essential feeling that
pervaded the twentieth century. It is a self that is banished,
scattered and multiplied. The etymology of the word 'exile' comes
from the Latin *ex*, 'away', and *ile*, deriving from *al*, meaning 'to

wander', which in turn comes from the Greek *alaomai*: to wander, stray or roam about. The term 'exiled self' can be applied to the self as plurality, which incorporates multiplication and othering of the self. In his early years, Pessoa experienced and cultivated a sense of exile – both exterior and interior – through language, existential alienation, landscapes and a nomadic existence. Pessoa wrote many years later in a letter to his only girlfriend, Ophelia: 'my exile – which is I myself'; Bernardo Soares calls himself 'Prince of the Great Exile'; Álvaro de Campos refers in one poem to his 'exiled, epidermically spirited heart', and in another writes that his 'inherent exile comes alive in the darkness'.[16] As an adult, Pessoa hardly ever travelled. Apart from his childhood years in South Africa, he never visited another country. He never even visited Porto in the north of Portugal, but with his imagination he could travel anywhere. Campos writes at the start of a poem: 'the best way to travel is to feel,' and another of Pessoa's heteronyms dreams of journeys to 'impossible countries' and has a room 'overlooking infinity'.[17] Pessoa evokes a feeling of exile within his outward reality of being ensconced in Lisbon in a poem called 'Navy' ('Marinha'): 'Orphan of a suspended dream/ By the ebbing tide'.[18]

Today on São Carlos Square there is a statue of Pessoa with his face covered by an open book. The figure has his back to the building of the apartment where Pessoa was born and faces the opera house – a fitting view for a self-declared 'dramatic poet'[19] and inventor of over a hundred personas, some of whom left only a signature and a fragment while others left mighty collections of poetry, biographies and correspondence with Pessoa and other heteronyms. Dublin has Joyce; St Petersburg has Dostoevsky; London has Dickens; Paris has Baudelaire; Alexandria has Cavafy; and Lisbon has Pessoa.

2

I Was a Poet Animated by Philosophy

Only poets and philosophers see the world as it really is, for only to them is it given to live without illusions.
Bernardo Soares[1]

Fernando Pessoa has the advantage of living more in ideas than in himself.
Álvaro de Campos[2]

On 20 August 1905 Pessoa returned to Lisbon. Physically he was alone. But in his imagination he was accompanied by invented friends, among them the heteronym Robert Charles Anon, whom he had created in 1903 and who had written a poem that was published by the *Natal Mercury* newspaper in Durban in 1904. Anon (meaning 'soon' or 'shortly', derived from *on an* in Old English, meaning 'into one' or 'continuously') was Pessoa's most prolific heteronym up to this time and had a personality that was both poetic and philosophical. On the cusp of Pessoa's adulthood, Anon described himself in a piece titled 'Excommunication': 'I, Charles Robert Anon, being, animal, mammal, tetrapod, primate, placental, ape, catarrhina, . . . man; eighteen years of age, not married (except at odd moments), megalomaniac, with touches of dipsomania, *dégénéré supérieur*, poet, with pretensions to written humor, citizen of the world, idealistic philosopher, etc. etc.'[3]

This text mirrors much of how Pessoa saw himself and what he might become. On 2 October Pessoa began studying at the University of Lisbon. He attended philosophy classes throughout

1906 and 1907 before abandoning his studies. In 1907 or 1908, reflecting on his formation as a poet and what it meant for him to be a poet, Pessoa wrote on a sheet of paper in English: 'I was a poet animated by philosophy, not a philosopher with poetic faculties. I loved to admire the beauty of things, to trace in the imperceptible and through the minute the poetic soul of the universe.'[4] During these first years back in Lisbon and this brief period at university, Pessoa would write various unfinished essays and fragments, nearly all of them in English, on philosophers and philosophical ideas such as rationalism, error, sensations, free will and the philosophy of science. In these it is possible to spot the deep philosophical themes and reflections that were later synthesized and condensed in Pessoa's mature poetry and in *The Book of Disquiet*. It was during this period of 1906–8 that Pessoa, as a young adult, first seriously explored the works of philosophers in his yearning to grapple with ideas in European culture and his attention turned away from solely reading literature. This is the background to Pessoa becoming not just a 'dramatic poet' but also a philosophical poet.

Though he quickly lost interest in attending university, this period permitted Pessoa some education in philosophy as he mimicked and copied ideas, jotted down notes, and responded to the insights and achievements of philosophers such as Spinoza, Plato, Aristotle, Lucretius, Bergson, Malebranche, Leibniz, Berkeley, Pascal, Rousseau, Kant, Hegel (whose philosophy Pessoa referred to as 'this cathedral of thought'[5]) and Nietzsche. But, as Pessoa clearly stated, he was not striving to be a philosopher. He was a poet 'animated by philosophy', not unlike other writers of his generation such as T. S. Eliot, Robert Musil, Franz Kafka, Virginia Woolf and James Joyce. This kind of writer is part of a modernist tradition that fuses the philosophical with the poetic, and in the twentieth century we can find the inverse in what could be called 'poetic philosophers' such as Heidegger, Unamuno, Benjamin, Adorno, Beauvoir, Sartre and Camus. The nineteenth century gave us the poetic philosophers Søren Kierkegaard and Friedrich Nietzsche, whose ideas were not really received until the twentieth century, and who profoundly

I was a poet animated by philosophy
not a philosopher with poetic faculties. I loved to admire the beauty of
things, to trace in the imperceptible ~~and in~~ through the minute the poetic
soul of the universe.

The poetry of the earth is never dead.
We may say that ages gone have been
more poetic, but we can say

Poetry is in everything – in land
and in sea, in lake and in river-
side. It is in the city too – deny
it not – it is evident to me here
as I sit: there is poetry in this
table, in this paper, in this
inkstand; there is poetry in the
rattling of the cars on the streets,
in each minute, common, ridiculous
nation of a workman who, the other
side of the street, is painting the sign-
board of a butcher's shop.

Handwritten page by Pessoa starting with the line, 'I was a poet animated by
philosophy'.

influenced a new generation of philosophers and artists alike in Europe.

According to Pessoa's heteronym Alberto Caeiro, poets dream and philosophers think.[6] But in Pessoa's case, the poets also think and the philosophers also dream and feel. From the same passage in English where Pessoa wrote that he was 'animated by philosophy', he went on to define poetry:

> Poetry is in everything – in land and in sea, in lake and in riverside . . . there is poetry in this table, in this paper, in this inkstand; there is poetry in the rattling of the cars on the streets, in each minute, common, ridiculous motion of a workman, who on the other side of the street is painting the sign-board of a butcher's shop . . . For poetry is astonishment.[7]

There are two important points in this passage about Pessoa's thinking on poetry and philosophy. First, the materiality of poetry is a deeply philosophical point for Pessoa. It questions the idea that poetry is simply the dream, and proposes that poetry is an expression of and articulated awe for the overflowing matter in the world. Poetry can be the thing in itself – like Kant's *Ding an sich* – and to write poems or create concepts is working to be as radical as reality itself. Second, the idea of astonishment evokes what it must have felt like to philosophize in ancient times. Philosophy began with wonder in antiquity but was driven by doubt in modernity. There almost seems to be an inversion here: Pessoa's poetry is riddled with doubt (led by Campos), but although a modernist, he thinks it should be driven by wonder like ancient philosophy. Alberto Caeiro seems to have succeeded in this endeavour, as he writes: 'The astonishing reality of things/ Is my discovery every day.'[8]

Ultimately, for Pessoa, the vocation of the poet is a more serious endeavour than that of the philosopher. The philosopher's work should be taken with a pinch of salt, at least until it perceives itself as an activity of experimentation, and is closer to being an art than a science, despite what many philosophers would have us think.

This is something akin to what Kierkegaard wrote in his diary regarding the German philosopher Hegel: 'If Hegel had written his entire *Logic* and said in the preface that it was merely a thought-experiment in which he had even shirked things in various places, he would no doubt have been the greatest thinker that ever lived. As it is he is comical.'[9] Commenting on the supreme philosophical work by Immanuel Kant, one of the most systematic and driest of philosophers, Pessoa writes: '*The Critique of Pure Reason* is literature.'[10] Like Beckett after him, Pessoa was very attracted to philosophical systems because of their precision and order in asking the most fundamental questions on life, death and the cosmos, and perhaps also as a kind of therapy to keep him from falling into the void of despair. But, at the same time, Pessoa also ridiculed them, which can be seen in the prose of Bernardo Soares and the poetry of Caeiro, the two most philosophical of Pessoa's literary heteronyms. Caeiro in particular encapsulates Pessoa's double approach to philosophy as the most philosophical heteronym and, at the same time, the most disdainful of the activity of thinking.

Pessoa's 'Thought-Poem'

Alain Badiou throws down the gauntlet to philosophers with these words about Pessoa:

> If Pessoa represents a singular challenge for philosophy, if his modernity is still *ahead of us*, remaining in many respects unexplored, it is because *his thought-poem inaugurates a path that manages to be neither Platonic nor anti-Platonic* . . . To this day, philosophy has yet to comprehend the full extent of this gesture.[11]

Pessoa's poetry thinks as well as feels. It is a mode of thought. Philosophy is yet to fully understand Pessoa's mode of thought in poetry because of its various layers and treatment of reality. Pessoa's major heteronyms engage directly with philosophy. Campos is really the closest to being Platonic, in seeking abstract realities and writing non-Aristotelian essays; he is a transcendental poet. In a poem called 'Original Sin', he states: 'What exists is the true world – not us, just the world./ We are, in truth, what doesn't exist./ . . . Our truth is what we never attained.'[12] On the other hand, Alberto Caeiro, the materialist poet, is completely anti-transcendental and anti-Platonic: reality is truth itself, and there is nothing behind reality. Thus, he writes: 'I feel my whole body lying down in reality/ I know the truth and I am happy.'[13] For Ricardo Reis, as the sad Epicurean and detached Stoic, the truth is already behind us, and we must accept with resignation the reality of our destiny. Bernardo Soares prefers 'reality to truth'.[14] Truth is something that we should not and cannot waste our time with any longer. Pessoa, as the creator of all these writers, assimilates both truth and untruth into reality. That is part of the conundrum for philosophy when reading Pessoa and his heteronyms and Pessoa's ability to have simultaneous selves and ideas.[15]

Álvaro de Campos interlinked poets and philosophers in his outrageous manifesto from 1917 called 'Ultimatum'. He declares that 'the greatest philosopher will be the artist of thought,' and that 'the philosopher will become the interpreter of crisscrossing subjectivities, with the greatest philosopher being the one who can contain the greatest number of other people's personal philosophies.'[16] And this appeal to the philosopher also calls to the artist, as he says the greatest artist 'will be the one who least defines himself, and who writes in the most genres with the most contradictions and discrepancies'. He goes on: 'No artist should have just one personality. He should have many, each one being formed by joining together similar states of mind, thereby shattering the crude fiction that the artist is one and indivisible.'[17] While this definition is widely accepted today when looking at artists and their work from Shakespeare to Bob Dylan, it is difficult to see it working convincingly for philosophers. However, this description might apply to Nietzsche, the modern philosopher as the overhuman (*der Übermensch*) – it is no coincidence that Pessoa made Álvaro de Campos's birthday fall on the same day as Nietzsche's. Or what of that other poetic philosopher of the nineteenth century: Kierkegaard?[18] Kierkegaard is a writer both of and against modernity, a thinker combating philosophy, a Christian against Christendom, a poetic mind and maestro of style critiquing aesthetic life, and a most likely celibate writer who captures in at least one of his works the passionate perspective of a grandiose *flâneur* and seducer of women. One of Kierkegaard's pseudonyms took on the guise of an upstanding married man writing one of the greatest defences of marriage by a philosopher, while Kierkegaard himself remained a bachelor all his life. In another book, his pseudonym is a radical faith-abiding and focused Christian, while in other pseudonymous works the narrators are tormented by doubt and indecision. When Pessoa writes as his 'semi-heteronym' Bernardo Soares, he is, to quote Richard Zenith, 'a prose writer who poeticizes, a dreamer who thinks, a mystic who doesn't believe, a decadent who doesn't indulge'.[19]

Alexander Search

In July 1906 Pessoa's family came to Lisbon from Durban, and in October he moved to the neighbourhood of Estrela to be with them. He missed exams because he was sick, and so he had to redo the whole year again in October 1906, but this time he added philosophy to his studies. It was also in 1906 that the name of the heteronym Alexander Search made its first appearance. Although he is English and only writes poems in his native language, Search shares the same birthday as Pessoa and was also born in Lisbon, bringing him closer to being a pseudonym than the heteronyms that Pessoa developed over the next few years. He completely took over from Charles Robert Anon, who disappears or was simply absorbed into the new heteronym. Search merges the activity of poetry with philosophical reflections, while also studying and writing both philosophy and poetry. We can call him the first significant major heteronym (certainly Pessoa's most prolific in the English language), as he is the author of more than 130 poems in English between 1903 and 1910, various texts and fragments, and a Gothic short story called 'A Very Original Dinner'. Again, in the ideas that are

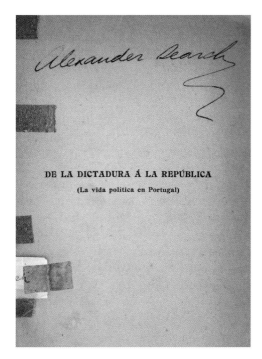

Signature of 'Alexander Search' on the book *De la Dictadura á la República* by Luis Morote.

DE LA DICTADURA Á LA REPÚBLICA

(La vida política en Portugal)

articulated in his poetry, this heteronym reveals what is to come in Pessoa's more mature work. His name evokes imperial, kingly resonances (Alexander the Great) and eternal questioning and searching (Search). There is also an implicit suggestion of the name Alexander Selkirk, the Scottish naval officer who was marooned on an island for four and a half years as a castaway, and who inspired the creation of the protagonist of one of the British Empire's most famous novels – *Robinson Crusoe* (1719) by Daniel Defoe. Giving more credence to this link between Search and Selkirk, the latter also turns up as a simile in Charles Dickens's novel *The Pickwick Papers* – one of Pessoa's favourite books when growing up in Durban, and which Bernardo Soares reminisces about many years later.[20]

Alexander Search lists books to read under the title 'Philosophy, etc.' such as Aristotle's *Organon* (his six collected works on logic),

Immanuel Kant's *Critique of Pure Reason* and Ernst Haeckel's evolutionary work *Die Welträtsel* (The Riddle of the Universe), which Pessoa owned in French. Search was to be a great intellectual heteronym: iconoclastic, anticlerical and a humanitarian. Part of this intellectual pursuit was the conscious connection to other insatiable mythical seekers (Faust) and givers (Prometheus) of knowledge. Pessoa's copy of the long poem 'Prometheus Unbound' by Percy Shelley was signed on the front page by Alexander Search. Like Faust, Search makes a bond with Satan. Search begins a pact dated 2 October 1907 with the words: 'Bond entered into by Alexander Search, of Hell, Nowhere, with Jacob Satan, Master, though not King, of the same place.' This is followed by four duties, all beginning with the absolute negation of the word 'never': never stop helping mankind; never write anything that would be of harm to mankind; never forget when attacking religion that it cannot be replaced; and never forget the suffering and ills of men. At the end of the text is the mark of Satan himself.[21]

The Myth of Faust, Doubt and Spinoza

Reminiscent of the opening speech of the scientist and alchemist Faust in Goethe's masterpiece, in 1907 Pessoa pondered how philosophical theories could be so vivid while he was ruminating on them, yet, more often than not, they would fade away into oblivion. It is as if, for Pessoa, philosophical ideas live in him as reality, which is also the dream. He wrote the following lines in English, perhaps meaning them to be attributed to Alexander Search:

> Thousands of theories, grotesque, extraordinary, profound, on the world, on man, on all problems that pertain to metaphysics have passed through my mind. I have had in me thousands of philosophies not any two of which – as if they were real – agreed. All the ideas I had if written down had been a great cheque on posterity; but by the very peculiar character of my mind, no sooner did the theory, the idea struck me that it disappeared, and after I ached to feel that one moment after I remembered

nothing – absolutely nothing of what it might have been. Thus memory, as all my other faculties predisposed me to live in a dream.[22]

On 14 December 1908 Pessoa wrote the first verses of his projected dramatic poem *Faust: A Subjective Tragedy*. Amazingly, Pessoa would continue to write verses for *Faust* until 1933, throughout nearly his entire adult life. It would turn out to be one of his most epic ruins: an unfinished and unorganized verse drama written in Portuguese and comprising texts on gazing into the unknown and the abyss, as the author suffered from simply thinking too much. The Devil is in fact really only present as the human intellectual mind itself. The transformation of the Devil from a physical entity into a psychological shadow within our being and experiences, memories and expectations is key to some of the great novels of twentieth-century modernity from Thomas Mann's *Doctor Faustus* to João Guimarães Rosa's *Grande sertão: Veredas*. Pessoa even wrote in 1935, at the end of an article he published defending secret societies, that Goethe's *Faust* was 'the greatest work of modern literature'.[23] The Faustian self divides, multiplies and disappears, wandering between myth and logic, trying to open up new forms of reality. The story of a person's quest to know and understand the riddles of the world, and to make a pact at whatever cost to gain insight, even if it leads them to the borders of madness, resonated throughout modern literature in works by writers from Christopher Marlowe to Mikhail Bulgakov.

The propensity to think too much or the addiction to pursuing an impossible metaphysics is the illness that Pessoa felt he had, and which his future heteronyms were sensitive to. For example, Soares writes: 'Metaphysics has always struck me as a prolonged form of latent insanity'; Campos remarks: 'metaphysics is a consequence of not feeling very well'; and the non-thinking philosopher-poet Caeiro writes: 'to think is to not understand' and 'philosophers are lunatics.'[24] Madness could be seen as getting lost in the void; it is something poets and seekers are wary of and yet have a need to draw from at the same time. They are also tormented by the image of a multiplicity of selves. Pessoa was exposed to this idea from an early age. He saw multiple personalities up close while living with his grandmother Dionísia, and then with his fellow travellers in literature such as Faust, Hamlet and Lear. Alexander Search, and later Campos and Soares, all suffer from lapses into madness and thinking without rest. Doubt plagues them, and Faust is the personification of doubt. The indecisions, contradictions and divisions in one's soul drive the tragedies of the various versions of Faust and, of course, Hamlet. Pessoa went on to create another heteronym called Antonio Mora, a Kantian and neopagan philosopher. On the relation between indecision and great minds, Pessoa has this to say when speaking of Mora: 'Indecisive, like all strong minds, he hadn't discovered the truth, or what he felt was the truth, which as far as I'm concerned is the same thing.'[25] In contrast to *Cogito, ergo sum* (I think, therefore I am), the dictum of René Descartes, who is often considered one of the founders of modern philosophy in Europe, Pessoa writes: 'I doubt, therefore I think.'[26] Alexander Search transfers his philosophical musings on Faustian themes of doubt and madness into poems such as 'Mania of Doubt', 'Flashes of Madness', 'Fragment of Delirium' and 'Epitaph', which were meant to be part of collections that never materialized called *Delirium*, *Mens Insana*, *Before Sense* and *Documents of Mental Decadence*.

For Caeiro, thinking is essentially to err.[27] Thinking with our eyes is the journey that Caeiro takes to liberate us from the striving and anxiety that plagues us as human beings. Like the religious prophets of old, he embodies that childlike quality of seeing in wide-eyed astonishment which we must open ourselves up to a second time as adults. Hence we encounter Caeiro's 'science of seeing'. Pessoa was reading the seventeenth-century philosopher Baruch Spinoza during his first years in Lisbon, and perhaps aspects of Spinoza's philosophy morphed into the figure of Caeiro. It is understandable that Pessoa, like other poets and writers, would have been drawn to Spinoza. Although he never wrote anything about aesthetics or art, Spinoza's philosophical system was a work of art in itself. To enter Spinoza's *Ethics* is to be confounded by a combination of extreme rationalism and some kind of underlying pantheistic mysticism. It is a philosophical voyage of immanence in the pursuit of freedom from anger, intolerance, suffering and inadequate passions. Spinoza's thought is thinking also with the body, and the realization that reality and perfection are the same. He is the counterpart to the insecure, doubtful and yearning Faust.

Spinoza was the son of a Portuguese Sephardic Jewish merchant in Amsterdam, but he was a heretic, cast out from the Jewish community. He wrote in Latin, spoke Portuguese with his family, and was fluent in Hebrew and Dutch. This heretical multilingual pantheistic philosopher, who saw God and nature as one and the same thing, greatly appealed to Pessoa. At the age of eighteen, Pessoa wrote down this passage on Spinoza, probably a quotation in his own translation in English from another book: 'Spinoza. Here at last the genius appears, true genius, having that which Descartes had not the fearlessness and the lack of respect for the established. Honours to the master-thinker who, prosecuted, hated, accurst, stood by truth, lived for truth, suffered for (the sake of) truth!'[28]

Ibis

On 25 April 1907, Pessoa's family returned to Durban. In May 1907 (almost two years after he had landed in Lisbon), Pessoa moved in with his great aunts Maria and Rita and his grandmother Dionísia on Rua da Bela Vista à Vista 17, also in the Estrela neighbourhood. The following year, on 1 February, King Carlos I of Portugal and his son were assassinated in broad daylight in downtown Lisbon. This catastrophic event marked the end of the almost three-hundred-year reign of the House of Braganza monarchy. The subsequent First Republic would endure for almost twenty tumultuous years. Alexander Search responds by reflecting on the tense and transformative political situation in Portugal and in 1909 prepares two political texts for the public: *The Portuguese Regicide and the Political Situation in Portugal*, on the topic of national decline, and *The Extent and Causes of Portuguese Decay*. Both Pessoa and Search approved of the assassination of the king of Portugal but not the more radical side of republicanism. Any political movement that had the potential to become a dogmatic mass movement did not meet with Pessoa's approval. Pessoa navigated the explosive twentieth-century rise of nationalism, fascism, communism and totalitarianism as a liberal, or even a conservative in the tradition of John Locke or Thomas Hobbes. For example, he was happy to see the end of the tsarist regime in Russia but thought Bolshevism was an abomination. For Pessoa, a proletarian revolution was a worse form of totalitarianism than a monarchy.

On 6 September 1907, Pessoa's grandmother Dionísia died and left him a sizeable inheritance. Pessoa used the money to set up a publishing company called 'Company Ibis – Printing and Publishing'. He started writing more poetry in Portuguese, and in November 1909 he travelled to the town of Portalegre in the Alentejo region of Portugal to buy a machine for his new publishing company. The idea was to publish some of Pessoa's favourite books in translation and also works by himself and his heteronyms. Working as a freelance translator and drafting letters for firms to earn some money, he also moved into his own apartment on Rua de Glória 4 and lived alone for the first time.

The name 'Ibis' has many connotations. As well as being a long-legged bird who wades in the waters of wetlands, forests and plains, the ibis is linked to Thoth, the Egyptian god of writing and wisdom (and of death), and is referred to by Joyce as 'the god of libraries, a birdgod, moonycrowned' and by the philosopher Jacques Derrida as the 'messenger-god' and 'signifier-god'.[29] Thoth has the body of a human and the head of an ibis. The name Thoth, written as *dḥwty* in ancient Egyptian and with a drawing of an ibis in hieroglyphs, literally means 'he who is like an Ibis'. The logo of the company was the image of an ibis standing on one leg. Pessoa would sign letters as 'Ibis' and adopted the symbol of the bird as an identity. It was even reported that he posed as an ibis on the street, lifting one leg and raising his arm to his mouth to create a beak. He would respond with this gesture when people he knew waved to him from across the street, declaring: 'I am an Ibis.'[30] In 1924 Pessoa wrote this little poem for his godchildren:

Pessoa in 1908, age twenty.

The Ibis, the bird of Egypt
Always lands on one foot
What it is
Weird.
It is a calm bird,
Because it goes nowhere.[31]

However, Pessoa's first attempt at setting up a publishing house was a financial disaster. Ibis closed after a year without publishing anything, while all the inherited money evaporated. Not only that, but Pessoa had to borrow money from the bank to pay off debts from this endeavour over the next four years. This was the first of many failed projects, nearly all of which led to financial disaster or were simply never fulfilled. But it also showed a new side to Pessoa – he was never discouraged by failure and he was interested not only in literature but in taking a chance with business ventures. Having the confidence and determination to write poetry and promoting his ambitions as a Portuguese and cosmopolitan writer were one and the same thing for Pessoa. This could be seen in the context of Portuguese commercial culture, relating to the history of

Document of 'Empreza Íbis, Typographica e Editora', showing the image of the bird.

a maritime empire: one of quixotic voyages, lucrative conquests and catastrophic shipwrecks. Two centuries previously, Daniel Defoe prefigured Pessoa's relationship to his literary and commercial enterprises:

> The Commerce of the World, especially as it is now carried on, is an unbounded Ocean of Business; Trackless and unknown, like the Seas it is managed upon; the Merchant is no more to be follow'd in his Adventures, than a Maze or Labyrinth is to be trac'd out without a Clue.[32]

The fiasco of the Ibis press venture reveals Pessoa's poor business acumen, analogous to his inability to complete most of his literary projects. He was certainly sailing on an 'unbounded Ocean' and remained within a 'Labyrinth'. But he would not be deterred, and would continue to concoct other business adventures and literary projects throughout his life that would crumble as Ibis did.

Pessoa moved away from reading philosophy, and in August 1910 he started writing Shakespearean sonnets in English (which he would later include in *35 Sonnets*, self-published as a chapbook in 1918). The First Portuguese Republic officially began on 5 October 1910. Because of his dire financial situation, Pessoa moved in with his aunt Anica on Rua Passos Manuel 24 in June 1911. Then, in 1912, Pessoa met Mário de Sá-Carneiro. He was a fellow poet and would quickly become Pessoa's best and only intimate friend, a confidante and equal in his life. Together they created a literary magazine called *Orpheu*, and ignited a new modernism and avant-garde in Lisbon that would leave its mark on Portuguese literature for the rest of the twentieth century.

3

Orpheu and the Birth of Modernism

We are Portuguese writing for Europe, for all civilization; we are nothing
as yet, but even what we are now doing will one day be universally
known and recognized. We have no fear that it will be otherwise . . .
We work away from Camões, from all the tedious nonsenses of
Portuguese tradition, towards the Future.

Fernando Pessoa[1]

Before looking more closely at the concept of heteronymy and
Pessoa's three most enduring invented poets, it is important first
to analyse the birth of modernism in Portugal and Pessoa's crucial
role in spreading its ideas and aesthetic. Modernism emerged out of
the ideas of the nineteenth century and accelerated and intensified
amid the chaotic and frenetic years in early twentieth-century
Europe during the First World War and its aftermath. Although he
was almost completely unknown outside Lisbon, Pessoa was at the
forefront of defining the modern world through his writing and
activities during turbulent and transformative years in Portugal –
the 'chaotic age', as literary critic Harold Bloom would later define
it.[2] The iconoclastic philosophers of the nineteenth century had
already warned us of what was to come. In the revolutionary year
of 1848, Kierkegaard, the philosopher of individual transformation,
had written in his journal of 'the age of disintegration'; and Marx
and Engels, the philosophers of collective transformation, had
written: 'All that is solid melts into air, all that is holy is profaned,
and man is at last compelled to face with sober senses his real
condition of life and his relations with his kind.'[3] And in the year

when Pessoa was born, Nietzsche wrote: 'What I relate is the history of the next two centuries. I describe what is coming, what can no longer come differently: the advent of nihilism,' while Engels commented on 'the necessity of total social change' in the preface to the 1888 English edition of *The Communist Manifesto*.[4] The twentieth century would witness an attempt, with brutal consequences, at implementing Nietzsche's 'revaluation of all values' and Marx and Engels's 'most radical rupture with traditional ideas' in art, politics and society at large.[5] The madman's declaration that 'God is dead' in Nietzsche's *The Gay Science* in 1882 really meant the death of the old value system in Western culture and civilization. It was a painful transition to let go of the old values and enter into a new epoch. There is a memorable sentence in Joyce's *Ulysses* from 1922 capturing this desperate moment: 'It is an age of exhausted whoredom groping for its god.'[6] In 1930 Bernardo Soares reflects that he was 'born in a time when the majority of young people had lost faith in God, for the same reason their elders had had it – without knowing why'.[7] In this context, Pessoa's shipwrecked, exiled and multiplied self in a peripheral landscape begins to make a lot more sense.

At the beginning of 1914, Pessoa was 25 years old. The Portuguese Republic was struggling through its fifth year of existence, while hanging on to its colonies in Angola, Mozambique, Guinea-Bissau and Cape Verde in Africa; the territories of Goa, Daman and Diu in India; and Macau and East Timor in Southeast Asia. During the next four years, the world would experience a series of upheavals: a global war with extraordinary advances of technology; the collapse of empires and old orders that would either disappear (such as the Hapsburg, Ottoman, Prussian and Tsarist) or be massively weakened (such as the British, French and Portuguese); the diaspora of displaced peoples and sudden rapid growth of the human population; the rise of new radical secular political and economic systems such as communism and fascism; new scientific breakthroughs spearheaded by Einstein's theory of relativity; and the explosion of the many '-isms' of various artistic movements across Europe. Álvaro de Campos would capture some of this chaos

and exhilaration in his ambitious odes, and wrote in one of them
that he was 'burning with all Europe' in his brain.[8]

The Age of '-isms'

From 1912 onwards, Pessoa was busy doing translations of his
favourite works, thinking about various literary projects and
starting new publishing houses, working as a copyist or copywriter,
and spending more and more time in the cafés in downtown
Lisbon reading local and international news and encountering
various other creative types. The meeting and friendship with
Mário de Sá-Carneiro was the most important of these encounters.
In October 1912 Sá-Carneiro moved to Paris, and he and Pessoa
began an intense and fruitful correspondence, sharing ideas as
equals, discussing their work and plans, and creating their literary
magazine *Orpheu*. New movements and modernist magazines were
in the making, and Pessoa, probably more than anyone else in
Portugal, tapped into the zeitgeist. He was aware of the modernist
literary magazines *Blast* and *The Egoist*. *Blast* was founded and
edited by Wyndham Lewis and published just two editions in the
summers of 1914 and 1915; *The Egoist*, founded by Dora Marsden,
lasted from 1914 to 1919 and was probably Britain's most important
literary periodical at the time as it published Eliot, Joyce, Ezra
Pound and D. H. Lawrence. Wyndham Lewis – writer, painter, critic
– created a London-based modernist art movement called Vorticism
and wrote most of the articles in *Blast*.[9] Vorticism was partly
inspired by Filippo Tommaso Marinetti's *Futurist Manifesto* of 1909,
with its celebration of speed, machines, violence, youth, energy,
progress and modernization.

As a teenager, Pessoa had already created imaginary literary
magazines, hoping to form a community of poets and eccentrics,
one example being *O Palrador* (which could be translated as
'tattler' or 'gossiper'). In this invented newspaper, conceived in
1902 while he was only thirteen years old, Pessoa created a host of
contributors such as Pip, Eduardo Lança, Dr Pancrácio and Diabo
Azul. Pessoa's own name was nowhere to be found. As an adult,

Pessoa involved himself in starting magazines and publishing houses or contributing poems, passages and essays to other people's magazines, as well as his own. These literary magazines (most of which had brief lifespans) included *Exílio*, *Centauro*, *Portugal Futurista*, *A Águia*, *A Renascença*, *Contemporânea* and *Athena*. In true modernist fashion, these projects were paradoxical as, on the one hand, they aimed to be cosmopolitan and for the world and yet, on the other hand, they were explicitly elitist and spoke only to the few. Pessoa actually said in the preface to *The Book of Disquiet*: '*Orpheu*

Mário de Sá-Carneiro, 1915.

speaks only to the very few.'[10] A tiny readership, however, is the fate of the avant-garde, and as pioneers and innovators of a particular period these publications went on to influence future generations.

By the end of the nineteenth century and the beginning of the twentieth, artistic movements such as Impressionism, Expressionism and Symbolism were starting to stick, and even more movements appeared in the early years of the twentieth century, such as Cubism, Formalism, Abstractionism and Futurism. It was during this period that the insatiably imaginative and intellectually restless Pessoa created his own new '-isms' of Portuguese literature, some of which were manifestos that were never completed while others were English and Portuguese documents of movements affiliated with particular heteronyms. Pessoa would conceive of Intersectionism (*Interseccionismo*), Atlantism (*Atlantismo*), Swampism (*Paulismo – paul* means 'swamp'), Neopaganism and, most importantly, Sensationism. He could well have gone further and created a movement of Impossibilism.[11] This was also a time when Pessoa had been meeting various other misfits from the worlds of poetry and painting, and they would regularly congregate at cafés in downtown Lisbon in Chiado's Café Brazileira (also spelled Brasileira), an emblem of modernist architecture which opened in 1905, for example, or Café Martinho da Arcada on the corner of Terreiro do Paço (now Praça do Comercio) facing the River Tejo – to scheme over potential literary projects. In later years, Pessoa spent a lot of his time at Café Martinho, writing poems and conversing with his literary friends, and today the table and chair where Pessoa used to sit are always kept empty out of respect for the poet of multitudes.

Swampism was a murky, ambiguous art and way of writing – Pessoa designates it in a notebook as an 'insincere cultivation of artificiality', but also inserted the word 'sincere' above 'insincere' without deciding which to use.[12] In his monumental biography of Pessoa, Richard Zenith defines the idea of Swampism as 'an exasperated symbolism, with suggestion, uncertainty, and mystery enveloping extravagant images in a shadowy world without time or geography'.[13] 'Swamps' ('Pauis') is the title of one of the first poems

Café A Brazileira, 1911.

Pessoa published in Portuguese as an adult. It appeared in February 1914 in *Renascença* literary magazine (which had only one issue) along with 'O Church Bell of My Village' ('Ó sino da minha aldeia'). Pessoa had written the poem 'Swamps' the previous year. It begins with the line: 'Swamps of yearnings brushing against my gilded soul', and gave rise to the movement of Swampism.[14] Sá-Carneiro liked the poem so much that he went on to master what he saw as the aesthetic of Swampism in his prose and poetry.

The Forest of Estrangement

In April 1912 Pessoa published his first text of criticism, titled 'The New Portuguese Poetry Sociologically Considered', in the literary magazine *A Águia* (The Eagle), which was based in Porto. The poet Teixeira de Pascoaes was a leading figure in *A Águia*. He subscribed to the doctrine of *saudosismo*, which has at its centre the concept of *saudade*, a kind of longing or nostalgia and perhaps the promise of a rebirth or renaissance of a new golden age for Portugal. In August 1913 Pessoa published a prose text called 'In the Forest of Estrangement' in *A Águia*. Not only was 'In the Forest of Estrangement' Pessoa's first published piece of creative prose, but it was the first one affiliated with *The Book of Disquiet*. It is written in the mode of Swampism – obscure and dreamy, and, like in the poem 'Swamps', many sentences trail off with an ellipsis. The reader also catches a glimpse of many of the recurring themes and preoccupations in Pessoa's writing over the next twenty years. Here is a selection of twenty key terms in Pessoa's oeuvre from this short text alone: lucid, dream, tedium, reality, landscape, 'brink of dawn' (*antemanhã*), *saudade*, nothing, disquiet (*desassossego*), feigning (*fingir*), contradiction, unknown seas, exile, absurdity, fog, madness, impossible, self, time's passage, death. Throughout its five pages, the seemingly exhausted narrator walks through a forest, accompanied by a shadowy woman, between sleeping and waking, in the interlude of things. This is the narrator and poet as living in between – in the interval, interlude, gap, chasm. He writes: 'this new reality – that of a strange forest – makes its appearance without effacing the reality of my warm alcove. The two realities coexist in my captivated attention, like two mingled vapours.'[15] In a forest, the logic of distinction falls away and all things intermingle, and we, as humans, cannot be certain of our senses.

Austrian poet Georg Trakl was another visionary who navigated between realities and conjured strange and disoriented visions in a dark forest. His poetry-in-prose piece called 'Dream and Derangement' feels like a German-language equivalent to Pessoa's 'In the Forest of Estrangement', which was published a few months before Trakl's text was written. Both texts were published on the eve of the First World War. Both narrators wander in a half dream through a dark wood, in a space where shadows reign supreme, and the human being is no longer in control as other lifeforms see, hear, smell, taste, touch and survive far better. That is the visceral way of nature, while the art of creation for Pessoa and Trakl is a form of magic, of conjuring magic, an attempt to become as radical as reality itself, to tap into and enter reality.

Intersectionism and Atlantism

Another movement or '-ism' conceived by Pessoa was
Intersectionism. He wrote an Intersectionist Manifesto and gave
it complete expression in a poem called 'Slanting Rain', which he
published in *Orpheu 2* in June 1915. In the one-page manifesto, he
pontificates over the definition and role of art, and also the meaning
of 'sensation', which is a prelude to his most enduring movement,
Sensationism. In answering the question 'what is art?', he writes:
'The attempt to give as clear and exact a notion as possible of
objects, understood not just as outer things but also as our thoughts
and mental constructions'.[16] This inclusion of 'objects' helps one to
understand what Pessoa is trying to get at with Intersectionism –
which is in fact art (at least it was for him while he was writing this
manifesto). The manifesto, never published during his lifetime,
concludes with the statement that Intersectionism is 'Intersection of
the Object with our sensation of it'.[17] He provides more intersections
for the reader when he writes, 'Reality, for us, is sensation. No other
immediate reality can exist for us,' and further on in the manifesto
he states: 'A sensation is composed of two elements: the object of
sensation and the sensation itself. All human activity consists in
the search for the absolute.' And finally: 'Art seeks Sensation in the
absolute. But sensation, as we've seen, is composed of the Object
of sensation and the Sensation itself.' Pessoa is obviously having
fun here with the typical jargon of the various artistic movements
of modernism, and, as usual, being stimulated by cerebral
philosophical gymnastics. But there is also something serious
going on behind this play – there is an interpenetration of reality,
art, the absolute and sensation. The most enthusiastic advocate of
Sensationism was Álvaro de Campos, who declared in his poem
'Time's Passage' ('Passagem das Horas'), which he was working on
in the previous year to 'Ultimatum', that we must 'feel everything in
every way'.[18]

   There was another, albeit very short-lived, movement called
Atlantism. This was swallowed up by Sensationism, but it is
worth considering for its influence on subsequent movements. It
is connected to the Atlantic Ocean – which links Ireland, North

and South America and the Iberian west coast, as well as being connected to all of West Africa, including the Portuguese colonies at the time such as Angola, Cape Verde and Guinea Bissau. However, Pessoa was of the opinion to let go of the African colonies, and he wrote in a notebook in 1915: 'Sell them off before they're taken from us.'[19] (The kind of empire that Pessoa was trying to forge and communicate is covered in Chapter Five.)

Sensationism

Intersectionism and Atlantism were assimilated or simply merged into Sensationism, to offer a more coherent vision of Pessoa's cosmopolitanism. There is a fascinating text that Pessoa wrote in English, probably in 1916, which could have been intended for Campos, or for one of Pessoa's minor heteronyms such as Sher Henay or the essayist and translator Thomas Crosse, who promotes Alberto Caeiro to the English-speaking world and is part of Sensationism's propaganda machine:

> The Portuguese Sensationists are original and interesting because, being strictly Portuguese, they are cosmopolitan and universal. The Portuguese temperament is universal: that is its magnificent superiority. The one great act of Portuguese history – that long, cautious, scientific period of the Discoveries – is the one great cosmopolitan act in history. The whole people stamp themselves there. An original, typically Portuguese literature cannot be Portuguese, because the typical Portuguese are never Portuguese. There is something American, with the noise left out and the quotidian omitted, in the intellectual temper of this people. No people seizes so readily on novelties. No people depersonalises so magnificently. That weakness is its great strength. That temperamental nonregionalism is its unused might. That indefiniteness of soul is what makes them definite.[20]

This passage is revealing in many ways. First, it shows how Pessoa is transforming a multiplicity of the subject into a fundamental characteristic of the Portuguese psyche. The passage mirrors Pessoa's own formation as a person and assigns to Portuguese identity the qualities of being dislocated and homeless and exiled in the transcendental and psychological sense ('nonregionalism'). It hints at the various imaginary personalities that accompanied Pessoa throughout his life ('depersonalises so magnificently'), and at the enigma, ambiguity and fogginess of the soul ('indefiniteness of soul'). It also highlights the ambiguity of being cosmopolitan. The Argonauts who sailed the unknown seas (who were followed by the argonauts of sensations, conquering the monsters in our imagination and in our consciousness) appropriated land, peoples and resources, and then divided these up or used them to the detriment of the colonized. The verb 'to explore' in Portuguese signifies this ambiguity and deception: *explorar* can mean both 'to explore' and 'to exploit'.

The cosmopolitan movement of Sensationism needed a literary outlet through which Pessoa could articulate and spread its universal and experimental literature. Pessoa was working on an 'Anthology of Intersectionism', which never came to fruition, when he turned to the idea of a magazine called *Europa*, which also failed to materialize. This was in 1914, a pivotal year for Pessoa and for Europe. Archduke Franz Ferdinand, and his wife Sophie, of the Hapsburg Empire were assassinated in Sarajevo, setting off a domino effect that undermined political allegiances and led to the First World War. Turning from social–political events to the personal level, the 'Triumphal Day' of Pessoa's life occurred on 8 March 1914, when he declared the appearance of Alberto Caeiro. Three months later, Álvaro de Campos and Ricardo Reis emerged. In November 1914 Pessoa rented a room on Rua de Dona Estefânia 127, and he and Sá-Carneiro (who was in Paris) began plotting the creation of the landmark literary magazine *Orpheu*. This avant-garde journal would be a futuristic counterpoint and provocative affront to Teixeira de Pascoaes and his circle and projects. Pessoa and Sá-Carneiro would only manage to publish two editions: *Orpheu 1* in March and *Orpheu 2* in June. But it was the first public documentation of the genius of Pessoa as a poet and feigner.

Orpheu

The name of the magazine is significant. Orpheus was the great bard of ancient Greek mythology whose playing could enchant anyone, even in the depths of hell. He was also an Argonaut who voyaged with Jason in the search for the Golden Fleece. He is credited with the composition of *Orphic Argonautica*. There is a Greek legend that tells of how Orpheus went down into the underworld of Hades to retrieve his dead wife, Eurydice. He was one of the few mortals to have been to the underworld and to return again to the surface. Even in the underworld his music was irresistible, and Hades and Persephone granted his request to return with Eurydice. But he could only do so if he walked ahead of her and did not look back until they had both reached the upper world. When he had made it to the surface, he turned around in his excitement, forgetting the condition, and Eurydice, who had not yet crossed over, disappeared forever. He is a tragic figure: after all the hard work had been done, he could not help himself and had to look back to see if his lover was still behind him, and so lost her. The writer Maurice Blanchot concluded a short piece on Orpheus by stating: 'Writing begins with Orpheus's gaze.'[21] The gaze is a symbol of desire. Everything is risked in looking back, more so than in descending into the underworld in the first place. In the story of Orpheus, we encounter faith, tragedy, daring, death, song and the descent into the subconscious of an artist. Eduardo Lourenço wrote in his essay 'Pessoa, or Reality as Fiction': 'Bearer of life for those excessively dead and death for those excessively alive, like Orpheus, he [Pessoa] performs for us a descent into the hell of modern subjectivity.'[22]

Orpheu elevated literary modernism to the avant-garde in Portugal. It is not only where some of Pessoa's finest pieces can be found, but it was also the first time the Portuguese public was faced with such audacious and experimental literature. Alongside Pessoa and Sá-Carneiro, various creative and political figures who debuted in the magazine went on to become famous in the country beyond the realm of literature, including Antonio Ferro, who later became director of the Secretariat of National Propaganda for the Estado Novo. Alfredo Pedro Guisado and José Almada Negreiros

Cover of *Orpheu 1* (1915), with a drawing by José Pacheco.

also contributed poems to *Orpheu*. The latter's famous modernist oil portrait from 1954 of Pessoa with a copy of *Orpheu 2* on his writing table was exhibited at Guisado's brother's café Irmãos Unidos, located in Rossio in downtown Lisbon. *Orpheu* contained an all-male troupe, except for one female contributor called Violante de Cysneiros. However, she was actually a fiction whose poems were written by Armando Cortes-Rodrigues at the behest of Pessoa, who

José de Almada Negreiros, *Fernando Pessoa*, 1954, oil on canvas.

wanted there to be a female collaborator in *Orpheu*. The avant-garde artwork of the Futurist painter Santa Rita Pintor appeared in *Orpheu 2* in four abstract quasi-geometrical pieces, and Sá-Carneiro published his groundbreaking poem 'Manicure'.

In the first issue, Pessoa's only completed play, *The Mariner* (*O Marinheiro*), was published alongside the first two poems by Álvaro de Campos – 'Opiary' ('Opiário') and 'Triumphal Ode' ('Ode Triunfal'). In the second issue, there is an experimental Intersectionist poem in six sections called 'Slanting Rain' ('Chuva Oblíqua') and Álvaro de Campos's operatic masterpiece 'Maritime Ode' ('Ode Maritima'). Despite the successful publication of the first two editions, the third issue was never completed. It might have turned out to be even more daring than the first two, as it was meant to include experimental Symbolist poet Camilo Pessanha (who was living in Macau and greatly admired by Pessoa),[23] the new rising star of painting Amadeo de Souza-Cardoso from the north of Portugal, and a wild homoerotic poem by Álvaro de Campos called 'Salutation to Walt Whitman'. However, the third issue was halted when it was almost ready to go to the printing press. Sá-Carneiro's father, who was living in Mozambique, financed the first two issues but refused to continue his support. Then there was Sá-Carneiro's

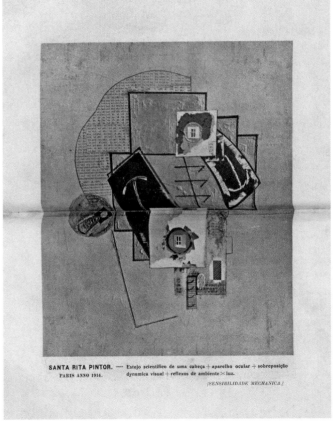

Santa Rita Pintor, *Scientific One-Head Case + Ocular Apparatus + Visual Dynamic Overlap + Ambient Reflections x Light (Mechanic Sensitivity)*, 1914, reproduced in *Orpheu* 2.

Cover of *Orpheu 2* (1915).

suicide the following year. Another factor in the closure of the magazine might have been Pessoa's persistent incapacity to stick at things. The publication's combination of poetic experimentation, punk attitude, sexual ambiguity, the celebration of instability and madness (one of the contributors, Ângelo de Lima, was in an asylum from 1901 until his death in 1921) and promotion of diversity and freedom enthralled a new generation of artists and poets while scandalizing the small literary establishment.

The shadow of death plagued the magazine. In 1916 Sá-Carneiro died at 25 years of age, while two years later, in 1918, Santa-Rita Pintor died of tuberculosis at the age of 28 and Amadeo de Souza-Cardoso died of the Spanish flu at the age of 30. Pessoa's play *The*

Mariner in *Orpheu 1* was dedicated to Carlos Franco, whose name was inscribed underneath the title. Franco was a painter and set designer, and quickly became good friends with Sá-Carneiro and Pessoa. Pessoa was writing the play when they met in 1913. With little work opportunity in Lisbon, Franco joined the French Foreign Legion, and died at the age of 29 in the Battle of the Somme in 1916. The two co-directors of the first issue of *Orpheu* died later in violent circumstances. The Brazilian poet Ronald de Carvalho died in a car

Amadeo de Souza-Cardoso, *Trou de la serrure PARTO DA VIOLA Bon ménage Fraise avant garde*, 1916, oil and pochoir on canvas.

crash in Rio de Janeiro at the age of 41 in February 1935, and Luís de Montalvor died in March 1947, also in a road accident, along with his wife and only son, who was driving the car in which they perished. The event is still shrouded in mystery, but the story is that they drove into the River Tejo and all of them drowned.

The etymology of *Orpheu* can possibly be related back to the word 'orphan' – which would resonate with the inner sense of absence, exile and loss experienced by both Pessoa and Sá-Carneiro. Although Pessoa was not an orphan, he did experience the death of his father at the age of five, and found himself on a ship sailing to the south of Africa at the age of seven. He was alone when he returned to Lisbon almost ten years later to begin life as an adult. Sá-Carneiro's mother died when he was two years old, and he was brought up by his grandparents. To be homosexual at that time, as Sá-Carneiro possibly was, would have meant a feeling of being different and an outsider and learning to wear a mask in public. To be a writer also entails learning to wear masks and to wander off the beaten track to return again with insight. It is no accident that the great novel of American modernity, *Moby-Dick*, ends with the word 'orphan' and begins with the word 'Call'. The call here could be a call or invocation of the poet as they begin their errant journey.

Pessoa's calling was to become the poet of multiplicities. He invented the concept of heteronymy from the feeling of being an absent and exiled soul, a kind of orphan facing the void of modernity and beyond. The printed pages of *Orpheu* give a glimpse of his imagination captured in poems such as 'Triumphal Ode' and 'Maritime Ode' and the play *The Mariner*. To explain Sensationism to the world, Campos wrote (in English, though only published posthumously): 'There are only two interesting things in Portugal – the landscape and *Orpheu*.'[24] After *Orpheu* folded, its status only grew and Pessoa's landscape expanded. The plurality of the subject continued with his three major heteronyms, who kept producing work as they conversed with each other and with Pessoa, exhibiting reality in fiction while fictionalizing reality.

4

Heteronymy and the Plurality of the Subject

And so I created a nonexistent coterie, placing it all in a framework of reality.

Fernando Pessoa[1]

To say that the poet only exists after the poem means that he receives his 'reality' from the poem, but that does not dispose of this reality except in order to make the poem possible. In this sense he does not survive the creation of the work. He lives by dying in it.

Maurice Blanchot[2]

Poets are tricksters, alchemists, seers of multiplicities. They feel, channel and condense our emotions into verse. 'O poeta é um fingidor.' So begins Pessoa's famous poem 'Autopsychography' ('Autopsicografia'), dated 1 April (April Fool's Day) 1931, which was published in 1932 in *Presença*, an important literary magazine founded by João Gaspar Simões (Pessoa's first biographer) and Branquinho da Fonseca and based in Coimbra, giving voice to modern poets in Portugal. *Fingidor* is a difficult word to translate. It could be rendered as faker, pretender, forger or deceiver. Following other readers and translators,[3] I will stick with 'feigner', as it alludes to Shakespeare's play *As You Like It*: 'No, truly; for the truest poetry is the most/ feigning; and lovers are given to poetry, and what/ they swear in poetry may be said as lovers they do feign' (III.3). For Pessoa, Shakespeare was the greatest and most enigmatic poet of them all, and in these lines we encounter both a negative and an assertion of truth in the first two words. This is followed

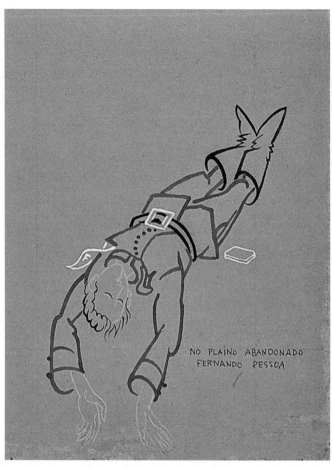

Pessoa lying down, with the words 'no plaino abandonado' (on the abandoned plain), mural painting by José de Almada Negreiros, one of the mural projects commissioned by the city of Lisbon between 1938 and 1956, on the entrance wall of the Faculty of Humanities, University of Lisbon.

by a paradoxical declaration that the truth of a poem lies in its feigning. It is similar to a line in Henrik Ibsen's play *Peer Gynt*: 'To speak, yet keep silent – confess; yet conceal,' says the protagonist, a feigner and shapeshifter who lived frivolously as if he was always in a play.[4] Bernardo Soares ponders a similar issue in *The Book of Disquiet*: 'The most abject of all needs is to confide, to confess . . . Be lucid: let expression, for you, be synonymous with lying.'[5] Peer Gynt and Bernardo Soares resonate with the monster in revealing and concealing at the same time.

The *Fingidor*

Following the trajectory of the poet-philosopher, we find the element of feigning and the link between concealing and revealing in figures from Kierkegaard to Nietzsche, Heidegger to Derrida. Kierkegaard began his first book, *Either/Or*, with the question: 'What is a poet?' His answer was: 'An unhappy person who conceals profound anguish in his heart but whose lips are so formed that as sighs and cries pass over them they sound like beautiful music'.[6] Mirroring the opening lines of *Either/Or*, the first verse of 'Autopsychography' goes like this:

> The poet is a feigner
> He feigns so completely
> That he even feigns the pain
> The pain that he really feels.

> (*O poeta é um fingidor
> Finge tão completamente
> Que chega a fingir que é dor
> A dor que deveras sente*.)[7]

'Autopsychography' is officially authored by Pessoa, but Kierkegaard's name is nowhere to be found in his eight-hundred-page literary-philosophical work. Instead, Kierkegaard's book is filled with pseudonyms with different points of view. Nietzsche often brings up the mask in his writings, and although he signs his books with the name 'Friedrich Nietzsche', he offers a multiplicity of perspectives and contradictory moods, not only in the different books but within the books themselves. For Nietzsche, after all, 'truth' is not fixed or stable, but rather a 'mobile army of metaphors'.[8] In *Beyond Good and Evil*, he writes: 'Every profound spirit needs a mask: what's more, a mask is constantly growing around every profound spirit, thanks to the consistently false (which is to say shallow) interpretation of every word, every step, every sign of life he displays.'[9] Later on in the same book, he concludes a section with: 'Every philosophy also *conceals* a philosophy; every opinion is also a hiding-place, every word also a mask.'[10] In the twentieth century, Heidegger explored the Greek word *aletheia*, meaning 'truth'. Heidegger dissects the etymology of the word to show it contains both revealment and concealment: *letheia* means 'conceal' and the prefix 'a' means 'un-', giving us 'un-conceal'. Ibsen's confess/conceal dynamic is also evident here. In the wake of Nietzsche and Heidegger, Derrida, a philosopher intoxicated with double entendres and dissolving the boundaries of fixed meanings, wrote: 'The god of writing is thus at once his father, his son, and himself . . . Sly, slippery, and masked, an intriguer and a card, like Hermes, he is neither king nor jack, but rather a sort of *joker*, a floating signifier, a wild card, one who puts play into play.'[11]

For an artist in modernity, the mask is often needed for protection and the liberation of expression, as writers such as Nietzsche, Kierkegaard, Wilde and Pessoa have found. Perhaps Sá-Carneiro lacked a mask, which might have made him vulnerable to the suicidal thoughts he eventually acted on. But Pessoa could assign suicidal thoughts to one of his heteronyms, who would do the deed so he could go on. For example, he created the Baron of Teive, who despaired of not being able to finish works or of creating works of perfection, and so committed suicide in his despair. Ever the mischief maker, Campos wrote in a one-page prose piece called 'Environment' ('Ambiente') that he published with *Presença* in 1927: 'To feign (*Fingir*) is to know ourselves.'[12] To live is to act and perform; we cannot help ourselves as humans. We often yearn for the life we cannot have, while fictional figures would like to have our lives. As a Hollywood executive says in Woody Allen's meta-film *The Purple Rose of Cairo* (1985): 'The real ones want their lives fictional, and the fictional ones want their lives real.'

In a recent text called 'Propositions on the Philosophical Nature of Poetry', Alessandro de Francesco writes that 'Pessoa's notion of *fingidor* gives fiction a meaning that differs from what Plato's idea of poetic truth intended: Pessoa's heteronyms disperse linguistic subjectivity to encounter the world.'[13] Pessoa, in coining the term 'heteronym' and creating this plurality of the subject in his literature, broke the spell of Plato more resolutely than Nietzsche did. Philosophy is still trying to catch up with Pessoa's ability to triumph in dissolution and create a new kind of selfhood rather than clinging to the ideal of a singular subjectivity. Examples of this are expressed in the heteronyms themselves. As early as 1915, in 'The Tobacco Shop', Campos writes: 'How should I know what I'll be, I who don't know what I am?/ Be what I think? But I think of being so many things!'[14] In 1932, Soares writes: 'Each of us is several, is many, is a profusion of selves. So that the self who disdains his surroundings is not the same as the self who suffers or takes joy in them. In the vast colony of our being there are many species of people who think and feel in different ways.'[15] In the same year, Pessoa begins a poem with the declaration: 'I am an anthology./ I write so variously.'[16] And as late as November 1935, two weeks before Pessoa's death, Reis begins an untitled poem with the line: 'Countless lives inhabit us.'[17] It seems that Pessoa and his 'non-existent coterie' were all coming to the same conclusion: they were a multiplicity of selves within their own selves.

For Pessoa, the real birth of the heteronymic universe began on 8 March 1914, or 'Triumphal Day', when Alberto Caeiro, the master heteronym, emerged for the first time, or as Pessoa wrote in a letter: 'my master had appeared in me.'[18] But it was only in December 1928 that Pessoa first mentioned the words 'heteronymity' and 'heteronomous' (the Greek root *hetero* means 'other' and *nym* means 'name'), in another one-page text he published in *Presença* called 'Tábua Bibliográfica' (Bibliographical Summary). Here he distinguished between the pseudonymous and the heteronymous: 'The pseudonymous work belongs to the author in his own person, except in the name that he signs; the heteronymous work is by the author outside his own person, it is of a complete individuality manufactured by him, like the words of any character in one of his dramas.'[19] In the same text, Pessoa famously wrote that his heteronymic universe is 'a drama in people, instead of acts'. Solidifying this idea, he wrote in a letter to João Gaspar Simões on 11 December 1931: 'The central point of my personality as an artist is that I'm a dramatic poet; in everything I write, I always have the poet's inner exaltation and the playwright's depersonalization.'[20] One can hear echoes of Shakespeare but also John Keats, the Romantic poet, in one of his letters to Richard Woodhouse:

> As to the poetical Character itself . . . it is not itself – it has no self – it is every thing and nothing – It has no character – it enjoys light and shade; it lives in gusto, be it foul or fair, high or low, rich or poor, mean or elevated – It has as much delight in conceiving an Iago as an Imogen. What shocks the virtuous philosopher, delights the chameleon Poet . . . A Poet is the most unpoetical of any thing in existence; because he has no Identity – he is continually in for – and filling some other Body – The Sun, the Moon, the Sea and Men and Women who are creatures of impulse are poetical and have about them an unchangeable attribute – the poet has none; no identity – he is certainly the most unpoetical of all God's Creatures.[21]

The poet is a Zelig-like persona: a sieve, incognito, nondescript, a multiplicity, changing with the colours it encounters. In a preface that he never published to a planned volume of his complete heteronymous works, Pessoa stated: 'The human author of these books has no personality of his own,' and he has 'nothing to do except as their publisher'.[22] Kierkegaard revealed something similar about his own relationship to his writing strategies in relation to his pseudonyms at the end of a large philosophical work which he had planned to be the last of his pseudonymous texts: 'Thus in the pseudonymous books there is not a single word by me. I have no opinion about them except as a third party.'[23] Kierkegaard also called his authorship here a 'polyonymity'.[24] Thus Kierkegaard's fictional authors are located somewhere between heteronymity and pseudonymity. At the end of the same letter on 'the poetical Character itself', Keats wrote: 'But even now I am perhaps not speaking from myself: but from some character in whose soul I now live.' Pessoa does a similar thing at the end of a letter (that he never sent) to an English editor: 'I was a pagan, however, two paragraphs above. I am no longer as I write this. At the end of this letter I hope to be already something else.'[25]

In a letter to Adolfo Casais Monteiro, editor, critic and translator, Pessoa wrote: 'I placed all my power of dramatic depersonalization in Caeiro; I placed all my mental discipline, clothed in its own special music, in Ricardo Reis; and in Álvaro de Campos I placed all the emotion that I deny myself and don't put into life.'[26] He sent the letter on 13 January 1935, the year of his death. At one point, Pessoa had a plan to publish a book presenting the panorama of his heteronymous universe, which would have included a philosophical

Pessoa's three heteronyms, mural painting by José de Almada Negreiros, on the entrance wall of the Faculty of Humanities, University of Lisbon, 1938–56.

introduction on Caeiro and neopaganism by Ricardo Reis followed
by the complete poems of Alberto Caeiro. The book would have
concluded with a text by Álvaro de Campos called 'Notes for the
Memory of my Master Caeiro', which recounted Campos's first
meeting with Caeiro and the philosophical conversation between
Caeiro and his disciples – Reis, Pessoa and Campos. The book
would also have included a horoscope of Caeiro cast by Pessoa.
This could have been Pessoa's finest achievement and one of the
masterpieces of the twentieth century. Alas, it was not to be. What
we have instead are Caeiro's poems, fragments and unfinished
texts from Reis's introduction, and parts of Campos's 'Notes for
the Memory of my Master Caeiro'. These unfinished 'Notes' were
written in the 1930s and offer a dazzling display of imagination
and philosophizing. They are also funny – an overlooked aspect of
Pessoa's writings. It was only from 1924 that the public first caught
a glimpse of the depth and width of Pessoa's heteronymic universe,
as the poems of Caeiro and Reis were published for the first time in
Athena, a magazine founded by Pessoa. Pessoa first thought about
setting up a magazine dedicated to neopaganism in 1915, but it did
not make its first appearance until 1924. He came up with the title
and was the magazine's literary editor, with the goal of bringing
paganism back to Portugal and showcasing his 'drama in people' via
his poems and essays.

Alberto Caeiro

For Pessoa, Alberto Caeiro was his most perfect creation because he
was entirely distant from his creator. Born in Lisbon on 16 April 1889,
Caeiro lived all his life in a whitewashed house in Ribatejo, an inland
region of Portugal, by the River Tejo (*riba* is the Portuguese word
for 'bank' or 'side' (of the river, for example)). Like Pessoa's father
and brother, Caeiro died of tuberculosis in 1915. He had little or no
education, and his poetry was simple in its use of vocabulary, syntax
and phrasal structures. It was not rhymed. But there is a deception
in this simplicity. In advocating the opposite of learning, Caeiro is
still greatly indebted to poets such as Walt Whitman and Cesário

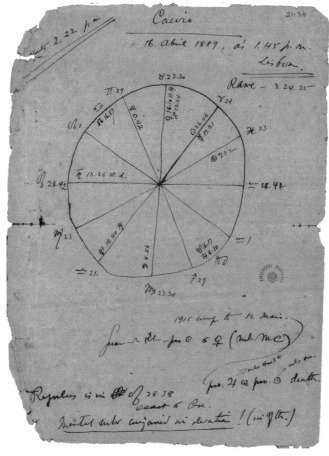

Pessoa's astrological chart for Alberto Caeiro.

Verde, and it is obvious that he has deep knowledge of Western philosophy and theology. But the poetry has a childlike quality, and it is immediately accessible to everyone.

Caeiro left behind a body of poetic work in three parts: *The Keeper of Sheep* (*O Guardador de Rebanhos*), *The Shepherd in Love* (*O Pastor Amoroso*) and *Uncollected Poems* (*Poemas Inconjuntos*). In the first poem in *The Keeper of Sheep,* he wrote that his soul is like a shepherd, knowing the wind and the sun, and walking hand in hand with the seasons.[27] The symbol of the shepherd has different connotations: as well as being nomadic and bucolic, it can also be religious and philosophical. In religion, there is the image of Christ as the Good Shepherd and the priest as the pastor of the faithful sheep. Many of the key Judaeo-Christian figures of the Old Testament, such as Abraham, Isaac, Moses and King David, were all shepherds. In philosophy, Plato's dialogue *Critias* uses the metaphor of humans being the cattle of the gods who guard and protect them.[28] Heidegger, who was born only a year after Pessoa, wrote of the task and claim on the human being as 'the shepherd of being'.[29] Both Heidegger and Caeiro offer a radical new conception of the shepherd. Caeiro wanted to start again, and forget all that he had learnt. Heidegger's shepherd aims to help us really philosophize by wandering strange paths in dark forests, by stepping off the beaten track (Heidegger used the word *Holzwege*[30]). Caeiro's shepherd also wants to help us. He wants us to see nature anew; to see the flowers and rivers again in reality; to be freed even from time, analysis and doubt; and to encounter innocence a second time.

In poems, the metaphor of sheep often relates to the scattered people that a shepherd will shelter, guide and protect. But many of these poems read as tautologies, and the 'sheep' in the poems are the poet's thoughts, which are in turn sensations, as stated in the ninth poem from *The Keeper of Sheep* ('The sheep are my thoughts/ And each thought a sensation').[31] The name 'Caeiro' itself has allusions to the sacrificial lamb and to a metaphorically disembodied animal. The word *Carneiro* means 'sheep' in Portuguese, so Caeiro could be read as a 'sheep' without the bones or flesh, as it lacks the two central consonants (Ca(rn)eiro). The name 'Caeiro' is also a nod to Pessoa's great friend Mário de Sá-Carneiro who, like Caeiro, died young. These early deaths bring to mind a saying by the Greek poet Menander: 'whom the gods love die young,' which Pessoa quoted in his eulogy to Sá-Carneiro in *Athena* in 1924 (it has also been quoted by Byron and Leopardi, whom Pessoa read and admired).[32] Finally, the name 'Caeiro' evokes the ram that symbolizes Aries, his star sign. Caeiro was born in spring, the time of the blooming of flowers, lambs and the resurrection of Jesus. He is a Zen-like, bucolic vision who is at the same time ancient and strikingly new; his writing resonates as a guide to both materialist philosophies and religions.

The cycle of poems known as *The Keeper of Sheep* opens with these words: 'I've never kept sheep/ But it's as if I had' (*Eu nunca guardei rebanhos/ Mas é como se os guardasse*). In the original Portuguese, the declaration starts with the words '*Eu*' (I) and '*nunca*' (never) – a first-person singular pronoun followed by an absolute negation – but the intensity of the sensations turns this absolute negation into an absolute reality beyond space and time. In the first two lines, we immediately enter key qualities of Pessoa's reality in the impossible, the nothing and the monster. Caeiro is a paradox, a disincarnated heteronym in the eternal present, who nonetheless declares himself to be a mystic but only with his body. He is the self-declared 'Discoverer of Nature', 'Argonaut of true sensations' and 'the only poet of Nature', because he 'noticed the Universe'.[33] Caeiro is depicted as the poet of the Sun, of the eternal present, living out in the countryside, unlearning everything that Western civilization has taught him, having 'no ethics except simplicity'.[34] Lourenço fittingly began an essay on Caeiro with a motto from Immanuel Kant's *Critique of the Power of Judgment*: 'An art of being naive is thus a contradiction; but it is certainly possible to represent naïveté in a fictional person, and this is a beautiful although also rare art.'[35] There is also a contradiction in Caeiro being the most philosophical heteronym as well as being the most critical of metaphysics, thinking and the activity of philosophizing. Caeiro goes one step further than Pessoa in his critique of Descartes' *cogito ergo sum*. Rather, for Caeiro, it would be: 'I think, therefore I am not.' For Caeiro, thinking paralyses, and to 'think about God is to disobey God'.[36]

Caeiro sits in the middle of Reis and Campos in both his year of birth (1889) and his location (Lisbon). But he is also in the middle in relation to time. Campos represents the future and Reis the past, while Caeiro represents the eternal present. Caeiro goes even further in saying that he does not even want the present, but reality itself: 'I want only reality, the things themselves, without any present.'[37] The thing in itself (*Ding an sich*), which is elusively referred to in

Kant's three Critiques, is the reality that simply is, after space, time and understanding have been articulated or postulated by human consciousness. But Caeiro is no Kantian; there is no separation between the object itself and its manifestation. Rather, for Caeiro: 'The astonishing reality of things/ Is my discovery every day.'[38] Caeiro is as radical as reality: 'Nothing returns, nothing repeats, because everything is real.'[39] There is no nostalgia, no resentment, no yearning. His poetry is a reversal of *saudade*.

For Caeiro, everything is real because everything is different. Different implies something singular, an animating essence which is perfect in itself. This relates to Spinoza's *Ethics*, in which he states: 'By reality and perfection I understand the same.'[40] Spinoza states in the final part of his system of philosophy: 'The more we understand particular things, the more we understand God.'[41] Caeiro attained reality by seeing things with the eyes and not with the mind. He made poetry from seeing a stone as a stone and nothing else. A philosopher tries to define it, see it as a representation of something, or as a subject or object of something. This also brings Caeiro close to the philosopher Henri Bergson, who took the view that conceptual thought cannot do proper justice to reality. As Caeiro explains to Pessoa, Campos, Reis and Mora in 'Notes in Memory of My Master Caeiro': 'The stone is not reality; it has reality. The stone is only stone.'[42] Caeiro's poetry is a kind of philosophy of vision, or what he called 'the science of seeing'. It is knowing how to see, and associating meaning with seeing. This can be understood in the common English sentence: 'I see what you mean.' Caeiro's wisdom is seeing nature as it is through our senses, seeing every aspect of reality as perfection, and seeing everything as different. It is not only in vision, but in all his sensations – his five senses are his thoughts, as he demonstrates in the ninth poem from *The Keeper of Sheep* where he thinks with his eyes, ears, hands, feet, nose and mouth, and writes: 'to think a flower is to see and smell it.' When asked by Campos what he was to himself, Caeiro replies, 'I'm one of my sensations.'[43] Caeiro attains and enters reality by feeling his whole body. He says in a fictional interview: 'I'm not a materialist or a deist or anything else. I'm a man who one day opened the window and discovered this crucial thing: Nature exists. I saw that the trees, the rivers and the stones are things that truly exist. No one had ever thought about this.'[44] The word and idea of 'window' is a poet's word; it is used throughout Caeiro's poetry, and is also present in the poetry of Campos. The Portuguese word for window is *janela*, which has a beautiful sound. The *janela* of Caeiro's solitary, whitewashed house on top of a hill has no curtains, which is like having no eyelids.

Ricardo Reis

The first of Caeiro's greatest disciples was Ricardo Reis, who was born in Porto on 19 September 1887. His star sign is Virgo, and he is the eldest of the three great heteronyms. His biographical details represent a lost past: the north of Portugal is where national consciousness and identity began. The astral sign Virgo is linked to antiquity: it is Latin for 'maiden' or 'virgin', and it is also the name for Persephone, the daughter of Demeter, the goddess of agriculture. Ricardo Reis is a classicist, a purist, a pessimist, a pagan and a monarchist. His philosophy is described by his brother Frederico as a 'sad Epicureanism'.[45] Campos has this to say about him:

> Ricardo Reis was a latent pagan, unable to grasp modern life and unable to grasp that ancient life into which he should have been born – unable to grasp modern life because his intelligence was of a different species, and unable to grasp ancient life because he couldn't feel it, for you cannot feel what isn't there to feel.[46]

Reis went to a Jesuit college, indicating a rigorous education that included the serious study of Latin and Greek thought and exposure to Christian catechisms. He is the opposite of Caeiro in terms of education and the level of sophistication in his use of language: his poems are strictly framed and he makes explicit references to other poets as well as to gods. He became a medical doctor who then emigrated to Brazil not long after the failure of a monarchical insurrection in Portugal in 1919. He only started writing poems after meeting Caeiro at the age of 25, mostly writing short odes in the style of Horace, the lyric poet of Roman antiquity. The quasi-Stoical poems are full of resignation. They are without hope and bow down to fate and are executed in a dignified and elegant manner. The poems have a cold, concise beauty to them; the words are painstakingly crafted in the Portuguese language, like chiselling finely shaped stones from rock. Reis begins one of his poems: 'I want my verses to be like jewels.'[47] But Pessoa would write: 'Reis writes better than I, but with a purism I find excessive.'[48] Reis was certainly transformed after meeting Caeiro. Once again, it is Campos who is entertaining and outrageous in recounting their meeting:

> Some physiologists say that it's possible to change sex. I don't know if it's true, because I don't know if anything is 'true', but I know that Ricardo Reis stopped being a woman and became a man, or stopped being a man and became a woman – as you like – when he met Caeiro.[49]

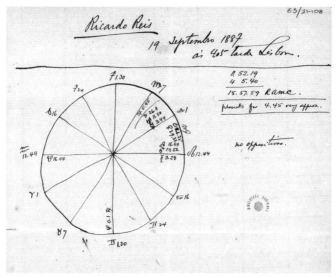

Pessoa's astrological chart for Ricardo Reis, with signature at the top.

Cover of *Athena*, 1/1 (October 1924).

Reis appeared for the first time in the public sphere in October 1924 in the first issue of *Athena*. Twenty odes of Reis were published, and the magazine would go on to publish half of the poems from Caeiro's *Keeper of Sheep* and sixteen poems from *Uncollected Poems*, two essays by Campos and twelve poems by Pessoa. Many of Reis's poems are speaking to one of his three ethereal muses – Lydia, Neera or Chloe. In the tenth ode published in *Athena*, Reis speaks of 'the three fates'. These three fates, knowns as *Moirai* in ancient Greek mythology, were the personifications of destiny. They were three sisters: Clotho (the spinner), Lachesis (the allotter) and Atropos (the unturnable, a metaphor for death). The words 'destiny' and 'nothing' permeate the poems of Ricardo Reis. The point is to see life from a distance, accept the fate of nothingness that awaits us, want nothing in order to be free, and in the meantime strive to create and capture beauty in verse. Greek and Roman gods appear throughout the poems, among them Apollo, Pan, Ceres, Neptune, Pluto, Adonis and Saturn. The fourteenth ode in the first issue of *Athena* is dedicated to Alberto Caeiro, Reis's master, whom he describes as 'like a god among singers,/ Who heard the voices that called from Olympus/ And hearing, listened/ And understood, is now nothing'.[50] In fact, for Reis, Caeiro enters the pantheon of pagan gods, as does Christ. But after Christ and before Caeiro, the gods disappeared. Many of his poems can only give resigned advice on living as death approaches, such as these two verses from a five-verse poem written in 1916:

> Follow your destiny,
> Water your plants,
> Love your roses.
> The rest is shadow of unknown trees.
> . . .
> But quietly imitate
> Olympus in your heart.
> The gods are gods
> Because they don't think
> About what they are.[51]

Álvaro de Campos

Álvaro de Campos – the youngest of the three central heteronyms – offers a stark contrast to Ricardo Reis. Campos accompanied Pessoa all his adult life from the moment he was conceived, and is the most productive and present of the heteronyms. He was born on 15 October 1890 in the old Arabic–Jewish village of Tavira in the Algarve, less than 30 kilometres (19 mi.) from the Spanish border. With echoes of the medieval myth of Ahasuerus, the so-called 'wandering Jew of despair', Pessoa notes that Campos is 'neither pale nor dark, vaguely corresponding to the Portuguese Jewish type'.[52] In his book *The Jewish Century*, the author Yuri Slezkine calls the twentieth century 'the Jewish Age', meaning that everyone is 'becoming urban, mobile, literate, articulate, intellectually intricate . . . learning how to cultivate people and symbols, not fields or herds'.[53] In essence, the age is modern and dynamic. Campos is urbane, mobile, an eternal wanderer, and suffers from a nagging despair that might be an implicit nod to Ahasuerus, whose myth Pessoa always had an interest in.[54] Campos means 'fields' in Portuguese. Álvaro de Campos has come from the fields, but will go on to embrace machines and the noise of modernity. His star sign is Libra, whose symbol of the scales represents oscillation, vacillation, doubt, double-mindedness and despair. He is bisexual,[55] and smokes opium, even though he says that he prefers thinking about smoking it rather than actually doing so. Being the youngest, Campos represents the future. He shares a birthday with Nietzsche, the philosopher of overcoming and the overhuman who declared that 'God is dead' and predicted that the next two hundred years would be an age of nihilism, who called for 'a tremendous multiplicity that is nonetheless the opposite of chaos',[56] and who said that he belonged 'to those machines which can explode'.[57] Campos himself would write in 1916: 'I am a great machine propelled by huge chains.'[58]

Being a sensationist, Campos wants to be and feel everything at the same time, and is eternally restless. It is worth quoting here a section from one of Campos's greatest yet lesser known poems (which has no title and remains unfinished). The words were probably written around 1916 in one of his moments of epiphany, capturing the character not only of Campos but of the philosophical and poetic vision of reality in Pessoa himself:

. . . the whole of reality is an excess, a violence,
An extraordinarily vivid hallucination
That we all share along with the fury of our souls,
The centre that draws in the strange centrifugal force
That is the human psyche when all its senses are in accord.

The more I feel, the more I feel like various people,
The more personalities I have,

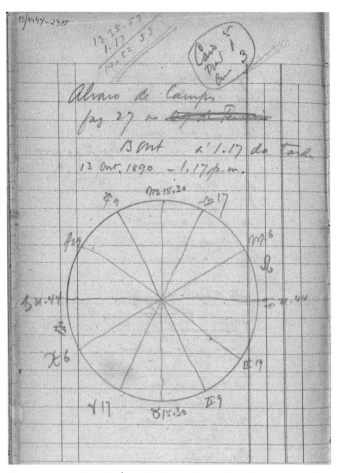

Pessoa's astrological chart for Álvaro de Campos. He would later change the date of birth to 15 October.

The more intensely, stridently, I have them,
The more simultaneously I feel with them all,
The more unifiedly diverse, disparately attentive,
That I am, feel, live, will be,
The more I will possess the total existence of the universe,
The more complete I will be in the whole of space . . .[59]

The ontology of Álvaro de Campos is succinctly expressed in his short prose piece 'Environment' in a deceptively simple sentence that is very difficult to translate: *Estar é ser*. Unlike the English language, Portuguese has two verbs for 'to be': that of permanence and that of change or movement. Thus this sentence could be translated, for example, as 'To be in flux is what it is to be,' or 'Where we are is who we are,' or 'To be is to exist.'[60]

Campos studies engineering in Glasgow: a fitting profession for a poet who represents the modern. The philosophy of engineering indicates productive operations and mechanics; the artist becomes an engineer, and the engineer becomes an artist. In studying naval engineering as well as mechanical engineering, Campos appropriates another trait of the Portuguese cultural soul. He goes off to work on ships and becomes a globetrotter, making his way down the Suez Canal on a steamboat and travelling to India and China. He works for some time in the shipyards in Newcastle upon Tyne, the most northerly city in England, before returning to Lisbon for good. Upon meeting Alberto Caeiro, he is inspired to create the movement of Sensationism. Campos declares in his unfinished magnum opus 'Time's Passage' that he wants 'to realize in oneself all humanity at all moments/ in one scattered, extravagant, complete, and aloof moment'.[61] The poems of Caeiro and Whitman are his inspirations to try to achieve this in his poetry, especially these lines by Whitman: 'Do I contradict myself?/ Very well then I contradict myself,/ (I am large, I contain multitudes.)'[62]

His poem 'Triumphal Ode' from *Orpheu 1* begins with these lines:

By the painful light of the factory's huge electric lamps
I write in a fever.
I write gnashing my teeth, rabid for the beauty of all this,
For this beauty completely unknown to the ancients.[63]

We are immediately brought into Campos's mind and vision of the world in 1915. In the third and fourth line we witness a break from the ancient world. Campos goes on to declare that the Greeks had no experience of the frenzy of the modern age of the twentieth century – in its speed, machinery, noise, electricity, mass production, mass media and communication, and the phenomenal growth of the human population around the world. The poem can be interpreted as a break or rupture with the authoritative foundation and official narrative of Western civilization represented by both Greek and Judaeo-Christian traditions. 'Gnashing my teeth' alludes to the descriptions of hell and damnation in the Bible, which Campos views as something to be relished in the feverish days of modernism. There is a fusion with something new. In 'Triumphal Ode' the narrator literally yells: 'If I could express my whole being like an engine!/ If I could be complete like a machine!'[64]

Campos uses engineering references to sign off two of his poems published in *Orpheu*. The first, 'Opiary', is signed off from the Suez Canal (an artificial waterway constructed by a feat of engineering in the nineteenth century); the second, 'Maritime Ode', is simply signed off as 'Álvaro de Campos, Engineer'. In the Portuguese language, the verb *engenhar* can also be translated as 'invent', 'contrive' or 'forge'. Campos inserts the verb at the end of 'Triumphal Ode' – which presents engineering as a construction, a creative machine from the modern world that contaminates and mingles with the empty inner self to find a new voice, or multiplicity of voices: 'I'm oblivious to my inward existence. I turn, I spin, I forge myself [*engenho-me*].'[65] Sonic effects contribute to the way the poems demand to be read aloud. Words morph into sounds in the fifth line of 'Triumphal Ode' ('r-r-r-r-r-r-r eterno'), and the penultimate line of the poem ('Z-z-z-z-z-z-z-z-z-z-z-z') is a prelude to the sound collage in the ecstatic sections in the middle of 'Maritime Ode'. 'Triumphal Ode' is signed off as 'London, June 1914'. In that year, London was the world metropolis and colonial capital of the world. In *Orpheu 2*, Campos composes his most ambitious and operatic poem, a thirty-page tour de force, 'Maritime Ode', which can be read as an attempt to conquer the oceans of his imagination. Eduardo Lourenço notes that this extraordinary poem is 'as vast as the sea itself'.[66] The poem was dedicated to Santa Rita Pintor, who died of tuberculosis three years after its publication. Campos tries to write even more audacious odes such as the incomplete 'Salutation

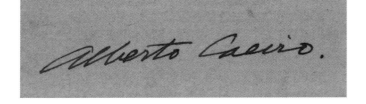

Lisboa, 28 de Fevereiro de 1922.

Pessoa's signatures (top to bottom): Pessoa, Caeiro, Campos.

to Walt Whitman' and 'Time's Passage'. But he overreaches and overstretches himself, becoming exhausted, which is what happens to the poet at the end of 'Maritime Ode', although that poet achieved the miracle of finishing and publishing the poem.

After the busy years of *Orpheu* and death of many of his collaborators, Campos fades into the background for a few years and goes almost silent before returning in a new resigned, reflective phase with the poem 'Lisbon Revisited: 1923'. From the second half of the 1920s onwards, Campos writes prolifically again and graduates to being an indolent, lonely idler in Lisbon. He is simply trying to be, but remains forever restless. While Caeiro resides in the realm of just 'being', Campos lives in the interlude of 'being' and 'doing'. He vacillates between embracing the machine's overactivity and the lack of necessity or will to do anything. Campos and Caeiro have diffcrent relationships to doing and being, and diverge in their response to the modern age of advanced technology and machines. Campos is a zeitgeist modernist poet alongside the industrialists, colonialists, capitalists and 'go-getters'. It is as if he is chasing after an exotic butterfly that flutters unpredictably in the breeze, but the chase is frustrated by the incessant noise and clumsiness of the chase. Alberto Caeiro, on the other hand, can be envisioned sitting down quietly or standing completely still, in Zen-like calm, letting the butterfly come to land on him, without noise, without chase, without seduction. He and the butterfly are simply located in reality.

Fernando Pessoa

The inventor of the heteronyms was a Gemini, the most playful and mutable of horoscope signs, which has the image of twins or a double. It is the chameleon sign that constantly juggles a variety of passions and interests. In 1913, before the emergence of his heteronymic trio of Caeiro, Reis and Campos, Pessoa wrote his only complete play (although there were many unfinished ones). It was *The Mariner*, and he published it two years later in the first issue of *Orpheu*. The subtitle is: 'A Static Drama in One Act'. Pessoa explained what he intended by static drama: 'as the one whose dramatic plot does not constitute action – that is, where the figures not only do not act, because they neither move nor talk about moving, but do not even have meanings capable of producing an action; where there is no conflict or perfect plot'.[67] The mysterious play is set in the dead of night, in a room in an old circular castle, with three speaking women who are watching over a female corpse lying in the centre of the room. There is a haunted fairytale quality and esoteric feel to the whole setting of the play. Is this a dream we are witnessing? Are these three watchers earlier versions of the three heteronyms who will be born one year later? There is talk among the watchers of a fifth character who is felt to be present with them. Is this fifth character their creator? Who is actually dead and who is alive, and how do we know when we are awake and when we are dreaming? The answers are not clear when reading the play, nor are they clear when listening to the watchers talk among themselves. One thinks here of two seventeenth-century plays: Calderón's *Life Is a Dream* (*La vida és sueño*) and Shakespeare's *The Tempest*, in which Prospero says: 'We are such stuff/ As dreams are made on, and our little life/ Is rounded with a sleep' (IV.1). In *The Mariner*, the First Watcher asks the question 'Why do people die?', and the Second Watcher answers, 'Perhaps because they don't dream enough.'[68] In his short story 'The Circular Ruins' (published five years after the death of Pessoa), Jorge Luis Borges wrote: 'In the dreamer's dream, the dreamed one awoke.'[69] This awakening in a dreamer's dream seems to be what happens in *The Mariner* when the Second Watcher tells the other two watchers of a dream she had of a mariner 'who seemed to be lost on a faraway island'. Is this a dream of reality or the reality of a dream? This question might be the answer to what the invention of the heteronyms is, which is an expression of the plurality of the subject, living simultaneous selves, articulating the three aspects of Pessoa's reality of the impossible, the nothing and the monster, and making poetry a mode of thought.

A small note by Campos ridiculing the play for being so dull and lacking any meaning reminds us of the humour and mischief that is present in Pessoa's work amid all this gloomy atmosphere, as well as the irony, intertextuality, modernism and postmodernism in this literary universe.[70] Once again, the invented one has the final word on the inventor. Campos's note was written in 1929 and published that year, but was given the fictitious date of 1915. Meanwhile, in November 1915 in South Africa, Pessoa's mother suffered a stroke that paralysed the left side of her body. Her mind was unaffected, and within half a year she was able to write letters again using her right hand. But the correspondence with her son was now far less frequent, due both to the pause in her letter writing after her stroke and to Pessoa's interior journeys and increasing distance in his outlook and relationship with his mother. In a piece called 'Aspects', which was another introduction to an unfinished volume on his heteronyms, Pessoa declared: 'I want to be a creator of myths, which is the highest mystery achievable by a member of the human race.'[71]

He is the empty vessel whose great myth-making achievement was the invention of the heteronyms Caeiro, Reis and Campos and their poetic output. Now, in the midst of a turbulent Europe of revolution, war, collapse of empires, new nations and despotic regimes, the second great myth-making objective was to provide the political and spiritual landscape in which his poets could flourish. What came next was to be a new renaissance, proclaimed by the myth of the Fifth Empire and Sebastianism.

5

Radical Politics and the Fifth Empire

I am, to be sure, a mystical nationalist, a rational Sebastianist. But I am many other things besides that, and even in contradiction to it.

Fernando Pessoa[1]

Throughout his life, Pessoa was a passionate social and political critic. He produced texts and articles, some of them published in newspapers, while political and societal events were unfolding. His opinions and perspectives would change, showing again the mutability and countless lives within even Fernando Pessoa himself, even though he invented no fully developed heteronyms to actually exclusively write on political ideas and current political affairs (although Álvaro de Campos dabbled in this arena as he did in everything else). Pessoa was an enthusiastic defender of the new republic in the first few years of its existence, but was then inspired by the 1917 *coup d'état*, which led to a military junta that lasted for a year. Pessoa wrote on such subjects as 'the non-latinity of Iberia', reflecting on Catalonia and Galicia, a theory of an aristocratic republic, liberal nationalism, Judaism, German culture and war, public opinion and tyranny.[2] In 1928, as Salazar was in the process of consolidating total power, Pessoa published a text on the necessity for dictatorship and tacitly accepted the Estado Novo (New State). But in the final year of his life, he criticized Salazar and repudiated his text on dictatorship, and called for universal humanity and liberty. In the background of all these events and changing opinions, there was the other reality that remained constant: the spiritual revolution of poets in his dream of the Fifth Empire.

Two things that did not change were Pessoa's quickness and astuteness of thought about the political situation of his time and his unwavering defence of free expression. On 5 April 1915, in between the publication of *Orpheu 1* and *Orpheu 2*, Pessoa published a text in a Lisbon newspaper called *O Jornal*. In it, he wrote: 'The sensibility and intelligence of a cultured and disciplined man are mirrors of the changing environment: he's a republican in the morning and a monarchist at dusk; he's an atheist when the sky is clear and sunny but an ultramontane Catholic at certain times of shadow and silence.'[3]

The shifting moods in this text show Pessoa's abiding love of contradictions and unwillingness to be pinned down. Pessoa never wanted to be aligned or committed to any party or dogma; the only thing he was sure of and would explicitly defend was the right to individual liberty. Groucho Marx's famous comment that he would not like to be a member of any club that would have him as a member is well suited to Pessoa. Three days later, in the same newspaper, Pessoa wrote: 'Let's cultivate, in ourselves, mental disintegration like a precious flower. Let's construct a Portuguese anarchy. Let's foster disorder and dissolution.'[4] This is not Campos or Soares speaking, but Pessoa in a daily newspaper during the fifth year of the republic, less than a year before the country entered the First World War when in March 1916 Germany declared war on Portugal. This reveals a destructive and decadent aspect of Pessoa, but his perspective might have been changing even as the piece was going to press. Pessoa was appalled by the takeover of Russia by the Bolsheviks. Extreme mass movements were an abomination to him, and he would later abhor Hitler and Stalin. But he was an articulate observer of the revolution and understood why these events occurred. In a text he wrote in English called 'The Military Dictatorship in Portugal' in *O Jornal*, more than ten years after these short pieces, Pessoa made some incisive observations on the revolutionary mind and state:

Revolutionary movements are formed, based on the general indignation and worked out by the more turbulent spirits . . . their positive existence is a negative one. Their life is what may be called a *critical* life, for their existence is involved and explained by the fact that they stand up against something and have life and being by virtue of that opposition . . . Once the revolution has triumphed, the critical attitude ceases, since the thing criticized has gone under. But, since the revolution has triumphed, the revolutionary spirit survives.[5]

The writing is neutral, clear and logical, while retaining ambiguity due to Pessoa's skill. In the same year, in 1928, Campos wrote 'The Tobacco Shop', whose original title was 'March of Defeat' ('Marcha da Derrota'). In this poem, the revolution is well and truly over, but the revolutionary spirit of the poet and his words are alive and well. The radicality of the poem's reality is executed with devastating effect, which can shake and inspire everybody – from the aspiring, imaginative, alienated student, to the intoxicated bohemian committed to the paradox of 'industrious indolence'[6], to the restless revolutionary who wants to violently overturn society.

Three Examples of a Civilized Nation

At the end of the day, Pessoa was more of a pragmatist in politics than he was in poetry. But Pessoa's admiration for ambiguous cosmopolitan political figures can be found in a brief note that he wrote in English between 1916 and 1918:

A nation which does not produce traitors can hardly be said to be civilized; a nation which produces too many cannot be said also to be. England is the example of a civilized nation, with such magnificent examples as the late Sir Roger Casement, Houston Stewart Chamberlain and Mr. Frank Harris.[7]

These three colourful and adventurous figures capture the contradictions of a nation and nationality, and also Pessoa's own shifting perspectives on civilization, on what it is and where it is going. Pessoa's choice of these three personalities reveals his psychological intelligence and uncanny and eccentric insights into European culture via seemingly marginal figures. The last, Frank Harris, was born in Ireland to Welsh parents in 1855. His father was a British naval officer. Harris proved himself an active vagabond from a young age, running away to New York as a penniless teenager, later becoming a cowboy outside Chicago, then studying law in Kansas. Growing tired of life in the United States, he returned to Europe and travelled around the Continent before settling in England. He became a journalist and a writer, publishing two books on Shakespeare, and befriending and writing biographies of Oscar Wilde and Bernard Shaw. During the First World War, he decided to return to the United States. A few years after Pessoa mentioned him as a member of a civilized nation, Harris gained fame and notoriety for publishing an autobiography called *My Life and Loves* (published in four volumes, 1922–7), which graphically described his sexual adventures – though he was famous for being a fabricator of his own life. He then returned to Europe and died in Nice in 1931. Both the sexual adventures and the fabrications would have deepened Pessoa's interest in Harris.

Houston Stewart Chamberlain was another mercurial, though more sinister, figure. He was born in England to English parents in 1855 and went to school in Versailles before attending an English boarding school. When he was an adult, he moved to Dresden, became obsessed with Richard Wagner and married the composer's daughter. He became interested in racial typology and botany, was a supporter of the Boers in the war in South Africa, and later became an influential and outspoken proponent of the idea of the Aryan race and antisemitism, mostly through his best-selling book *The Foundations of the Nineteenth Century*, published in 1899. He called himself an 'Evangelist of Race' and was a fully fledged Germanophile and passionate supporter of the German Empire during the First World War. He later befriended Hitler, calling him 'Germany's saviour' in the 1920s. Chamberlain died in Bayreuth in 1927 and was cremated there. Hitler was present at the funeral.

And then there is Roger Casement, an Irishman born in 1864 in Dublin to a Catholic mother and a Protestant father who served as a captain in the British Army, fought in the Afghan Campaign of 1842 and volunteered to fight in the Hungarian Revolution of 1848. Casement's father was a lover of Irish fairytales and supporter of Home Rule for Ireland. Casement grew up in England and the north of Ireland. Both his parents died when he was young, and as a teenager he started working as a clerk in a shipping company in Liverpool. He was soon off to Africa, where he ended up working in many capacities for the British Empire – initially helping to set up trading posts on the Congo River and then on special missions during the Boer War. In 1899 Casement was in Durban for a few weeks at the same time as Gandhi, Churchill and Pessoa. What a quartet! It was in South Africa that Casement began to have serious doubts about the moral authority of the British Empire. Casement would become famous all over Europe when his 'Congo Report' was published in 1904, exposing the atrocities being perpetrated in the Belgian Free Congo in the brutal system of extracting raw rubber in the jungle under the reign of Leopold II. In 1906 he sailed to Brazil, where he was posted as British consul in Rio de Janeiro, and while there travelled much of the country before producing another pioneering report, this time exposing the horrors being enacted in the rubber trade along the banks of the Putumayo River deep in the heart of the Amazon. Today, Casement is recognized as a pioneering activist in universal human rights. He was knighted for his exposé work in the Putumayo, but in 1913 he retired from the British service and joined the effort for Irish independence. He was eventually hanged as a traitor in 1916 for bringing arms from Germany in a submarine that landed off the southwest coast of Ireland. His moral reputation was destroyed as sections of his diaries, which aimed to show he was homosexual, were shared among the elite and his former allies and colleagues during his public trial. These particular diaries became known as the 'Black Diaries', and to this day scholars argue over their authenticity and whether they were tampered with or forged. Casement makes up the trio of figures who were adventurers, eccentrics, sexually ambiguous, feigners, manifestations of the multiplicity of the self, and traitors. They were cosmopolitan and cultured. They switched loyalties and redefined what it meant to be part of a nation. All of these facets combined would have delighted Pessoa.

'Ultimatum'

In October 1917 Campos published a sixteen-page manifesto called 'Ultimatum' in the one and only issue of *Portugal Futurista*. The magazine, which was organized by *Orpheu* collaborator Santa Rita Pintor, miraculously passed the censors but was seized by the police a month after publication. The manifesto was published in the same month as the Bolsheviks took power in St Petersburg and during the worst year of the First World War. It shows Campos at his wildest, most vitriolic and most political. In the first part of the manifesto, Campos rampages along, mocking famous contemporary writers, and damning all European nations for being traumatized by the collapse of European empires only thirty years after the continent of Africa was divided up among the leading powers of Europe at the infamous Berlin Conference of 1884. In the second part, he proposes a wild vision for the future of society. The two parts are divided by the outburst *MERDA!* in capital letters, meaning 'Shit!' The first part begins with the line: 'Eviction notice to the mandarins of Europe! Get out!' and from then on Campos never takes his foot off the pedal. Here is another example of the kind of language in 'Ultimatum': 'You, German culture, a rancid Sparta dressed with the oil of Christianity and the vinegar of Nietzscheization, a sheet-metal beehive, an imperialistic horde of harnessed sheep!'[8] Campos is the quasi-Nietzschean but at the same time stands against his generation's interpretation of Nietzsche. He ends the second part of the manifesto by describing what 'the Superman' will be: not the strongest, but the most complete; not the toughest, but the most complex; and not the freest, but the most harmonious. In this satire and tirade, what Campos has actually done is predict how Nietzsche will be read over a hundred years later.[9] When, in the second part, Campos declares that a philosopher should be an artist of thought and that no artist

Cover of *Portugal Futurista*, no. 1 (1917).

should have just one personality, he is closest here to what Nietzsche strove to show in his philosophy of experimenting with oneself and going against oneself in the art of endless becoming.

Campos outlines his desired political system in 'Ultimatum': '*In politics*: A Scientific Monarchy that will be antitraditionalist, antihereditary, and absolutely spontaneous, since the Average-King may appear at any time.'[10] One can never take Campos at his word – his words are sensations and his philosophy is a form of hysteria – but this 'Average-King' may well be an obscure, ambiguous, messianic, Sebastian-type figure who inspires all.

At the end of the year when the manifesto was published, on 5 December 1917, there was a *coup d'état* in Portugal and a charismatic general called Sidónio Pais became dictator. However, nine days later Pais was assassinated, setting off a cult of Sidonism in which Pessoa became active. Pessoa was growing tired of the republic, and now it became a case of Sidonism or Bolshevism. For Pessoa, Bolshevism was just a worse form of Christianity; both doctrines advocated slavery, a mass democracy of stupidity, and a curbing of the aristocratic liberalism and radical individualism that he ultimately desired. By 1919 Pessoa was playing the role of a full-blown reactionary, and began a collaboration with *Acção* (Action), a Sidonist journal, which was fiercely critical of the republic. He wrote pieces advocating Sidonism as a great symbol for Portugal, and in February 1920 wrote a long unpublished poem celebrating the cult of Sidónio Pais in which he envisions Pais as an incarnation of King Sebastian.[11] Here is an example of one of the many obscure, messianic verses:

Tall flower of the parish swamp [*paul*],
Brink of dawn [*Antemanhã*] of the great redemption
At a certain hour embodied by his highness
Don Sebastian.[12]

Meanwhile, in Pessoa's family life, his stepfather died in Pretoria on 7 October 1919. Almost six months later, at the end of March 1920, Pessoa's mother and her three grown children moved back to Lisbon. Maria Madalena would remain in Lisbon for the rest of her life, while Pessoa's two half-brothers moved to England. Pessoa, his half-sister Teca and their mother moved to Rua Coelho da Rocha 16 in the neighbourhood of Campo de Ourique. Pessoa would live there until the end of his life. After moving apartment over a dozen

Pessoa walking on the streets of Lisbon, 1920s.

times in twenty years, Pessoa would now spend the next fifteen years living in one place. Today, this address is the Museum of Fernando Pessoa (Casa Fernando Pessoa), which houses his personal library and is a haven for study and events related to Pessoa.

The Anarchist Banker

While living through these trail-blazing days and societal transformations in Europe, Pessoa's endlessly restless and creative mind kept shifting and experimenting. He was always up to date with current affairs and the latest innovative literature. In 1922 Pessoa wrote and published twelve poems and a short story called 'The Anarchist Banker' in the journal *Contemporânea*.[13] This was a key year in both literature and politics: Joyce's *Ulysses* was published, along with T. S. Eliot's *The Waste Land*, Hermann Hesse's *Siddhartha*, Carl Schmitt's *Political Theology* and the first part of *Sodom and Gomorrah* from Marcel Proust's *In Search of Lost Time*; Ludwig Wittgenstein's *Tractatus Logico-Philosophicus* was published in an English translation, and Rainer Maria Rilke wrote *Sonnets to Orpheus*. It was also the year when Mussolini marched on Rome and formed a fascist government in Italy, and Stalin became general secretary in the Soviet Union. In exile in Vienna, the Hungarian Marxist Georg Lukács finished probably the most famous and influential work of Western Marxism of the twentieth century – *History and Class Consciousness* – which was published in 1923, the same year as Sigmund Freud's *Ego and the Id*. Lukács's biographer Arpad Kadarkay comments on these two publications: 'Both works express, in their own way, the crisis of the modern soul, whose alphabet was written by war and revolution.'[14] His words could apply to nearly all the groundbreaking works of 1922.

'The Anarchist Banker' is Pessoa's only complete short story in Portuguese (though he also had a lifelong interest in writing detective stories). The twenty-page story is a showcase for Pessoa's contradictions and political stance as an aristocratic liberal. The 'anarchist' element represents the part of him that was against capitalism and mediocre order; the 'banker' is the part against mass movements. He referred to the story as a 'dialectical satire' in an unsent letter to the editor, José Pacheco.[15] In Hegelian–Marxist dialectics, opposites fuse together, out of which something new emerges, but this story is also a satirical jab at both working-class movements and our idea of what a banker is. Behind the mundane, self-contained, bourgeois banker, we might meet a Kierkegaardian 'knight of faith' or a radical individualist–nihilist of the Max Stirner type.[16] For the anarchist banker, social fictions are everywhere, and the banker and his interlocuter are most used to the bourgeois system. What the anarchist banker wants, like Pessoa himself, is freedom for himself and for all humanity, and to expose all social fictions. The anarchist banker explains that 'the "fight" isn't against the members of bourgeois society but against the body of social fictions on which the society is founded.'[17] And yet he has never helped others, for as he explains: 'that would infringe on their freedom, which is likewise against my principles.'[18] For the anarchist banker and for Pessoa, creative individuals transform societies, while mass movements and stupidity do not. Here is another glimpse of Pessoa's aristocratic liberalism: an aristocrat without the monarchy, and a liberal without being enslaved to democracy, Christianity or other more extreme mass movements.

O Estado Novo

As the 1920s wore on, the republic lost its popular support. Eight presidents were inaugurated and there were 44 cabinet reorganizations and 21 revolutions before the government was finally toppled by a military *coup d'état* on 28 May 1926. The new regime called itself a 'National Dictatorship', and included a little-known finance minister called António de Oliveira Salazar. This period was in effect a dictatorship, which lasted until 1974.

   During the 1920s and '30s, Pessoa continued to write a diverse array of texts on politics and society, culminating in a booklet called *The Interregnum: Defence and Justification of Military Dictatorship in Portugal*, which he published in March 1928. Mussolini, the triumphant exponent and inventor of the word 'fascism', had already been in power for six years in Italy, while Hitler was five years beyond his failed Munich putsch and five years away from becoming the Führer of Germany. Pessoa intensely disliked both because of 'the absolute banality of their ideas' and the fact they were driven by instinct rather than intelligence.[19] He described Mussolini as 'an overgrown child governing one of the first empires on which the sun could not set', and disdained Hitler's lack of a sense of humour, writing that 'his very moustache is pathological.'[20] In another note, written in English sometime in 1929 or 1930, Pessoa wrote that fascism 'is not action nor reaction, but mere partisan savagery'.[21] After drawing up a new constitution in 1933, the National Dictatorship in Portugal changed its name to Estado Novo, and Salazar became the dictator of the country for the next 36 years. He died in 1970, but the regime carried on through the height of the Cold War until 1974, when there was another military

Title page of
Fernando Pessoa,
O Interregno (1928).

coup d'état primarily due to the brutal and chaotic colonial wars that had being going on for over a decade in Angola, Guinea Bissau and Mozambique.

Pessoa defined his political stance in his 'Resumé' (1935): 'An English-style conservative, meaning that he is liberal within conservatism, and absolutely anti-reactionary'.[22] Pessoa became disenchanted with the Salazar regime, though he had never been that enthusiastic about it in the first place. As time went on, he saw that dictatorships held a hatred of the individual and were enemies of liberty, intelligence and humour. After Salazar's speech on 21 February 1935 on the Estado Novo's 'moral and patriotic principles', Pessoa wrote explicitly anti-Salazar poems. Instead of Salazar's famous declaration of 'Nothing against the Nation; everything for the Nation', Pessoa jotted down: 'Everything for Humanity; nothing against the Nation'.[23] In the last year of Pessoa's life, he repudiated his booklet *The Interregnum*. He had completely rejected communism, fascism and Salazar. When Italy invaded Ethiopia on 3 October 1934, Pessoa wrote and published an article denouncing Mussolini's regime: 'what are we all in this world if not Abyssinians?'[24] This was a far cry from Pessoa's earlier flirtation with supporting colonialism. A month before he died, Pessoa was calling out for freedom not just for the aristocratic liberal but for Abyssinia – the Ethiopian Empire. In the spring of the same year, Pessoa wrote a poem called 'Freedom' ('Liberdade'). There are two points in this poem that are worth considering in detail. The first is that Pessoa is responding to Salazar's speech from 21 February where the dictator had quoted these lines from Seneca: 'All kinds of orations and histories, on shelves reaching up to ceiling, adorn the home of the lazy man.' But Seneca had also famously written (in his Epistle 51 to Lucilius): 'You ask what freedom is? It means not being a slave to anything.' This sums up Pessoa's attitude, via his shifting points of view on society through an age of radical politics. This in a way is the response of a creative mind to political turbulence, with the intention of remaining true to freedom of thought. Pessoa could be accused of political escapism in his ideas of the Fifth Empire and Sebastianism, but his common sense and liking for British conservative liberalism would never permit him to embrace the Estado Novo and other such regimes that curbed and censored freedom of thought and expression. The second point is in the third verse: 'How much better, when it's foggy,/ To wait for King Sebastian,/ Whether or not he ever shows!'[25] This was the dream of the Fifth Empire and Sebastianism which had some playfulness but was more enduring, profound and closer to Pessoa's heart and mind than all the noise and fads of the day-to-day activities in the political arena.

The Dream of the Fifth Empire and Sebastianism

Eleven of the Twelve poems published in *Contemporânea*, which includes one of his most well-known poems, 'Mar Português' (Portuguese Sea), would later be included in the only book in

Cover of the first edition of *Mensagem* (1934).

António Ferro (left) and António de Oliveira Salazar (centre right), October 1933.

Portuguese that he published in his lifetime. The book came out on
1 December 1934 and was called *Mensagem* (translated as *Message*).
Antonio Ferro, an old friend from the *Orpheu* days, pushed and
encouraged Pessoa to publish a book and put it forward for a prize.
Ferro became director in chief in the bureau of the Secretariat of
National Propaganda in the Estado Novo in 1933. The prize was
granted by the Secretariat, but Pessoa only won second place. First
prize went to a largely forgotten book, *A romaria* (The Pilgrimage)
by Vasco Reis, a Franciscan priest and missionary. It was hugely
disappointing and surprising to Pessoa that he had not won, and
he began to regret having published the book, especially given its
association with the Estado Novo. This work became his most well
known over the next fifty years. *Mensagem*, which was called *Portugal*
right up until the moment of publication, contained 44 poems about
Pessoa's vision of mystical nationalism, providing many epitaphs
to the various kings, princes and navigators of the so-called 'age of
discoveries'. The final sections of the book travel further into the
mystic, with titles such as 'Fog', 'The Hidden One', 'The Desired One',
'Portuguese Sea', 'King Sebastian', 'Brink of Dawn' and 'The Fifth

Empire'. The third poem of the book is called 'Ulysses'. Pessoa was drawn to the myth of Ulysses because of an old and most likely false reading of Lisbon as the name of the port town which Odysseus was fabled to have founded. Pessoa famously began the poem with the sentence: 'Myth is the nothing that is everything.'[26] This may well be Pessoa's revolutionary vision for Portugal and for himself. It certainly relates to the invention of the heteronyms and his lifelong interest in the occult and esoteric writings.

The seventeenth-century Jesuit priest, diplomat and writer Antonio Vieira, who was born in Lisbon and moved to Brazil when he was six years old, first came up with the idea of the Fifth Empire. Vieira was perhaps Pessoa's favourite prose writer in the Portuguese language, and his book *The History of the Future* recounts a prediction by Gonçalo Anes Bandarra, a sixteenth-century shoemaker and prophetic poet, of 'a hidden king' who would bring a glorious period to Portugal. This would only happen after the fall of four previous empires (Babylon, Persia, Greece and Rome), and the evidence of this prophecy and of these four empires was supposedly to be found in the Old Testament Book of Daniel, chapters 2 and 7. However, for Vieira, 'the hidden king' would be Portuguese, and this would lead to the Fifth Empire. Thirty years before Vieira was born, King Sebastian of Portugal led his troops into the Battle of Alcácer Quibir (Battle of the Three Kings) in northern Morocco. The Portuguese forces were wiped out and the king disappeared into the fog. Sebastian was only sixteen years old, his body was never found and he had no heir, and for the next sixty years Spain ruled Portugal.

Over the centuries, Portugal's fortunes as a world power continued to decline, and King Sebastian became known as 'the hidden one' or 'desired one'; it was said he would return in Portugal's greatest hour of need, reappearing during a foggy dawn. To this day, when in the early morning Lisbon is enveloped with fog from the vapour rising from the River Tejo, some people say that King Sebastian is returning on a white horse. This is the messianic myth of Sebastianism, whose symbol extended into Brazil. At the end of the nineteenth century, thousands of peasants, vagabonds, bandits, ex-slaves and desperados gathered in a remote town called

Cover of Joaquim Correia da Costa, *Dom Sebastião* (1923).

Canudos in northeast Brazil, in the interior of the state of Bahia, in a backlands region known as the *sertão*. The mass movement of people to this settlement was led by a Christ-like figure called Antônio Conselheiro. He was known simply as the Counselor, and he preached the myth of Sebastianism to this rapidly growing community of poor and marginalized people. This group of outcasts rose up against the godless state of the new Republic of Brazil, which had come into power in 1889, a year after the end of the monarchy and abolishment of slavery in Brazil. A terrible war ensued between the community of Canudos and the republican army of Brazil that ultimately led to the complete annihilation of everyone in Canudos, including Antônio Conselheiro, and the town itself was burnt to the ground. Pessoa made a note on the leader:

> To the memory of Antônio Conselheiro, madman and saint, who, in the *sertão* of Brazil, died, as an example, with his companions, without surrendering, fighting them all, the last of the Portuguese, in the hope for the Fifth Empire and the coming when God wanted, of King Sebastian, Emperor of the World.[27]

In *Mensagem*, in the section called 'The Warnings' ('Os Avisos'), there are three poems dedicated to three poets who want to help bring about the Fifth Empire and the return of King Sebastian. The first poem is 'Bandarra', the second is 'António Vieira' and the third poem is simply called 'Third' ('Terceira'). The unnamed third poet is most likely Pessoa, who writes in the last verse of this poem and section:

> Ah, when will you want, returning,
> Turn my hope into love?
> From fog and longing when?
> When, my Dream and my Lord?[28]

For Pessoa, this Fifth Empire was to be a spiritual empire. He ventured to rearrange the four previous empires according to his idea of civilization. But there is always more than one idea or perspective for Pessoa. There is the Pessoa of India, and the Pessoa of Persia and the Rubaiyat. But the Pessoa of the Fifth Empire is a European Pessoa, and his four spiritual empires are the motors of European civilization: Greece, Rome, Christianity and Europe. Pessoa was quick to recognize that in the material world, the Fifth Empire is probably the British Empire; but in the immaterial world, it is Portuguese. Pessoa's task is to ensure a spiritualization of humanity. Changing the title of his only book in Portuguese from *Portugal* to *Mensagem* allows him to make a connection with a sort of pantheistic and alchemistic line from Virgil's *Aeneid*: 'Mens agitat molem' (The mind or spirit moves the material).[29] In a hermetic gesture, when one joins the first six letters of the Latin line with the last two letters, the word 'mensagem' is formed (*mens ag*[*itat mol*] *em*). Bernardo Soares had stated that in another age the Portuguese had mastered the physical ocean, now they would 'master the psychological ocean, emotion, mother human nature, thereby creating intellectual civilization'.[30] However, it is neither the priest nor the philosopher who will take on this task, but the poet. In the preface to the first edition of *Leaves of Grass* Walt Whitman writes: 'There will soon be no more priests. Their work is done.'[31] And in the same paragraph, he states: 'Through the divinity of themselves shall the kosmos and the new breed of poets be interpreters of men and women and of all events and things.'[32] So the poets will bring in a new sense of divinity, and there will be for Pessoa an empire of poets: Pessoa and his heteronyms!

Without the spiritual element, an empire cannot exist for Pessoa. So he writes: 'Any Empire not founded on the Spiritual Empire is walking Death, a ruling Corpse.'[33] Going further, Pessoa declares: 'The imperialism of poets endures and wins out; that of politicians passes on and is forgotten, unless the poet remembers it in his songs.'[34] Both in myth and in history, every hero (factual and fictional) needs a poet, and perhaps vice versa: Achilles and Odysseus had Homer, Hamlet and Romeo had Shakespeare, Vasco da Gama had Camões, Don Giovanni had Mozart, and Abraham had Kierkegaard. Portugal as the Fifth Empire, in this case the hero, will have as its poets Pessoa, Caeiro, Campos and Reis. This is the dream of Pessoa, and it may be a fool's dream. But a poet is a fool who chases after the reality of the impossible, the nothing and the monster. In a poem called 'Gazetilha' (translated as 'Squib' by Zenith), Campos writes:

Only a fool who makes poems
Or a mad inventor of philosophies

Or an eccentric geometrician
Will survive the vast unimportance
Of what's left behind, in the dark,
And which not even history remarks.
For tomorrow belongs to today's fools![35]

It is not military or political power that will ultimately reign, but cultural and poetic power. The poems are a gesture towards Pessoa's dream of the Fifth Empire. In Campos's poem, the trio that survives is made up of the poet, the philosopher and the geometrician. These are the three who grapple with the cosmos.

Even though the twentieth century was plagued by total war and the radical politics of extremes, Badiou still calls it the century of the poets. It is perhaps for that reason too that Badiou became so passionately interested in the poetic universe of Pessoa and dedicated a chapter of his book specifically to Campos's poem 'Maritime Ode'.[36] Badiou also calls the century of poets 'the threshold-century, a century without a crossing' that is caught in the middle of things, in Pessoa's interlude to be explored in the final chapter.[37] Pessoa's poets are of his own making, and he never lost his capacity for play and tomfoolery, even within the serious task of creating a mythology to surpass that of the practical politics of change, upheaval and stagnation. Pessoa believed in everything and nothing at the same time, without losing the vocation of poetic inspiration and awe. The book *Mensagem* ends with these words:

All is uncertain and final
All is scattered, nothing is whole.
O Portugal, today you are fog . . .
The Hour has come![38]

The poem is signed off as 'Valete, Fratres', literally meaning 'Be strong, Brothers', which the Romans used to say. 'Valete' also appears in esoteric Rosicrucian rituals, which is where Pessoa got it from.

6

The Esoteric Journeys of the Soul

I believe in the existence of worlds higher than our own and in the
existence of beings that inhabit those worlds.
Fernando Pessoa[1]

. . . All Matter is Spirit,
Because Matter and Spirit are merely vague names
Given to the great shadow that drenches the External in dreams
And plunges the Excessive Universe into Night and Mystery!
Álvaro de Campos[2]

Let us now enter the fog to encounter the occult and esoteric worlds
that Pessoa travelled in. These worlds were an essential component of
his spiritual and philosophical development and outlook and of his
formation and pulse as a poet. Alchemy already lay beneath many of
the poems in *Mensagem*, and the task of alchemy has always been for
the spirit to move the material, for the dream to change reality and
our conception of reality, and to uncover a reality behind a reality.
Pessoa had a lifelong interest in diverse spiritual traditions around
the world, and also in occult societies of alchemy and initiation.

In 'Fragments of an Autobiography', in a paragraph that may
have originally been meant for *The Book of Disquiet*, Pessoa writes:
'First I was engrossed in metaphysical speculations, then in scientific
ideas. Finally I was attracted to sociological [concepts]. But in none
of these stages of my search for truth did I find relief or reassurance.'[3]
The word 'esoteric' comes from the Greek *esoterikos*, meaning further
(*térō*) within/inside (*ésō*), and 'belonging to the inner circle'; it refers

to something that is usually secret or intended to be communicated only to the initiated. Pessoa was an expert in drawing astrological charts; he acted as a medium with the dead and practised automatic writing; he owned various books on magic, Freemasonry and other esoteric subjects;[4] and he wrote many esoteric poems under his own name. His first published esoteric poem, 'A Múmia' (The Mummy), appeared in *Portugal Futurista* in November 1917, and two of his finest esoteric poems are worth mentioning here – 'O Ultimo Sortilégio' (The Last Spell) and 'Eros e Psique' (Eros and Psyche), which Pessoa published in *Presença* in 1930 and 1934, respectively. Zenith writes: 'In all of Portugal there was no one better versed than he in the intricacies of Western esotericism.'[5] In a paragraph dated 1931, Bernardo Soares writes: 'I've always felt that virtue lay in obtaining what was out of one's reach, in living where one isn't, in being more alive after death than during life, in achieving something impossible, something absurd, in overcoming – like an obstacle – the world's very reality.'[6] Various levels of reality exist here, and by delving into the realm of the esoteric, Pessoa may have wanted to access other realities, or a reality behind this 'world's very reality'. In his book *Ka*, Roberto Calasso defines the esoteric as 'the thought closest to the vision things have of themselves'.[7] This is not too far from viewing Pessoa as attempting to get to a place of 'being as radical as reality itself'. Towards the end of *The Keeper of Sheep*, Caeiro refers disparagingly to 'The Great Mystery'.[8] Caeiro's nature is an assemblage and not a totality. His 'great mystery' is that there is no mystery, and the greatness for him is that he has shown us nature and has been faithful to nature. Nature, the so-called 'great mystery', is the reality, in all its parts, of the visible world and nothing more. But the 'mystery' that Campos and Pessoa (as author of *Faust*) speak of is different from Caeiro's concept of reality, as, for them, it is something we cannot reach or uncover fully. Reality, whether elusive and invisible or visible and before us, is what the poets try to express, or as Blanchot wrote in his essay 'Literature and the Right to Death': 'Literature is a concern for the reality of things, for their unknown, free, and silent existence.'[9]

Conversing with the Dead, Astrology and Neopaganism

From 1914 to 1915 Pessoa lived with his aunt Anica and her daughter Maria on Rua Pascoal de Melo 119, and together they started organizing séances. From these séances, Pessoa started producing automatic writings dictated by astral spirits. This was not unusual for the time. In fact, it was a fashionable practice for the elite and the aristocracy, at least among artists and sophisticated bohemians across Europe. Pessoa's contemporary William Butler Yeats regularly engaged in automatic writing, and his wife Georgie acted as a medium so he could speak with the dead in order to develop and deepen his poetic output. Yeats produced several key works from this experience, including *A Vision* (1925), his most baffling book. Other works were *Michael Robartes and the Dancer* (1921), a collection of poems on contemporary politics and the mystical; his long esoteric poem *The Gift of Harun al-Rahid* (1923); and two poetry collections, *The Tower* (1928) and *The Winding Stair and Other Poems* (1933), which were perhaps his most focused and finest modernist works. Yeats's interest in the esoteric realm was present from the very beginning of his writing output. As early as 1901 he was working on an essay called 'Magic', which begins with the words:

'I believe in the practice and philosophy of what we have agreed to call magic, in what I must call the evocation of spirits, though I do not know what they are, in the power of creating magical illusions, in the visions of truth in the depths of the mind when the eyes are closed.'[10]

Yeats was also a member of the Dublin Theosophical Club and the Hermetic Order of the Golden Dawn.

In 1915 and 1916 Pessoa completed six translations of theosophical books by the likes of Helena Blavatsky and Annie Besant, among others, which were all published at the time. Most of Pessoa's astral communications as a medium were in English, and his first and most prolific contact was with a figure from the grave called Henry More. More was an English philosopher and rationalist theologian of the Cambridge Platonist school who lived in the age of the Rosicrucian Enlightenment, from 1614 to 1687. More was against Cartesian dualism, wrote about a fourth dimension, and was quoted by Blavatsky in her book *Isis Unveiled: A Master-Key to the Mysteries of Ancient and Modern Science and Theology* (1877). Pessoa's interest in communicating with historical figures from beyond the grave illuminates the movement of Sensationism. When Henry More communicated that 'Sensationism is occult on account of the inspiring deities,' Pessoa jotted down his words in automatic writing.[11] During the years in the wake of Sá-Carneiro's death, through séances and automatic writing, More encouraged Pessoa's reading of Rosicrucian texts and prophesied his impending fame. He also gave advice on love, on masturbation, on ending a 'monastic life', and on marriage and having sex.

It was also while living with Aunt Anica that Pessoa began to make his first astrology charts, a skill he would go on to master. In December 1915, a heteronym called Raphael Baldaya emerged. He was an astrologist with a long beard who was meant to write two texts: a small book titled *A New Theory of Astrological Periods* and a work in Portuguese called *A Treatise on Negation*, though Pessoa only wrote a few pages of each. There are eleven points in the treatise, and in the last point, Baldaya writes: 'All the worlds affirmed by theosophists do really exist, but they are within Illusion, which is, for as long as it lasts, Reality.'[12] This statement that illusion is reality again reveals the various realities that Pessoa was immersed in. From 1914 onwards, Pessoa drew dozens of charts of historical and literary figures, and also made astrology maps for his friends and for Caeiro, Campos, Reis and himself. He even made astrology charts for the birth of the magazine *Orpheu* (26 March 1915) and Portugal's declaration of war on Germany (10 March 1916), and other events in his life and in the world.

Whether Pessoa actually believed in astrology and esotericism is open to debate. But in studying his vast and varied corpus, one can see that it was a central passion for him, and it was useful, as it was for Yeats, for his creative output. At the beginning of the last year of Pessoa's life, Campos revealed the uncertainty of these studies in a

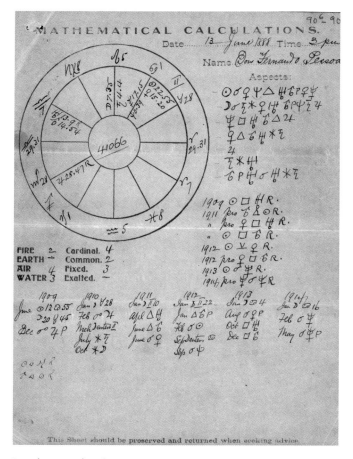

Pessoa's own astrology chart.

poem: 'I don't know if the stars rule the world/ Or if tarot or playing cards/ Can reveal anything/ . . . But I also don't know/ If anything is attained/ By living the way most people do.'[13] The idea of believing in everything and nothing, and the feeling of living in between worlds, pervaded Pessoa's entire life. There is an incisive sentence from Jean-Jacques Rousseau, another contradictory writer whom Pessoa admired, that is pertinent here: 'It is hard to prevent one from believing what one so keenly desires.'[14] This quote is from the book *Reveries of the Solitary Walker*, which Pessoa had in the original French (*Les Rêveries du promeneur solitaire*) in his personal library. The book links with Pessoa's own wanderings in three ways: first, 'reverie' relates to delirium or madness, but can also be a wandering vision or dream – imagining a dream into a reality – second, the reverie is done by someone who is wandering alone; and, third, the book remained unfinished (it would have been Rousseau's last work). On 5 May 1934, Pessoa wrote an untitled poem with three stanzas. The first one goes:

> This great wavering between
> Believing and not quite dis-
> Believing troubles the heart
> Weary of knowing nothing.[15]

The grappling with belief and unbelief, or even believing in unbelief, was a lifelong preoccupation for Pessoa. Campos, Reis and Soares also articulated this struggle – Soares admitted his 'vital habit of disbelieving everything'.[16] In the last year of his life, Pessoa wrote a two-page 'Resumé' in which he was a 'Gnostic Christian, and thus flatly opposed to all organized religions, especially Roman Catholicism'.[17] Again, going with the mood of the times, Pessoa was also looking for a new religion, or at least playing with the idea of formulating one. Many of his generation sought to find meaning in new philosophies and new political structures, but also in new spiritualities. Pessoa wrote about neopaganism with the help of his heteronyms Caeiro, Reis and Mora.

Pessoa's heteronym António Mora first emerged in 1909, but only became active in 1914. A disciple of Caeiro and an avid reader of Kant, Mora was a philosophical advocate of neopaganism, and a supporter of the German Empire during the First World War. Mora was meant to write three books – *The Foundations of Paganism*, *Prolegomena to a Reformation of Paganism* and *The Return of the Gods* – but Pessoa only left us fragments. Mora is present at the famous meeting recounted in Campos's 'Notes on My Master Albert Caeiro', but he is the only one who does not speak, preferring to listen to everything instead. Campos notes that that particular conversation inspired Mora 'to write one of the most astonishing chapters of his *Prolegomena* – the chapter on the idea of Reality'.[18] While most of the other '-isms' of Pessoa were within the new climate of modernism, neopaganism was, according to Pessoa scholar Antonio Cardiello, 'a commitment to reviving the cult of polytheism and the Hellenic model of civilization'.[19] Except that Pessoa, through his heteronyms and his own writings, was advancing this vision even deeper in incorporating Christ into the pantheon of pagan deities, both spiritually and materially, and transforming the human self or idea of selfhood into a multiplicity.

Reality is Multiple

The pagan gods of antiquity celebrated, represented and embodied beauty, freedom and plurality – nature itself. Pessoa's engagement with nature began with Alberto Caeiro, who wrote, 'Nature is parts without a whole,' which is a foundation for the neopaganism that Mora and Reis attempt to articulate.[20] For Caeiro, there is no nature, but there are hills, valleys, flowers and trees. His poetry displaces knowledge, and it is immersed in reality and the real. In *The Return of the Gods*, Mora states: 'Paganism is the one religion that springs directly from nature, that's born from the earth, from attributing to each object its true reality.'[21] But what is this 'true reality'? Mora gives us the answer and offers a key to Pessoa's whole oeuvre via his spiritual and esoteric writings: 'Reality, when it first appears to us, is multiple.'[22] To be pagan is to collapse the subject and the object: Caeiro is an absolute objectivist with a Zen-like demeanour, while Campos has a hysterical personality and is a subjectivist pursuing absolute forms. In this studied treatise of neopaganism we find the conundrum that Badiou presented to philosophers of Pessoa inaugurating 'a path that manages to be neither Platonic nor anti-Platonic', which is neither realist nor anti-realist. From reading Pessoa, it appears that he is against separation in the Cartesian sense of mind–body distinctions and the modern science of specialization while at the same time conceding that 'there is no system of the Universe.'[23] And nature is 'parts without a whole'. Nature is plural and the gods are multiple. Thus, Mora and Reis want to restore the cosmos to paganism, not to humanism. Ever the great feigner, Pessoa proposes that to believe in the gods is a lie, and yet he writes: 'In the eternal lie of all the gods, the only truth is in all the gods together.'[24] The gods, like the supreme artists, are false, but they are part of or emerge from nature, which is reality. Or, as Mora says it: 'The gods are the artifices (or the artists) of the real things.'[25]

The eighth poem from *The Keeper of Sheep* stands out from all the other poems by Caeiro. First, it is by far the longest poem that Caeiro ever wrote, and, second, it was written and published on its own in *Presença* in 1931, many years after the so-called 'Triumphal Day' of 8 March 1914. It is explicitly blasphemous to Christianity as Christ mocks his father and the Holy Spirit, and it is implicitly heretical in bringing Christ closer to the pantheon of pagan gods alongside Pan, Dionysius and Apollo. In this provocative, free-flowing, unrhymed melodic poem, Caeiro sets the stage in the opening lines:

> One midday in late spring
> I had a dream that was like a photograph.
> I saw Jesus Christ come down to earth.[26]

There are many components that connect to the vision of neopaganism and to Caeiro. The poem occurs in the middle of the day, when the Sun is in the centre of the sky. The season is on the cusp of change, and nature is in full bloom. Caeiro's dream is a snapshot; it is the Kierkegaardian moment or *Øieblik* – 'that ambiguity in which time and eternity touch each other',[27] where one feels a giddiness and where the 'science of seeing' shocks one into a standstill. It is where history stops and reality begins. The poem's narrative depicts Christ coming back down to earth, revealing the materiality of neopaganism. He is the Eternal Child, a god and a poet, and he thinks and attains knowledge through his five senses. For Caeiro and for Pessoa, Christ is part of nature like many of the pagan gods, he moves instinctively and freely, he acts and is present like a child, and he is detached from material things. In this blasphemous poem, he is reminiscent of the god Pan (albeit without the sexual escapades). Christianity had long distorted the image of Pan, associating him with Satan when goat legs appeared in Christian depictions of the Devil. Reis wrote a poem for Pan in the summer of 1914, which begins: 'The god Pan is not dead.'[28] Pan was denigrated and erased more than the other pagan gods. But in one of the final fragments of *The Return of the Gods*, Mora cries out: 'The Great Pan is reborn.'[29]

On 8 February 1925 Pessoa's uncle Henrique Rosa died. Although Pessoa had grown distant from his uncle during his adult years, Henrique had encouraged Pessoa's creative inclinations as he was growing up, so his death would have been a blow. One month later, on 17 March, even more catastrophically, Pessoa's mother died. Now nearly all of the closest people in his life were gone. Towards the end of the most fallow period of Pessoa's writing life, he wrote a book in 1926 in English called *Lisbon: What the Tourist Should See*, an English-language travel guide for foreigners, which was only published in 1992. What one would have thought could have been a fascinating guide is actually one of Pessoa's most forgettable and dullest pieces of writing. Campos's poetry entered a new nostalgic and solitary phase in the last years of the 1920s, as he penned some of his greatest poems such as 'Lisbon Revisited: 1926', 'Clouds' ('Nuvens'), 'Deferral' ('Adiamento'), 'The Tobacco Shop' ('Tabacaria'), 'English Song' ('Canção à Inglesa') and 'Note' ('Apontamento'). From 1929 onwards, during the last six years of his life, Pessoa's study and interest in the esoteric and occult journeys of the soul intensified. He kept a close interest in the Kabbalah, Rosicrucianism, the Knights Templar and Freemasonry. In the realm of initiation (the action of admitting someone into a secret society), in 1931 or 1932, Pessoa attained the grade of 'Adeptus Minor' – which is awarded to those able to conquer the love of life and the fear of death. A year later, Pessoa claimed to have attained the grade of Master of the Atrium. Pessoa wrote an essay on initiation in 1933: 'But the real meaning of initiation is that this visible world we live in is a symbol and a shadow, that this life we know through the senses is a death and a sleep, or, in other words, that what we see is an illusion.'[30]

Alchemy

In the famous letter to Monteiro, Pessoa explained that there are three paths towards the occult: magic, the mystical and alchemy. Of the three, Pessoa placed alchemy the highest, describing it as 'the hardest and most perfect path of all, since it involves a transmutation of the very personality that prepares it, not only without great risks but with defenses that the other paths don't have'.[31] This journey into the occult and the appropriation of ideas from the esoteric realm had a significant influence on the variety and depth of Pessoa's poetic thought. It is an aspect of his work that is frequently overlooked compared to his relationship with Portuguese and anglophone literature and Western philosophy. But for Pessoa, to think about magic and alchemy was to think about poetry. Alchemy is a poetic enterprise, and poetry is a form of magic – a kind of conjuring and initiating.

Alchemy was potent at the end of the sixteenth century and into the beginning of the seventeenth. This is the fascinating period when the mysterious cult of Rosicrucianism was founded, when Shakespeare was writing, when natural science was emerging and when the modern tenets of liberalism were forming. It was the age of Galileo, Descartes, Newton, Hobbes, Locke, Spinoza and Leibniz, but also of John Dee and Robert Fludd. It saw superstition displaced by a science of verification. It was a transition period in that, for example, Newton was both an alchemist and a natural scientist (and later was in charge of running the Mint in London). Spinoza wrote his *Ethics* in the form of the geometric method, and yet some readers received it as a mystical experience and developed an interest in pantheism. Alchemy is a fusion, a coagulation, a process of mixing and melting into something new. It is a form of interpenetration, a way of being in the middle, a unity in opposites and contradiction leading to transcendence that resonates in the Renaissance hermetic philosophy of Giordano Bruno and reappears in a covert way in the philosophy of Hegel (in the dialectical transformations in *The Phenomenology of Spirit*) and Marx (in the dialectical materialism and what he calls 'the metabolic process' in *Capital*[32]). Alchemy unites matter and spirit – two contradictory aspects of the universe – into a third thing. Marx and Engels write in *The Communist Manifesto*: 'all that is solid melts into air.'[33] This sounds like it could have been lifted from Shakespeare's play *The Tempest*, when the magician Prospero says:

> Our revels now are ended. These our actors,
> As I foretold you, were all spirits and
> Are melted into air, into thin air:
> And, like the baseless fabric of this vision,
> The cloud-capp'd towers, the gorgeous palaces,
> The solemn temples, the great globe itself,
> Ye all which it inherit, shall dissolve
> And, like this insubstantial pageant faded,
> Leave not a rack behind. We are such stuff
> As dreams are made on, and our little life
> Is rounded with a sleep. (IV.1)

Shakespeare plays are shrouded in magic and alchemy, particularly *Macbeth*, *A Midsummer Night's Dream*, *A Winter's Tale* and *The Tempest*. He is an example of the poet as alchemist as well as being the inventor of the modern human. Pessoa conceived of Intersectionism as a form of alchemy, 'the sensationism that takes stock of the fact that every sensation is really several sensations mixed together'.[34]

Rosicrucianism

Rosicrucianism was another of Pessoa's esoteric influences. It aimed to reach the intellect via the senses. Pessoa's personal library contained key Rosicrucian texts. He owned copies of Arthur E. Waite's *The Brotherhood of the Rosy Cross* (1924), Frans Wittemans's *Histoire des rose-croix* (1925) and Hargrave Jennings's

The Rosicrucians: Their Rites and Mysteries (1870) – which is heavily notated by Pessoa. Pessoa revealed something of his own trajectory, thought and style by underlining a passage in the preface to the third edition of Jennings's book: 'The haughty Philosophers [the Rosicrucians] forbade disclosure – this, of either their real doctrines or intentions, or of their personality.'[35] Pessoa's copy of the book included the preface to the second edition, which begins with 'The authors of this important Book', and Pessoa also underlined the letter 's' in the word 'authors'. Jennings also mentions Henry More in a list of authors who were profoundly adept in Rosicrucian philosophy.[36] The appearance of More here might have given Pessoa the idea to reach out to him via astral communications.

There are three key texts from the hermetic tradition of Rosicrucianism written by a mysterious Brother R.C., who was supposedly born in 1378 and lived for 106 years. There are two manifestos – the *Fama Fraternitatis* (1614) and *Confessio Fraternitatis* – and a work called *The Chemical Wedding of Christian Rosencreutz* (*Chymische Hochzeit Christiani Rosencreutz*) (1616), which is a German romance, fantasy novel and occult message rolled into one. The two manifestos are likely a hoax – any number of people could have been behind their creation and appearance, though a real figure called John Dee might have been the author. Dee was a collector of books, a builder of scientific instruments and a composer of codes and cyphers. He was a Renaissance figure of introspective saturnine melancholy and an esoteric political visionary who was fascinated by alchemy. He brings to mind both the mythological Merlin from the tales of King Arthur and the Germanic figure of Faust. The mingling of alchemy and the sciences, the crossover between the political and the spiritual, and the birth of an esoteric movement forever shrouded in mystery would all have appealed to the playful imagination of Pessoa and his abiding attraction to the occult for his own poetic journey.

In an essay on Pessoa and the more occult aspects of his writings, Lourenço writes that 'negation is nothing other than the vision embodied in Rosicrucian Pessoa: the world as originary unreality.'[37] In 1935 Pessoa wrote a poem called 'At the Tomb of Christian

Rosenkreutz'. It begins with an epigraph containing eight lines from the *Fama Fraternitatis*, describing a beautiful dead corpse with a book written in gold in his hand. In the poem, the poet asks: 'Will we finally know the hidden/ Truth about all that exists or flows?'[38] His answer is no. But that does not stop Pessoa from keeping up the search. In his *Faust*, Pessoa writes: 'The secret of Seeking is that nothing's found.'[39] And Pessoa concludes his poem 'At the Tomb

'The Invisible College of the Rose Cross Fraternity', illustration from Daniel Mögling, *Speculum Sophicum Rhodostauroticum* (1618).

of Christian Rosenkreutz' with the words: 'Our Rosy Cross Father knows, and says nothing.'[40] There is a fabulous drawing from 1604 by Theophilus Schweighhardt (a pseudonym of the alchemist and Rosicrucian Daniel Mögling) called 'The Invisible College of the Rose Cross Fraternity', which shows a fortress-like building moving on wheels surrounded by various symbols and ciphers. Symbols of the rose and the cross are placed on either side of the door of the illustration, and the word 'MOVEMVR' (Let us move) is written over two lines directly below the door and entrance. Sá-Carneiro wrote in a letter to Pessoa: 'Beautiful is all which provokes in us a sensation of the invisible.'[41] Sá-Carneiro died within a few months of writing these words, but they describe an aesthetic that appealed to both men, and Pessoa continued to chase and probe this 'sensation of the invisible' until his own death.

An Encounter with Aleister Crowley

Pessoa's journey through esotericism leads to a curious encounter with Aleister Crowley, a painter, poet, writer, mountaineer, practitioner of black magic and infamous trickster. During 1929 and 1930, Pessoa corresponded with Crowley, who was thirteen years older. Edward Alexander Crowley was born in 1875 in Warwickshire in the Midlands of England into a wealthy, fundamentalist Christian family. He was a self-proclaimed prophet and ceremonial magician, and supreme master of the Hermetic Order of the Golden Dawn. There are rumours that he may have been a double agent or some kind of spy during the First World War. For a time he was also a Tibetan monk – and a great mountain climber, almost making it to the summit of K2 in the Himalayas – and was a connoisseur of ancient Mexican religions and founder of a new religion called Thelema. He lived by his motto of 'Love is the law, love under will'. He published books including *The Book of the Law* (1909), *The Book of Lies* (1912), *Magick* (1913), *Confessions of Aleister Crowley: An Autohagiography* (1929) and *The Book of Thoth* (1944). He regularly engaged in kinky sex and drug taking. Many people who became intimate with him were destroyed or destroyed themselves, and

Photograph of Aleister Crowley from *The Equinox*, 1/3 (March 1910).

the British newspapers referred to him as 'the Wickedest Man in
the World'.[42] A very macabre version of Crowley was captured in
the Gothic novel *The Magician* (1908) by Somerset Maugham, who
met him several times. In the preface to the novel, Maugham writes
of Crowley: 'He was a fake but not entirely a fake.'[43] Crowley was
delighted by the book and wrote a positive review of it in *Vanity Fair*
and then signed off as the character he was modelled on (whom
Maugham had called Oliver Haddo).

Crowley and Pessoa had an odd affinity: both were obsessed with
initiation, secret societies and the role of magic; both believed in

Cover of The Master
Therion (Aleister
Crowley), *Magick in
Theory and Practice*,
Book IV, part III
(1929).

MAGICK

THE MASTER THERION

absolutely everything and absolutely nothing at the same time; both
were master feigners or *fingidores*. But they also differed greatly in
their personalities and the types of lives they lived. Crowley was a
globetrotting exhibitionist immersed in black magic satanism and
sex rituals, while we can think of Pessoa as a kind of white magician,
taking, as Zenith puts it, 'the divine road of chaste androgyny'.[44]
Pessoa already had a copy of Crowley's book *777=777*, which was
published in 1909, and when Pessoa heard about Crowley's new
autobiography (*Confessions of Aleister Crowley*), he wrote (on
18 November 1929) to the publisher inquiring about the book and
requesting the first volume along with Crowley's *The Stratagem*. The
publisher, Mandrake Press, responded immediately and sent out the
two books. Less than two weeks later, Pessoa wrote another letter
to Mandrake Press thanking them for their rapid response. He told

them that he had received the books and that there was an error in Crowley's horoscope in the *Confessions*. Pessoa even offered some advice in the letter on how to correct the mistake. One week later, Pessoa received his first letter from Crowley, who addressed him as 'Frater' and began with the sentence: 'Do what thou wilt shall be the whole of the Law.' Crowley expressed gratitude for Pessoa's remarks and suggestions, and in his letter asked Pessoa for more information on his situation regarding the horoscope. He signed off the letter as 'Master Therion χ§ς' – which means 'The Great Beast 666'. Pessoa

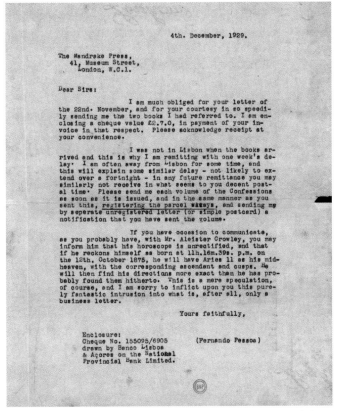

4th. December, 1929.

The Mandrake Press,
   41, Museum Street,
      London, W.C.1.

Dear Sirs:

       I am much obliged for your letter of the 22nd. November, and for your courtesy in so speedily sending me the two books I had referred to. I am enclosing a cheque value £2.7.0, in payment of your invoice in that respect. Please acknowledge receipt at your convenience.

       I was not in Lisbon when the books arrived and this is why I am remitting with one week's delay. I am often away from Lisbon for some time, and this will explain some similar delay – not likely to extend over a fortnight – in any future remittance you may similarly not receive in what seems to you decent postal time. Please send me each volume of the Confessions as soon as it is issued, and in the same manner as you sent this, registering the parcel always, and sending me by seperate unregistered letter (or simple postcard) a notification that you have sent the volume.

       If you have occasion to communicate, as you probably have, with Mr. Aleister Crowley, you may inform him that his horoscope is unrectified, and that if he reckons himself as born at 11h.16m.39s. p.m. on the 12th. October 1875, he will have Aries 11 as his midheaven, with the corresponding ascendant and cusps. He will then find his directions more exact than he has probably found them hitherto. This is a mere speculation, of course, and I am sorry to inflict upon you this purely fantastic intrusion into what is, after all, only a business letter.

                                 Yours faithfully,

       Enclosure:
       Cheque No. 155095/6905   (Fernando Pessoa)
       drawn by Banco Lisboa
       & Açores on the National
       Provincial Bank Limited.

Pessoa's letter to Mandrake Press on receiving *Confessions of Aleister Crowley* and *The Stratagem* and on Crowley's mistake, 4 December 1929.

then proceeded to send three of his English chapbooks of poems to both Crowley and Mandrake Press. Crowley responded a week later thanking him for the poems, saying that he found them 'very remarkable for excellence'.[45] At the bottom of the letter, Crowley added a handwritten note that said he saw the arrival of Pessoa's poems 'as a definite Message', and that he would like to come to Lisbon and see him, but that they must not tell anyone.[46] This must have given Pessoa some anxiety to say the least, given the radically different lives of the two men. Pessoa delayed his response and tried to keep Crowley at a distance, but Crowley did not give up on him.

A little less than a year later, in September 1930, Crowley decided to come to Portugal. His visit was triggered by the arrival of a new woman in his life, Hanni Jaeger, a beautiful nineteen-year-old whom Crowley met in Berlin. He designated her his new 'Scarlet Woman', calling her 'Monster' and 'Anu'. He had just left his wife (who soon entered a mental asylum) and wanted to take Jaeger with him to Portugal and engage in sex magic in their hotel. It would also be an opportunity to meet Pessoa. Crowley genuinely thought highly of the poetry that Pessoa had sent, but also seemed to have had some kind of plan for Pessoa in his occult system, maybe to set up the Portuguese sector of the esoteric order – the Ordo Templi Orientis (OTO) – or be part of sex initiations. On 2 September 1930 Pessoa met Crowley and Jaeger off their ship at the port, and accompanied them to their hotel in Chiado in the centre of Lisbon. The three of them sat down in the hotel, had drinks and chatted. Crowley swiftly realized that Pessoa was not one to be engaged in kinky sex or any kind of sex magic rituals, but he nonetheless wanted to continue to meet up with him and talk about a publishing collaboration and expanding his occult societies. They met again on 7 September in Estoril, a rich international resort on the outskirts of Lisbon, where Crowley and Jaeger were now staying for a few weeks. They agreed to meet for a third time two days later, this time in Lisbon, as Crowley and Jaeger had to come in to collect their post. This time Pessoa brought along his eccentric friend Raul Leal (who had written some of the most unhinged poetry for *Orpheu*), who was also passionate about the occult and was very interested in meeting

Crowley. They met at the Café Martinho da Arcada but Crowley took a dislike to Leal, writing in his diary later that day: 'Met Leal. Don't like him. There's something very definitely wrong with him.'[47] The day after that meeting, Pessoa wrote what could be his only erotic heterosexual poem in the Portuguese language, obviously inspired by the lust he felt for Hanni Jaeger after spending time with her at the café. Here is how it starts:

Her very being surprises.
A tall, tawny blonde,
It delights me just to think
Of seeing her half-ripe body.[48]

After this, Pessoa kept his distance and made excuses to avoid meeting up again in Portugal. Jaeger literally ran away from Crowley a few days later, and fled to Germany. She was reported to have had some kind of hysterical attack in the hotel. She committed suicide a year later. Her distress has unsettling echoes of Somerset Maugham's novel *The Magician*, published 22 years earlier, and its descriptions of the sinister, albeit fictionally hyperbolic, sides to Crowley's personality when it came to his dealings with women.

This strange episode in Pessoa's life concluded when Crowley famously faked a suicide off the cliffs of the Boca do Inferno (which means Mouth of Hell), close to Sintra and Estoril. It was a final act of being a *fingidor* with the aim of creating some fake news before leaving Portugal once and for all. Pessoa was a willing participant in the deception. Crowley had supposedly left a suicide note by the Boca do Inferno, but actually left it with Pessoa. Pessoa, in turn, got his journalist friend Augusto Ferreira Gomes to take a picture of the suicide note to try and get the story onto the front page of the newspaper in Lisbon. Pessoa and Gomes fabricated an interview about the event and the story did make the news in Portugal. However, the British newspapers did not buy it, knowing what Crowley was like, and the story soon dropped out of the newspapers in Portugal. By this time Crowley had left the country and reunited with Jaeger in Berlin. Pessoa made plans to write

Drawing of Hanni Jaeger, nicknamed 'Anu', by Aleister Crowley.

a detective novella based on the event called *The Mouth of Hell*. Crowley even wrote from Berlin making some suggestions for the novella, and Pessoa made a rough draft with ten chapters but, once again, he did not manage to complete the text, and we are left with pages and fragments of yet another unfinished project. The initial idea seemed exciting, but as Pessoa advanced, the novella lost its momentum and slowed, and he lost interest. Crowley continued to live a decadent life in Berlin, but in 1932 he returned to London. Meanwhile, Pessoa delved further into the esoteric and continued to write poems of the occult. Crowley and Pessoa's correspondence became less frequent, mainly because Pessoa stopped responding. He did, however, translate Crowley's most famous poem, 'Hymn to Pan', into Portuguese and even published it in *Presença* in the July–October 1931 edition.

In the last year of his life, Pessoa became virulently opposed to Salazar's regime. This was partly motivated by a new law banning Freemasonry and other secret societies, and the censorship of a sexually graphic poetry book called *Canções* (Songs) by his friend António Botto, who was homosexual. These prohibitions touched on two aspects that were fundamental to Pessoa and so close to his heart: first, secret societies must be allowed to exist, and, second, there should always be complete creative freedom and expression for the artist.

7

Love, Sex, Friendship and Self-Fecundation

We can die if all we've done is love. We've failed if we've amused ourselves.

Bernardo Soares[1]

To feign [*fingir*] is to love.

Bernardo Soares[2]

While Pessoa thought of himself as incapable of loving, he retained a longing within himself for love. Pessoa received a lot of love from his mother – he had no doubt that she loved him – and the other members of the family doted on him, which he appreciated. He had many male friends throughout his life who maintained a genuine affection for him; he often conversed with his advisor from the dead (Henry More) in his automatic writings on the possibility of marriage and sex; and he was loved by a woman in real life. The woman, Ophelia Queiroz, would have devoted herself to Pessoa if he had allowed her to. But by the end of Pessoa's life, it seems that Pessoa could only give his abiding love and commitment to literature and his heteronyms. And, once again, it was his heteronyms who seemed to express more authenticity and honesty when writing about love than Pessoa himself.

In one of his automatic writings, Pessoa wrote these two sentences: 'Love is the monster' and 'Love is a mortal sample of immortality.'[3] Perhaps he describes love as the monster because it reveals the self – relationships between humans certainly reveal parts of ourselves which we may not want shown, and love reveals our limitations. But, at least according to the second sentence above, love is also a yearning for eternity, a taste of immortality in a moment. Pessoa could never make that leap from the dream into consummated love with another person because of the possibility of the shutting down of endless daydreaming and no longer being able to give himself over entirely to literature. His reality would ultimately lie elsewhere. Nietzsche once wrote that 'a married philosopher belongs in comedy,' but many of the great poets throughout history experienced love, sex, romantic relationships and marriage.[4] This was not the case with Pessoa, whose life seems more aligned with the unmarried (and male) European philosophers, such as Heraclitus, Plato, Descartes, Spinoza, Leibniz, Hobbes, Locke, Hume, Kant, Schopenhauer, Kierkegaard, Nietzsche and Wittgenstein. In the opening line of a poem dated 27 August 1930, Pessoa writes: 'My wife, whose name is Solitude'.[5] In 1916 Pessoa's séance communicator, More, encouraged Pessoa to lose his virginity and to abandon his 'monastic life'.[6] Pessoa channelled a woman called Margaret Mansel, and his automatic writing captured her definition of him as an 'onanist'; she went further, exclaiming: 'You masturbator! You masochist! You man without manhood! . . . You man without a man's prick! You man with a clitoris instead of a prick!'[7] However, despite More's encouragement and Mansel's damning accusations, Pessoa remained celibate and continued instead to give birth to more heteronyms. Pessoa used the term 'self-fecundation' (writing it in English) to describe the process of inverting his sexual prowess and longing, and directing them into himself to create or self-fertilize, thus giving rise to the heteronyms.[8] However, in the last year of his life, Pessoa expressed an understanding and appreciation of the greatness and necessity of love in another untitled poem of just six lines, which begins: 'What matters is love./ Sex is just an accident.'[9]

Ophelia Queiroz

Pessoa's only romantic relationship with a woman began on 8 October 1919, the day after his stepfather João Rosa died, when a nineteen-year-old girl called Ophelia Queiroz was interviewed for the job of secretary at the firm Felix, Vallada, & Freitas, Ltd, on the second floor of Rua da Assumpção 42 in downtown Lisbon. This was one of the firms for which Pessoa worked, drafting and copy-editing letters in French and English. Within a few weeks, the two of them were sharing glances and flirting at the office. Pessoa was 31 years old. He was quite isolated at this time – he had not seen his mother in well over a decade, and three of his closest friends from *Orpheu* (Sá-Carneiro, Santa Rita Pintor and Amadeo de Souza-Cardoso) had died in the last three years – so the arrival of an attractive, intelligent and empathetic young woman at the office who showed interest in him must have been a welcome surprise. And to be called Ophelia, like the sweet, overwhelmed and ultimately tragic character from *Hamlet*, would have been all the more enticing for Pessoa the Shakespeare fanatic.

On 22 January 1920 there was a power cut in the office and everyone left except Pessoa and Ophelia. As she was putting on her coat to leave, Pessoa went over to her and quoted Hamlet: 'O dear Ophelia, I am ill at these numbers; I have not art to reckon my groans: but that I love thee best, oh, most best, believe it.'[10] Then he put his arm around her waist and kissed her. Pessoa wrote about this first passionate kiss, and there were more secret kisses and an exchange of notes over the next few months, but the relationship was never made public and Pessoa never introduced Ophelia to his family.

On 28 February 1920 Ophelia wrote a letter to Pessoa requesting a written statement of his intentions. And so Pessoa wrote his first love letter on 1 March 1920. At the end of that month his mother moved back to Lisbon and they moved in together on Rua Coelho da Rocha. In an exchange of letters with Ophelia between March and November of that year, Pessoa showed he had a playful, funny, emotionally expressive side, and also revealed yearning, depression and loneliness to another human being. Ultimately, however, he remained reticent and resistant to real intimacy with a real woman. In his first love letter, he wrote: 'I myself would think it was funny, if I didn't love you so much, and if I had the time to think of anything besides the suffering you enjoy inflicting on me,

Ophelia Queiroz at around eighteen or nineteen years old.

although I've done nothing to deserve it except love you, which doesn't seem to me like reason enough. At any rate . . .'[11] In his love letters, he would call her by names such as 'baby', 'beastly baby', 'wasp', 'terrible baby', 'naughty little baby', 'baby angel' and 'dear sweet love'. Ophelia affectionately called Pessoa 'Ninhinho' in her letters – literally meaning 'little boy'. Pessoa called her 'Ninhinha' sometimes, and began one letter with 'Dear Ibis,'[12] which perhaps reveals a bit of mirroring and narcissism, as he often referred to himself as Ibis. Ophelia's birthday was one day after Pessoa's, a fact that would have appealed to him. It is possible that Pessoa was merely experimenting with the art of love letters and allowing himself to try a new form of writing, but the letters also indicate a genuine affection for and attraction to Ophelia. The first phase of their relationship ended with a love letter dated 29 November 1920, after which Pessoa stopped communicating with her. They had both moved firms, which may have made it easier for Pessoa to break off the relationship, but this letter must have been hurtful to Ophelia as Pessoa divulged the possibility of his love being only an idea, rather than a concrete reality or the basis for a real relationship:

> My love has passed. But I still feel a steadfast affection for you, and you can be sure that I'll never, never forget your delightful figure, your girlish ways, your tenderness, your goodness, and your lovable nature. It's possible that I fooled myself and that these qualities I attribute to you were my own illusion, but I don't think so, and even if they were, it did no harm to have seen them in you.[13]

After nine years of silence, the secret relationship resumed. In 1926 Pessoa had met and befriended the young poet Carlos Queiroz, who initially acted as a kind of scout for *Presença* to find modernist Lisbon poets of quality to publish. Queiroz also happened to be Ophelia's nephew, and lived with her and her mother in Rossio. One day Pessoa gave Carlos a recent photo of himself standing by his favourite bar called Abel's, drinking a glass of wine. Carlos showed Ophelia the photo. She asked him to ask Pessoa for another copy. Pessoa guessed

immediately that the request was from Ophelia and gave Carlos
a second photo. She wrote him a letter of thanks and said he was
welcome to write to her. Pessoa responded immediately on
11 September 1929. He wrote: 'Your letter reached my exile – which
is I myself – like joy from the homeland, and so it's I who should
thank you, dear girl.'[14] So the second phase of their relationship
began, with love letters from Pessoa over the next few months that
again used affectionate names for Ophelia. The couple again took
walks together, rode on the tram and exchanged secret kisses. But the
tone of Pessoa's letters in this phase was darker, lonelier and more
erratic, and he often sounded drunk. His communication petered out
rather quickly this time, and he wrote his last letter to her on
11 January 1930. Tragically, Ophelia continued to write letters to
Pessoa for more than a year but got no reply. In all, Pessoa wrote
around fifty letters to Ophelia while she wrote more than four or five
times as many letters and postcards to him.

The photograph of
Pessoa from 1929
that Pessoa gave
to Carlos Queiroz,
which he then
showed to Ophelia.

At one point Ophelia went along with Pessoa's version of reality by blaming his heteronym Campos for preventing the relationship between her and Pessoa from flourishing. She received a letter from Campos himself on 25 September 1929, telling her that Pessoa was mentally unwell and more or less that she was better off without him. He concluded his letter by writing: 'my own advice to you is to take whatever mental image you may have formed of the individual [Pessoa] whose mention is sullying this reasonably white paper and to throw it down the drain.'[15] Understandably, she was not fond of Campos at all. The last dated poem that Campos wrote (on 21 October 1935) begins with the words: 'All love letters are/ Ridiculous.'[16] He derided the act of writing love letters, but, being the vacillating Libra that he was, and also revealing a deep humanity in the absurdity and glorious activity of love letters, he also wrote these lines in the poem: 'But, in the end/ Only the creatures who've never written/ Love letters/ Are those that are/ Ridiculous.'

In 1935, when Ophelia got word from her nephew that Pessoa had died, she was deeply shocked and saddened. She married three years later and it was a happy marriage, although she admitted late in life that Pessoa was the only great love of her life.[17] Her husband died in 1955 and Ophelia passed away in 1991 at the age of 91; she was buried in Alto de São João Cemetery in Lisbon. They had no children. In 2016 her remains were brought to Prazeres Cemetery not far from the Pessoa family vault. But by that time Pessoa had moved again: in 1985 his remains had been taken to the Jeronimo Monastery in historical Belém, at the mouth of the River Tejo where the navigators from Portugal had set sail for Africa, Asia and Brazil. Even in death, Pessoa had managed to slip away from her.

The Shepherd in Love

A surprising and rather beautiful part of Pessoa's oeuvre is the eight love poems by Caeiro that were gathered under the title *The Shepherd in Love*. This is what Campos had to say about them in 'Notes for the Memory of My Master Caeiro':

The Shepherd in Love is a futile interlude, but the few poems that make it up are among the world's great love poems, for they are love poems by virtue of being about love and not by virtue of being poems. The poet loved because he loved, and not because love exists, and this was precisely what he said.[18]

So the Zen-like shepherd and bucolic poet, who lived on a hill and possessed Spinoza-like clear-sightedness and independence, had gone and fallen in love! These eight poems read as genuine yearning, desire, suffering, disorientation and transformation – mirroring the experience of love itself. Caeiro wrote: 'Love is a company./ I no longer know how to walk the roads alone/ For I'm no longer able to walk alone.'[19] Reading these poems, there seems to be more authenticity and feeling in them than in a lot of the letters that Pessoa wrote to Ophelia. The poems are carefully constructed and unrhymed as usual, and the language is simple and direct. Campos was perturbed and annoyed by these poems, because his master had lost focus and become distracted by another human being. He wrote about how Caeiro's sense of smell had become stronger than his power of seeing, despite his philosophy of the 'science of seeing'. Campos wrote in the third poem: 'Now sometimes I wake up and smell before I see.'[20] Caeiro saw the face of his beloved everywhere in nature: 'All of reality looks at me like a sunflower with her face in the middle.'[21] His longing for another human being was a reminder of the animate and inanimate things all around him, and of nature itself – a lover's smile is described in these terms: 'her teeth gleam like the river's stones.'[22]

By falling in love, Caeiro's thinking had become confused to the point that 'to love is to think,' whereas before, 'to think was not to understand.'[23] Now that he had entered the world of human relationships, he began to suffer and become contaminated and blinded by time, memory and everything around him. When he fell in love, the anxiety of yesterday and tomorrow emerged. He knew that the self of longing was intertwined with time and temporality. Where once Caeiro had warned that 'remembrance is a betrayal of Nature,'[24] now he had become lovesick, and nature was full of memory for the one he loved. He had started to feel and not to see. In the last of the eight poems, Caeiro admits that he has even lost his staff and cannot find it again, and that his sheep (which are his thoughts and each of his thoughts sensations) are scattered along the slopes of the hill. He concludes by stating that he sees everything: 'All of reality, with the sky and air and fields that exist,/ And he felt the air reopen, with pain, a freedom in his chest.'[25] Because his love is unrequited, this is a particularly acute and juvenile pain, but also the vivid experience of being alive to reality. It is interesting to see when these poems were actually written. The first two were composed on 6 July 1914, not long after the 'Triumphal Day' of Pessoa's life, when Caeiro, Reis and Campos emerged. But the other six poems were written much later: one of them on 18 November 1929, three on 10 July 1930 and two on 23 July 1930. The November poem is the longest of the collection and was written towards the end of Pessoa's romance with Ophelia. In its opening lines, Caeiro discloses a rare moment of doubt and vulnerability: 'Perhaps those who are good at seeing are poor at feeling/ And do not enchant because they don't know how to act.'[26] Once again, Pessoa put his real sense of longing and disorientation into some magnificent poetry rather than into the messiness of human attachment and commitments.

All this makes one wonder what kind of pain Pessoa was transferring to Caeiro, and how this compares with his treatment and experience of love in his other two great heteronyms, Campos and Reis. Ricardo Reis is a poet of desire who writes yearning odes to his eternal muses Chloe, Lydia and Neara, but remains in an isolated bubble of resignation and pessimism as he tries to stoically accept mortality and maintain detachment from intimacy with other humans. Álvaro de Campos never really knows how he feels, as he yearns for all sensations. But what is present in his poetry, especially in his early masterpieces 'Maritime Ode' and 'Salutation to Walt Whitman', is a rampant erotic desire and sexual violence. On the outside, Pessoa could easily be considered prudish and repressed, but 'Maritime Ode' is a sexually explicit poem where Pessoa transfers an erotic explosiveness into the voice of Campos.

Erotic Fantasies

Operatic in its sweep, the middle of 'Maritime Ode' turns into a
kind of Portuguese version of the Walpurgis Night from Goethe's
Faust, where a festivity of the witches' sabbat occurs and there is sex,
carnage and magic, and, in moments, it is reminiscent of Berlioz's
Symphonie fantastique, which also reaches a climax where the
protagonist, who is full of sexual desire, enters into a terrifying and
exhilarating dream of a witches' sabbat where he meets his end. The
language in Campos's most ambitious poem is vivid, provocative
and full of ruptures and passionate outbursts; the poem ebbs and
flows dramatically as the reader follows the imagined journey of the
poet as he reacts, acts, explodes, scatters and dissipates. He urges
his body on. His mind fills with excessive desires. He yearns to be
raped by pirates. We find lines such as 'the flesh of my adventure!';
'To be in my submissive self the female who needs to be theirs!'; and
'My imagination the body of the women you rape!'[27] The rhythm
and expression of the poem reach what can be interpreted as a
sexual climax at the end of the middle section. Then the reader
enters the denouement, the calm after the storm, the winding down
and catching one's breath after orgasm. In this final section of the
poem, Campos suddenly feels sad and nostalgic, and is reflective,
nihilistic and finally exhausted. He ponders: 'How far I am from
what I was a few minutes ago,' and 'Everything in me suddenly
beholds a night at sea/ Full of the vast and utterly human mystery
of the nocturnal waves.'[28]

Campos goes further in his homoerotic outpourings in his
unfinished 'Salutation to Walt Whitman', in which he eulogizes
Whitman, who is consciously excessive in his writing, and is an
obvious model and inspiration. Campos writes of him as:

Passionate mistress of the scattered universe,
Great homosexual who rubs against the diversity of things,
Sexualized by stones, by trees, by people, by professions,
Full of lust for passing bodies, chance encounters, mere
observations.[29]

Further on in the poem he describes Whitman as 'Pimp of the whole Universe,/ Slut of all solar systems, pansy of God!'[30] Campos admits in the poem on the same page that he has 'an indirect, abstract erection' in the depths of his soul. This 'abstract erection' represents the sexually charged creativity of Campos and Pessoa, though Pessoa could be said to have channelled all his sexual energy into his writing. It is also part of Pessoa's 'mild sexual inversion' (*inversão sexual fruste*), as he called it.[31] The word *fruste* here means something that relates to a mild or incomplete form of a disease. It is not too far away from the word 'latent' (*latente*), which is something that is concealed and not yet developed or manifest. Pessoa was fond of the word *latente*, and it turns up, for example, in his description of Reis as a 'latent pagan'; it appears in the 'latent tendencies' of Campos, the 'latent throbbing energy' of nature and the 'latent insanity' of metaphysics.[32] To help Pessoa justify his 'mild sexual inversion', or at least not feel that he is alone in it, he made comments and notes and reflections on other writers who he presumed were homosexual or bisexual, including Walter Pater, Oscar Wilde and Shakespeare. Pessoa expressed to João Gaspar Simões that 'Shakespeare's homosexuality' is 'so clearly and constantly affirmed in his sonnets'.[33] Pessoa might have seen himself in these moments in the role of 'the new womanly man', which is how Joyce describes Leopold Bloom in the brothel scene in the Circe episode of *Ulysses* – the episode that has been called 'the unconscious of the novel'.[34] Perhaps this is a reach, but Pessoa does have this to say about himself in a short text that seemed to be intended as part of a preface to a work on Shakespeare:

> I can define myself without any trouble: I'm female by temperament, with a male intelligence. My sensibility and the actions that derive from it – my temperament and its expression, in other words – are those of a woman. My associative faculties – intelligence and the will, which is the intelligence of our impulses – are those of a man.[35]

Even an advertising slogan that Pessoa wrote for Coca-Cola in 1927 can be interpreted as a kind of homoerotic innuendo. It reads: 'Primeiro estranha-se, depois entranha-se', which could be translated as, 'First it feels strange, but then it gets into you.' The reflexive verb *entranhar-se* could be translated as 'dive into' or 'devote oneself', while *entranhar* without the reflective *-se* means 'to pierce'. This may be an unconscious homoerotic allusion, or nothing at all, but taking into account Pessoa's interest in ambiguous sexual impulses and preferences, it could easily be a demonstration of his humorous and provocative side. In the preface to his unrealized work on Shakespeare, Pessoa wrote a striking self-definition in the same text on 'being a female by temperament': 'I liked being passive. I wanted to be active only insofar as it was necessary to stimulate and keep alive the love activity of the person who loved me.'

Two Love Poems: Antinous and Epithalamium

Pessoa planned to write a series of five poems on the history of love. They were to be called: 1 Greek – Antinous; 2 Roman – Epithalamium; 3 Christian Era; 4 Modern Era; and 5 Future of Love – Anteros. Pessoa only completed the first two, while the theme of the fifth makes up a fragment for *The Book of Disquiet*. Anteros was the Greek god of unrequited love. It was also a misfortune suffered by Pessoa's last heteronym, a nineteen-year-old girl called Maria José – Pessoa's only female heteronym – who emerged from his imagination in 1929 or 1930. Maria José was dying from arthritis and tuberculosis, and wrote just one text called 'A Letter from a Hunchback Girl to a Metalworker'. It is a letter of unrequited love for a man she sees by her window who will never know she exists. It was only published for the first time in 1990.[36]

The two poems from the planned series of love poems that were completed are 'Antinous' and Epithalamium'. Perhaps Pessoa's greatest poem in English, the long homoerotic 'Antinous' was written in 1915, certainly one of Pessoa's most creative years. 'Antinous' was later revised and published by Pessoa's new publishing house and commercial agency Olisipo (which he had set up in 1920 with a vision

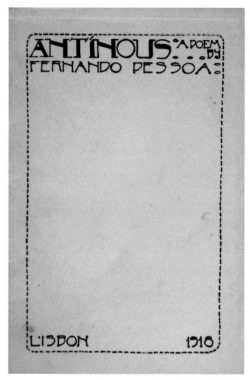

of creating a publishing empire) in December 1921 in the chapbook *English Poems I–II* (one of the pamphlets that so impressed Aleister Crowley). In the same month, Olisipo published the other long love poem, 'Epithalamium' (written in 1913), in the chapbook *English Poems III*, this time dealing with heterosexual love. The two poems are written in English under Pessoa's name, are over fifteen pages in length and are titled with Greek names. This pair of poems again reveals Pessoa's splintered personality, his condition of wanting everything and wanting nothing.

'Antinous' means 'opposite in character, resisting' in ancient Greek, and the poem tells of Hadrian's love, desire and despair for his young male lover Antinous, who is dead and lies naked on a couch. Pessoa's verse is precocious and vivid:

O lips whose opening redness erst could touch
Lust's seats with a live art's variety!
O fingers skilled in things not to be told!
O tongue which, counter-tongued, made the blood bold![37]

The reader encounters an androgynous corpse ('O bare female–male body'). There is a slight hint of necrophilia ('He runs his cold lips all the body over'). But Hadrian sees his young love in death as a god now: 'The god is dead whose cult was to be kissed!' At the end of the poem, the body of Antinous is taken away by the gods. The word 'love' appears a staggering 48 times, and the word 'lust' is used 19 times in the poem (which perhaps gave Crowley the idea that he might be able to recruit Pessoa for his sexual schemes). Antinous is a symbol of male homosexuality, not only in Pessoa's poem but in earlier and later works by other writers: he is mentioned in *The Picture of Dorian Gray* (1891) by Oscar Wilde, and appears in *Memoirs of Hadrian* (1951) by Marguerite Yourcenar.

'Epithalamium' means 'nuptial chamber' in ancient Greek. In Greek and Roman antiquity, poems were written on the theme of 'epithalamium' to be sung at the door of the nuptial chambers as a song of praise to the bride and bridegroom on their first night together. This tradition continued through the Renaissance and into modernity in both poetry and music. Pessoa was familiar with several composers and poets who produced epithalamium verses, including Edmund Spenser, Ben Jonson, John Donne, Alfred Lord Tennyson and Richard Wagner. Shakespeare's play *A Midsummer Night's Dream* could be described as an epithalamium. And Percy Shelley, one of Pessoa's favourite poets as a teenager, wrote a poem called 'Epithalamium' in 1821. Pessoa's 'Epithalamium' is not as powerfully executed as 'Antinous', but nonetheless presents a picture of the act of sex and the body as an object of desire. Like 'Antinous', it keeps to an exacting rhyme, but the poem is split up into 21 sections headed by Latin numbers. The poem includes the word 'lust' five times and 'love' ten times as it describes the first night of sexual intercourse mostly from the bride's perspective. It contains sexually explicit lines:

The bridegroom aches for the end of this and lusts
To know those paps in sucking gusts,
To put his first hand on that belly's hair
And feel for the lipped lair,
The fortress made but to be taken, for which
He feels the battering ram grow large and itch.[38]

In the poem, Pessoa demonstrates a flair for the English language, but it lacks emotional intensity and sometimes drags along in an artificial and placid manner. Pessoa mostly presents the female point of view, which continues an approach in Campos's 'Maritime Ode'. There is the sense that the woman is being raped. And there is Pessoa's 'self-definition' of being 'a female by temperament'.

Friendships

A final word should be said about Pessoa's relationship with his friends – virtual and of flesh and blood. His literary and political friends were an important and regular presence in his life. One may be forgiven for thinking from reading *The Book of Disquiet* or some of his most famous poems that Pessoa was utterly alone, but the reality is that he was in company and conversation with others in Lisbon probably nearly every day of his adult life. Perceived as outwardly shy and reserved, Pessoa remained all his life a subversive and eccentric figure who also felt more comfortable surrounded by oddball literary types. His friends and the people he gravitated towards informed his outlook on singularity, sexuality and self-fecundation. Jack Kerouac had famously written, when it came to finding company, that the only people for him were 'the mad ones, the ones who are mad to live, mad to talk, mad to be saved'.[39] Though Kerouac and Pessoa lived very different lives, perhaps this instinct for seeking out marginal companions applies to Pessoa too. Pessoa was attracted to eccentric types (such as, for example, Aleister Crowley and the wandering Russian poet Eliezer Kamenezky,[40] among others), all his friends were male, many were bachelors, and some were openly homosexual – a

Pessoa sitting with António Botto, Raul Leal and Augusto Ferreira Gomes (standing) at Café Martinho da Arcada, from *O Notícias Ilustrado*, 23 December 1928.

courageous and rebellious act in the early twentieth century, not least in conservative, Catholic Portugal. Pessoa's closest and perhaps only true friend of flesh and bone, Sá-Carneiro, was possibly homosexual, and also his fellow poets and friends Raul Leal and António Botto were homosexual, and Álvaro de Campos was most likely bisexual. Botto wrote explicitly homosexual poems and Pessoa admired him for this, seeing it as an audacious expression of freedom. In November 1922 Pessoa's Olisipo published a second and expanded edition of Botto's poetry book *Canções*, which was accompanied by a sensual photo of the poet.[41] In 1923, Leal's homoerotic book *Sodoma Divinizada* (Sodom Divinized) was also published by Olisipo, and was to be its last publication.

During Pessoa's last years, after Ophelia had given up on him, new and old friends came to seek out his company in the cafés and bars of downtown Lisbon, perhaps to ask for help with a poem, write a preface for a collection or ask for advice on how to get published. They might try out a theory with him, inquire what he was working on himself or encourage him to publish his work. But ultimately it was his virtual friends who stayed with him, who sat up with him late into the night. As early as 1920, Pessoa wrote (in another unfinished preface to a volume of poetry and prose that never came to fruition): 'No one knew me personally except Álvaro de Campos.'[42] It was Campos who interfered in his life, who perhaps spoke more honestly than Pessoa to Ophelia, and it was Campos who continued to write poetry right up until the last month of Pessoa's life. But it was Bernardo Soares who was most like Pessoa, and who kept him company during the witching time of night. At some unspecified time, Pessoa encountered a virtual friend called Vicente Guedes in a restaurant in Lisbon, and the two began talking about literature, *Orpheu* and a book that Guedes had been writing since 1915. From 1929 onwards, this book was attributed to Bernardo Soares. For the next five years Pessoa dedicated himself to Soares, though he failed to live up to his promise to the author to publish this cracked masterpiece of the modern age. Publication would happen posthumously.

8
The Ruin of Disquiet

Nothing, nothing, part of the night and the silence and what I share
with them of vacancy, of negativity, of in-betweenness [*intervalar*], a gap
between me and myself, something forgotten by some god or other.
Bernardo Soares[1]

Writing is like the drug I abhor and keep taking, the addiction I despise
and depend on. There are necessary poisons, and some are extremely
subtle, composed of ingredients from the soul, herbs collected from
among the ruins of dreams, black poppies found next to the graves of
our intentions, the long leaves of obscene trees whose branches sway
on the echoing banks of the soul's infernal rivers . . . To write is to lose
myself, yes, but everyone loses himself, because everything gets lost.
Bernardo Soares[2]

Desassossego is a serpentine five-syllable word which is usually
translated as 'disquiet' in English. For non-Portuguese speakers,
it takes more than a few attempts to pronounce it correctly and
catch its rhythm, where the first 's' in the word has a 'z' sound.
Desassossego can be a feeling of discomfort or unease, of something
unsettling or disturbing, of anxiety and restlessness, and even of
something akin to the uncanny as in Freud's *unheimlich*. Pessoa
wrote the word *desassossego* in capital letters in the margins
of a poem on 20 January 1913. That year he also wrote and
published, under his own name, the Symbolist text 'In the Forest
of Estrangement', which is the first text attributed to the *Livro do
Desassossego*, translated as *The Book of Disquiet*.

Desassossego captures both the singular spirit of Pessoa and the universal spirit of disquiet of the twentieth century. The word and feeling provide a stark contrast to Alberto Caeiro, who, on the surface, is the poet of *sossego* (tranquillity, calm), and who, in the first poem of *The Keeper of Sheep*, describes his sadness as *sossego* or 'soothing', 'because it's natural and right'.[3] For a moment, the creator of the poem thought about using the word *alegre* (joyful), but scribbled it out and wrote *sossego* instead.[4] That said, Caeiro's calmness and certainty contain within them a rupture, a shock and, at times, something disquieting.

Pessoa is both explicitly and implicitly present throughout the pieces that are collected in *The Book of Disquiet*. He writes the preface to the work and recounts meeting the author, who declares himself to be one of those rare people who reads *Orpheu*; there are ruminations on literature that sound like Pessoa's opinions and reflections on Pessoa's favourite authors; there is much philosophizing and lucid daydreaming; and there are detailed observations of the streets of downtown Lisbon. Made up of everything from notes scribbled on the back of letters to typewritten papers, this is a mesmerizing collection of passages that contains some of Pessoa's finest prose. It examines the interior universe of a solitary human self, rendering it as an exterior universe and landscape for readers of each generation to travel through and be astonished by. We, as disquieted humans in the modern age of acceleration, encounter our own fears, desires, doubts, anxieties and regrets reflected back at us as we wade through *The Book of Disquiet*. It is Pessoa's prose masterpiece.

Pessoa's 'Demon of Reality' stalks *The Book of Disquiet* via three authors – Fernando Pessoa, Vicente Guedes and Bernardo Soares. The heteronyms write into being the three aspects of the impossible, the nothing and the monster. This book, if we can even call it that, was never finished, and had at least two lives during Pessoa's lifetime and more lives after his death. It was written between 1913 and 1934 and begins under the name Fernando Pessoa. Vicente Guedes takes over from 1915 to 1920, but then goes silent forever. The name Bernardo Soares emerges in 1920 as a writer of short stories, but is put aside until 1929, when he suddenly becomes the author of *The Book of Disquiet* and writes more than half of the texts for the book before he too disappears in 1934. A year later, Pessoa was also gone, and thus begins the slow afterlife of one of the great literary artefacts of the twentieth century. Reflecting on the transformative shifts in the construction, writing and intervals of the book, Lourenço writes: 'The reality and the written trace in which that metamorphosis-rupture has taken place we call modernity.'[5] The texts for *The Book of Disquiet* feel pertinent and fresh today, almost as if they were written for a generation disorientated by information overload, idiotic political leaders and a feeling of powerlessness in what seems to be the self-destructive and irreversible path of humanity.

Lourenço calls *The Book of Disquiet* a 'suicidal text', 'a kind of non-book' and an 'impossible book'.[6] In his introduction to one of the Portuguese editions, Zenith calls it an 'anti-book', while Jerónimo Pizarro, the editor and compiler of another edition, calls it 'at least two books', with the author Guedes being 'the more decadent' and Soares 'the more modernist'.[7] Pessoa himself, in the early stages of writing *The Book of Disquiet*, refers to it as 'this gentle book'.[8] Every edition of *The Book of Disquiet* is different because Pessoa left it unfinished and in complete disorder in a wooden trunk. The first edition of the book was not published until 1982, 47 years after his death. And since then, more complete editions (almost twice the size of the first) have been published. Zenith organized his edition thematically to try to give it some kind of fluidity and rhythm, inserting most of the early symbolic-style texts with their titles at the end of the book. A few years later, Pizarro organized his edition as chronologically as possible. The two editions work well side by side, particularly if one holds dear *The Book of Disquiet* and wishes to return to it again and again. This pair of editions gives the reader the eyes of Argus – which always change upon awakening and see in a multiplicity of ways – so they can enter the book both quasi-thematically and chronologically.

The Authors and Phases of *The Book of Disquiet*

The Book of Disquiet began in 1913 with Pessoa's Symbolist texts with titles such as 'Our Lady of Silence', 'Painful Interval', 'Peristyle', 'The Lake of Possession', 'A Voyage I Never Made', 'Aesthetic of Indifference', 'In the Forest of Estrangement', 'The Art of Effective Dreaming', 'Milky Way' and 'Absurdity'. But its first real (heteronymous) author was Vicente Guedes, who actually emerges in 1909 (or might even have been conceived in 1908) as a collaborator in Pessoa's first short-lived publishing venture, Ibis. Guedes goes on to write short stories and poems, and translates various classic works of English literature by Lord Byron, Percy Shelley and Robert Louis Stevenson, among others. He is also attributed as the Portuguese translator of Alexander Search's short story 'A Very Original Dinner'. But he really gets writing when he takes on the role of author of *The Book of Disquiet* in 1915. Guedes was an office clerk working on the fourth floor of Rua dos Retroseiros 17 (the street is now called Rua da Conceição). Reflecting on Guedes, Pessoa described him as 'the definite creator of inner aristocracy', 'one of the most subtly passive souls and one of the purest, most profligate dreamers that the world has ever known' and 'a dandy in spirit'. For Guedes, 'to dream was a religion' and he 'took languid pleasure in having no ambition at all'.[9] In conclusion, Pessoa wrote: 'This book is not by him: it is him!' Guedes describes himself as a 'stagnator of life' and 'a chiseller of inexactitudes'.[10]

Around 1916 Pessoa wrote in a text in English: 'The Sensationists are, first of all, Decadents.'[11] Guedes is no aristocrat, nor does he gravitate in any way towards bodily pleasures, material goods or gastronomical delights, but he still belongs to the lineage of *fin de siècle* decadence with his musings on the aesthetics of abdication, discouragement and indifference. He is part of a Europe that was languishing in an age of decadence in the aftermath of Nietzsche's 'death of God'. In 1920, the year when Pessoa began his love affair with Ophelia, Vicente Guedes suddenly disappears. The writing of the book resumes again just before the second break between Pessoa and Ophelia, but now the author is Bernardo Soares.

In the second phase of *The Book of Disquiet*, many of the entries were given dates, and the style moved away from the Symbolist period to appear more as diary entries; it started to read more like a novel. The second dated piece of writing appears under the heading 'L. do D.'. It is dated 22 March 1929 and begins with the words: 'In the cove on the seashore, among the woods and meadows that fronted the beach, the fickleness of inflamed desire rose out of the uncertainty of the blank abyss.'[12] In this passage, the author goes on to write of 'the magic power of words' in isolation or joined together with the trees and with landscapes, while also mentioning 'Moorish ladies of folklore' and 'princesses from other people's dreams'. So much of Pessoa is found in this passage: it contains his love and mastery of words and the architecture of constructing beautiful sentences, his inability to refrain from entering into reverie, the interpenetration of language and landscape,[13] the conjuring of a fairytale mood and, of course, the always shadowy presence of the abyss. Almost exactly one year later, the author wrote one of the most famous entries of 'L. do D.' on being born in a time when the majority of young people had lost faith in God (which was quoted at the beginning of Chapter Three). This passage is the first entry in the first edition of *Livro do Desassossego* that was published in Portugal in 1982, and in Zenith's edition in both Portuguese and English. It begins the second section (which comprises the entries of Bernardo Soares) of Pizarro's edition. Pessoa himself marks it as 'beginning passage'. The narrator declares that he does not accept the concept of Humanity and instead embraces Decadence, and that the author will not completely give up on God, at least not give up on being open to the mystery of things, then dramatically says: 'Could it think, the heart would stop beating.'[14] This phrase captures something of the vision of its author, who is often attempting to feel through concepts and to think through feelings. Pessoa's thinking was suffused with feeling, and his emotions were often interrupted by his intellect. Or, to put it another way, Pessoa's supreme rationality is often disturbed by intense feeling, while his poetry of overflowing sensations is often interrupted by philosophical reasoning.

Soares refers (most likely in 1929) to the work as his 'factless autobiography' and his 'lifeless history'. He writes: 'These are my Confessions, and if in them I say nothing, it's because I have nothing to say.'[15] Pessoa described Soares in 1935 as a 'semi-heteronym' because his personality was not different from his but 'a mere mutilation of it'.[16] Soares lives in a rented room on the fourth floor of Rua dos Douradores and works for a firm on the same street called Vasques & Co. His job is to fill in ledgers. Pessoa worked as a freelance translator between 1922 and 1935 in an office building on Rua da Prata 71, very close to Rua dos Douradores. *Douradores* means 'goldsmiths', and a *dourador* is a gilder. There is an obvious link here with alchemy, but, as Ronald W. Sousa points out, a gilder 'merely coats the outside of a base metal with a gold surface'.[17] It is as if these texts are not real gold but merely a surface that covers emptiness; they are written by a poet who writes prose in an age where what once was thought sacred is now very much in doubt, has been profaned, or has faded away into oblivion. The street is one of the narrowest in Baixa. The sun's rays do not stay for long, it is difficult to see the other end of the street, and after a working day it is quiet and empty. Rua dos Douradores is reality for Bernardo Soares, and is an integral part of *The Book of Disquiet*. Today, one of Soares's sentences is inscribed on the ground halfway down the street: 'I will always belong to the Rua dos Douradores, like all of humanity.'[18]

Throughout *The Book of Disquiet*, Soares proves to be a supremely gifted prose writer with a talent for philosophy, literary criticism and social observation. He is an abstemious *flâneur* of urban landscapes and a master of lucid daydreaming. He is another everyman of modernism, alongside Kafka's tortured protagonists, Musil's Ulrich, Proust's narrator and Joyce's Bloom. These characters from modernist literature often descend into a nihilistic mood. They do not stand out from the crowd and are not heroes in the traditional sense, yet they observe everything in great detail with the eye of a poet and the sensibility of a mystic. Soares reflects on his own appearance: 'I look like a nondescript Jesuit. My gaunt and inexpressive face has no intelligence or intensity or anything else to raise it out of that lifeless tide of faces.'[19] At another moment, he describes himself as 'the character of an unwritten novel'.[20] In the text that was probably intended for the beginning of *The Book of Disquiet*, Soares writes: 'Taking nothing seriously and recognizing our sensations as the only reality we have for certain, we take refuge there, exploring them like large unknown countries.'[21] Soares informs the reader that his mother died when he was only one, and his father committed suicide when he was just three years old, making him an orphan from a very early age.[22] Soares judges suicide to be a cowardice because 'it is to surrender ourselves completely to life.'[23] Adrift, exiled in himself and alone, Soares is an invisible secret writer, walking, working and sleeping on the Rua dos Douradores.

Reading and Absorbing Writers

Bernardo Soares at one moment admits: 'Literature is the most agreeable way of ignoring life.'[24] The authors he gravitates towards throughout *The Book of Disquiet* give another indication of the kind of person and artist he is, and how close he is to Pessoa himself. Five Portuguese authors offer a good guide to the architectonics of the book. First, there is Cesário Verde, the father of modern Portuguese poetry, with whose writing Soares thinks he shares 'the identical substance'.[25] Then there is António Vieira, his 'master',[26] a Jesuit priest, educator and writer, whom Pessoa calls 'Emperor of the Portuguese language' in his book *Mensagem*.[27] Third, there is António Nobre, the poet of a collection called *Só* (Alone), a book that Soares says will no longer be the saddest book in Portugal once *The Book of Disquiet* is published.[28] Fourth, there is José Valentim Fialho de Almeida, a writer who embraced decadent ideals and who was very sensitive and careful in the use of grammar and syntax in writing a sentence.[29] Finally, there is Alberto Caeiro, whose lines of poetry Soares thinks 'seem to spring into being on their own' and make him feel free and inspired.[30]

French writers also have an influence, such as the Viscount of Chateaubriand – 'a great soul that diminishes'; Henri-Frédéric Amiel and his posthumous book *Fragment d'un journal intime*; and Jean-Jacques Rousseau – 'the modern man' who possessed 'the intelligence of a creator and the sensibility of a slave'.[31] The usual suspects from British and Irish literature are present: Charles Dickens and Thomas Carlyle; Shakespeare, 'the reckless playwright';[32] and Oscar Wilde, particularly his idea that most of us are someone else. Philosophers are engaged with too, both explicitly and implicitly: Hegel, Kant, Edmund Spenser, Francisco Sanches, Rousseau, Plato and Scotus Erigena are all named, and there are allusions to Spinoza and Schopenhauer, among others. Then there are reflections on the Persian poet Omar Khayyám, revealing Soares's (and Pessoa's) fascination with the concept and experience of 'tedium' and the idea of the East. In the earliest stages of *The Book of Disquiet*, even before Vicente Guedes takes on the task of writing it, an entry in the text reads: 'My Imagination is a city in the Orient,' though this would now be seen in terms of Orientalist essentialism.[33] Within his outward loneliness, there is a rich inner creative conversation with all of these dead authors whose words gleam like pearls, and Soares at one point fantasizes about how his own prose might turn out: 'The sensibility of Mallarmé in the style of Vieira; to dream like Verlaine in the body of Horace; to be Homer in the moonlight.'[34]

Ruins

The theme of ruins pervades *The Book of Disquiet*. It was written during years of catastrophe, chaos and enormous ruptures in literature, philosophy, politics and science in Europe. The era is defined by colossal ruins of books, or at least ones that remain unfinished and open-ended. Walter Benjamin started writing *The Arcades Project* in 1927 and continued carrying it around with him until his death by suicide in the Pyrenees in 1940 (it was only published for the first time in 1983). There are Kafka's unfinished posthumous novels. Then there is Wittgenstein's *Philosophical Investigations*, which he worked on for over fifteen years. He did manage to finish it six years before he died, but it was only published posthumously. In the preface, he calls it 'an album' rather than a book, and defines the philosophical remarks as 'a number of sketches of landscapes'.[35] Even Heidegger only managed to complete a third of *Being and Time*, a major work of twentieth-century philosophy. It was written quickly and published in 1927, but the final section trails off with three questions. Theodor Adorno's final work, *Aesthetic Theory* (1970), was left unfinished as he died in the final stages of writing the book, although the nature of his great philosophical work on aesthetics meant that it could not be finished as it was a study of how art, music, literature and society had become totalities of ruins. Adorno wrote elsewhere that 'in the history of art, late works are the catastrophes.'[36] The same could be said of Pessoa's *The Book of Disquiet* – both works encapsulate the philosophical problem of modernism, which had become a 'culture of rupture'.[37]

Writers in this era were grappling with a rupture of time, and what it means to exist and communicate as a human being in modernity. The protracted writing and publishing process seems to have been part of this struggle. Other delayed masterpieces of European literary modernism include Proust's *In Search of Lost Time* (1913–27), which had not been fully published by the time of the author's death, and Robert Musil's colossal *The Man without Qualities* (1930–43), which remained unfinished. Meanwhile, Joyce dedicated sixteen years to writing his final work, *Finnegans Wake* (1923–39), and thought about quitting on a few occasions, or at least getting someone else to finish it.[38] Unlike Pessoa with *The Book of Disquiet*, Joyce did manage to complete *Finnegans Wake*, but it remains one of the most fractal and impenetrable works in the history of literature. In contrast, *The Book of Disquiet* is easy enough to read. Its profundity and sophistication do not lie in a radical deconstruction and invention of language but rather in precise writing, concise descriptions and the succinct capture of profound ideas in wondrous ways.

Pessoa, Guedes and Soares were architects and creators of ruins, building fragments upon fragments. As Pessoa himself wrote, probably as early as 1913, in a text for 'L. do D.': 'I'm the ruins of buildings that were never more than ruins, whose builder, halfway through, got tired of thinking about what he was building.'[39] Five years later, Vicente Guedes writes: 'The only true art is that of *construction*. But the present-day milieu makes it impossible for constructive qualities to appear in the human spirit.'[40] It was the age of Werner Heisenberg's 'uncertainty principle' from 1927. And in the previous century, Marx already knew of the ruins at the heart of the modern world and described how capitalism thrives in these ruins – his books *Grundrisse* and *Das Capital* can be added to the list of masterpieces of ruins. *Grundrisse* was not published until 1939, but it was written in the winter of 1857–8 in the British Library, and is a laborious eight-hundred-page study that enters new territory for Marx in his attempt to find a new method and approach to a critique of political economy. He abandons the book but it is really a work that he was writing for himself before moving on to his most important text. *Das Capital* is a sprawling and ever-expanding analysis of capitalism over thousands of pages. Marx worked for three decades on it but only saw the publication of the first volume in 1867.

Pessoa was surrounded by an atmosphere in Europe where everything seemed to be lacking solid ground. Álvaro de Campos, the engineer and poet of the modern age, also began to construct ruins, such as the unfinished odes 'Time's Passage' and 'Salutation to Walt Whitman'. Another great ruin is Pessoa's book on Faust, where at one point among the rubble of passages is written: 'All is scattered, nothing is whole.'[41] Yet another ruin is a short incomplete work called *The Education of a Stoic* by Pessoa's penultimate heteronym, the Baron of Teive. Conceived in 1928, the baron kills himself, with the reason for this action given in the subtitle of the book: 'The Impossibility of Producing Superior Art'. The first Portuguese edition of only these passages in a single book was not published until 1999.

All of these works, with *The Book of Disquiet* at the top of the heap, are good examples of *disjecta membra* or 'scattered fragments'. Pessoa was fond of this term, which was used first by Horace and later by Carlyle – crucial writers for Reis and Soares respectively. The term is mentioned in a small text called 'The Man from Porlock', which Pessoa wrote and published in 1934. In this piece,

Pessoa reflects on the 'unknown interrupter' (a man from Porlock) who knocked on Coleridge's door when he was in the middle of writing down the great poem 'Kubla Khan', which came to him in a dream. With this interruption, the middle of the poem was lost forever because when the poet returned to his writing table, he had forgotten the middle section. What is left is an example of *disjecta membra*, just the beginning and end of the poem. As Carlyle wrote: '*Disjecta membra* are all that we find of any Poet.'[42] Throughout *The Book of Disquiet* we can see how the poet tries to communicate between the abyss and life. In *The Waste Land*, perhaps the most famous twentieth-century English-language poem, T. S. Eliot writes: 'These fragments I have shored against my ruins.'[43] Thus even the finished works can be fragments or remnants of the dream, but very substantial remnants. Pessoa is well aware of this as he reflects on Shakespeare's *King Lear* in an early pre-Guedes/pre-Soares text for *The Book of Disquiet*, seeing it as 'a monstrous defect' and 'a broken Greek statue'.[44] In a piece written in English called 'The Task of Modern Poetry', Pessoa writes of Shakespeare as 'the monstrous phenomenon'.[45] Shakespeare, *magister ludi*, overreaches himself, creating a colossal uneven work, the great play of the void, full of errors alongside some of the finest moments in English literature. It is Shakespeare who shows (*monstrare*) the self, who, for some, has invented the human.[46] In another note on Shakespeare, Pessoa wrote that the great dramatist and poet lacked 'balance, sanity, discipline' – attributes that Pessoa would have thought he also did not have.[47] Access to profound knowledge and to the mystery of things can be accompanied by melancholy, imbalance and lunacy.

Finally, in relation to ruins, the image or metaphor of the shipwreck is pertinent and vivid in the cultural memory of Portugal's history of seafaring voyages, and in Pessoa's writings as the Argonaut of disquiet who took 'the abstract path to the world's void'.[48] Again, in one of the earliest texts for *The Book of Disquiet*, Pessoa wrote: 'Shipwrecks? No, I never suffered any. But I have the impression that I shipwrecked all my voyages, and that my salvation lay in interspaces of unconsciousness.'[49] There is a double metaphor of the shipwreck of the modern mind and the shipwreck of the Portuguese Empire and its vision for a future. But Pessoa, echoing the philosophy of Walter Benjamin, wrote in an inverted affirmative manner: 'The beauty of ruins? That they are no longer good for anything.'[50]

The King of Gaps

Another central aspect running through *The Book of Disquiet* is the concept and experience of being in between. Words such as interval (*intervalo*), interlude (*interlúdio*), intermission (*entreacto*) and gap (*lacuna*) are scattered throughout Pessoa's writings. There are at least two simple definitions of interval: the space between two points or two objects; and the space of time between events, artistic shows, dates or epochs. In Western thought, interval can also signify a temporary messianic interruption: St Paul's *rhipé* (twinkling of the eye), which Martin Luther translated into the word *Augenblick*, and subsequently Kierkegaard's *Øieblik* (the moment) and Heidegger's version of *Augenblick* (moment of vision).[51]

Pessoa wrote as early as 1910: 'I hate the beginnings and the ends of things, for they are definite points.'[52] The middle point is the crack, the access to the void – where the poets, seekers and shamans must traverse and dwell. It is perhaps there, in the middle of things, where the grappling with negation occurs and the nothing is encountered. It is the space of creativity and transformative thought. Nineteenth-century philosophers such as Hegel and Kierkegaard commented on this state and activity. Hegel wrote in the preface to his first major work, *Phenomenology of Spirit*: 'tarrying with the negative is the magical power that converts it into being.'[53] Kierkegaard, under the guise of his philosophical pseudonym Johannes Climacus, wrote of keeping 'open the wound of negativity', which sums up much of his writing endeavour.[54] This leads us to Keats's famous idea of 'Negative Capability', which Pessoa, among many other poets and thinkers, was drawn to:

at once it struck me what quality went to form a Man of Achievement, especially in Literature, and which Shakespeare possessed so enormously – I mean *Negative Capability*, that is, when a man is capable of being in uncertainties, mysteries, doubts, without any irritable reaching after fact and reason.[55]

Being in this negative capability, tarrying with the negative, entering the wound of negativity, being in the middle of things that are nowhere and nothing – that is where Pessoa, Campos and Soares often find themselves or where they feel they must go. This middle is the dolorous interval, the gap, the play within the play, the interlude. It is where the creative mystery is, and where the poem and voyage begin. Dante perhaps said it most eloquently in the exquisite opening line of *The Divine Comedy*: '*Nel mezzo del cammin di nostra vita/ mi ritrovai per una selva oscura,/ ché la diritta via era smarrita*' (In the middle of the journey of our life I came to myself within a dark wood where the straight way was lost).[56]

Some of Pessoa's poems explicitly dwell in the interval, such as 'Intervalo' in Portuguese from 1935 and 'Meantime' in English (translated as 'Intervalo' by Jorge de Sena), which was published in *The Athenaeum* in 1920, and is the only poem Pessoa published in Britain even though it is nowhere nearly as good as much of his other poetry.[57] 'The King of Gaps', a poem in English from his collection *The Mad Fiddler*, opens with these lines:

> There lived, I know not when, never perhaps –
> But the fact is he lived – an unknown king
> Whose kingdom was the strange Kingdom of Gaps.
> He was lord of what is twixt thing and thing,
> Of interbeings, of that part of us
> That lies between our waking and our sleep . . .[58]

There are lots of poems by Campos expressing the ontological experience of the interval, such as the undated, untitled poem where he wrote: 'It is in the interval that I exist.'[59] 'Lisbon Revisited (1926)' is one of his greatest poems, and includes the lines: 'At intermittent intervals I understand;/ I write in respites from my weariness; And a boredom bored even of itself casts me ashore.'[60] In 'Maritime Ode' the interval is implicit throughout, beginning with the dramatic opening verses in the image of the gap between the wharf (*cais*) and the ship (*navio*) that set the scene and allusions for this epic, imaginative adventure in piracy, homoeroticism and the reckless life of a seafarer. Many years later, Campos wrote a seven-line poem with no title or date that appears on the page like a shipwrecked version of the earlier poem. The poem begins dramatically with these lines: 'I'm beginning to know myself. I don't exist./ I'm the gap between what I'd like to be and what others have made me,/ Or half of this gap, since there's also life . . ./ That's me.'[61] In 1929 Pessoa came up with the title 'Fictions of the Interlude' for his projected book series on his three major heteronymous poets.

The interval was also of interest to Pessoa's friend Sá-Carneiro, as can be seen in his poem 'Inter-Sonho' (Inter-Dream) from 1913. Sá-Carneiro ends the poem with explicit reference to the interval: 'I envision a great interval/ I go wild in all the colours/ I live in purple and die in sound . . .'[62] In this poem we see that the interval is not only connected to dreams, but plays an important role in the structures in music, which is relevant to its literary usage in the dreamscapes of *The Book of Disquiet*.

The word 'interval' turns up over thirty times in *The Book of Disquiet*, with some passages beginning with the title 'Dolorous Interval'.[63] Soares confesses: 'I'm the gap between what I am and am not, between what I dream and what life has made of me, the fleshly and abstract average of things that are nothing, I being likewise nothing.'[64] Everything is in a state of in between in *The Book of Disquiet*: between the death of God and the birth of a new humanism, between the dream and the waking life, between the writer and the public. There is a gap between life and death, truth and fiction, philosophy and poetry (which becomes elliptical prose) and thought and expression. Reality is that which lies in between; it is that which is disquieting. It is also reality that mixes and muddles all these seeming opposites and dichotomies, and the reader experiences this in the mix of ruinous and rigorous prose. Reality is in the interlude, in the middle, *in medias res*; it is what the poet highlights to us. It is where Dante begins his journey into hell, where the play Hamlet begins, and where Soares and Campos keep returning. In *Grande sertão: Veredas*, the Brazilian masterpiece of modernist literature that was published 21 years after the death of Pessoa, João Guimarães Rosa writes: 'the real is not in the setting out or in arriving: it reveals itself to us in the middle of the journey.'[65]

Dream – Death – Darkness

The Book of Disquiet is the story of a dreamer of quotidian reveries. His dreams occur in interiors and in exteriors – in the office where the author works and along the streets of downtown Lisbon where the author wanders. It is impossible not to dream or get distracted in a city. And with the onslaught of increasing speed and population, cacophonic noise, crowds of people, public and private transport, electricity and new technologies, the poet's writing cannot help but be radically transformed and moulded by the city. The authors of *The Book of Disquiet* are dreamers who want lucidity, who are attempting to dream while awake. This will be achieved through the articulation of the dream through language converted into literature. The authors of this lucid dreaming sometimes step into deathlike landscapes, which can be expressions of paralysis, images of statues or instances of non-participation in life. Like other modernists, Pessoa and his coterie were writing for no one and everyone at the same time. As Claudio Magris wrote in his intellectual and poignant journey along the Danube many years later: 'But it can also be an advantage in literature to write for no one, now that wherever one goes the machine of organised culture falsely claims to represent everyone.'[66] This sentiment was already expressed in the previous century in the subtitle of Nietzsche's *Thus Spoke Zarathustra*, which reads: 'A Book for None and All'. Guedes admits that he has never done anything but dream: 'This, and this alone, has been the meaning of my life. My only real concern has been my inner life.'[67] And sixteen years later, Soares explains that it is the tedium of his boss and his work and his office that allows him to dream majestically: 'Having Vasques as my boss, I can enjoy dreaming of kings; having the office on Rua dos Douradores, I can enjoy the inner vision of non-existent landscapes.'[68] For Soares and Pessoa, actually going in actual life to a mysterious country – which is how Pessoa thought of India, for example, would just be a pale imitation of infinite dreams.

In *The Book of Disquiet* there is a Symbolist text by Guedes titled 'Funeral March for Ludwig II, King of Bavaria'. Called the 'Swan King', the 'Mad King' and 'the Fairy Tale King' (*der Märchenkönig*), Ludwig II was a self-exiled creator of beautiful and useless castles and a supporter of Wagner's grandiose operas. Bordering on madness, he was a melancholic, sickly loner who pined for a woman who did not love him, and a king of deathly things and dark dreams who, like Ophelia from Hamlet, drowned in a river, and on 13 June 1886 – the same day as Pessoa's birthday! He was the perfect muse for Pessoa. The section on King Ludwig II is an example of a celebration of lost causes, a fetish for fairytale worlds and the feeling of melancholy, and speaking with the dead:

> Sovereign King of the Watches, knight errant of Anxieties traveling on moonlit roads without glory and without even a lady to serve, lord in the forests and on the slopes and, a silent silhouette with visor drawn shut, passing through valleys, misunderstood in villages, ridiculed in towns, scorned in cities![69]

Guedes declares King Ludwig II to be an 'Emperor of Death and Shipwreck', a 'Shadow King who despised light' and a 'Dream King who rejected life'.[70] Thus, although much of *The Book of Disquiet* takes place during the day, in the office and on city streets, a darkness pervades the writing. Pessoa, in the preface, says the author 'spent his nights at home . . . writing'.[71] And it is by night that the author says that he really comes alive, or as he says with a mix of biblical and Gothic allusion: 'By day I am nothing and by night I am I.' Elsewhere, the author wrote of his 'night-time walk to the lonely shore of the sea', and other passages contain phrases such as 'the nocturnal waters of my disquiet'; 'Everything around me is the naked, abstract universe, consisting of nocturnal negations'; and 'Nocturnal glory'.[72] *The Book of Disquiet* could be categorized as a 'nightbook', alongside other modern works of the

Neuschwanstein Castle in Bavaria, c. 1890–1906.

dark, such as, for example, Louis-Ferdinand Celine's *Voyage au bout de la nuit* (Journey to the End of the Night), James Joyce's *Finnegans Wake*, Arno Schmidt's *Zettel's Traum* (Bottom's Dream), Julian Rio's *Babel de una noche de San Juan* (Larva: A Midsumer Night's Dream) and John Moriarty's *Night Journey to Buddh Gaia*, among others.[73] Pessoa's predecessor Cesário Verde wrote his own night work, his masterpiece *O sentimento dum occidental* (The Feeling of a Westerner). The poem, published in 1880, is divided into four parts: Vespers, After Dark, By Gaslight and the Dead Hours. It begins with the lines: 'On our streets, as night falls,/ There is so much gloom/ there is so much melancholy . . . (*Nas nossas ruas, ao anoitecer,/ Há tal soturnidade, há tal melancholia*).[74] In the nightbook, to quote a line from a poem by Álvaro de Campos, Soares's 'inherent exile' also 'comes alive in the darkness'.[75]

Tedium and the Spy of Nothing

Tedium (*tédio*) is a key word in *The Book of Disquiet*. It is an ontological category and an experience of existing in the modern age, 'a continuity in nothingness' that the poetic philosophers

Kierkegaard and Heidegger have tried to articulate through philosophical discussion about what it is to be a human being existing in time.[76] One could approach and view tedium in various ways. There is the feeling of tedium as being in the office day in, day out and the inevitability of repetition; there is the metaphysical feeling of tedium as weariness and exhaustion in the wake of the 'death of God' where tedium 'is a lack of a mythology';[77] and there is the general existential experience of tedium as boredom in the facticity of one's existence, one's struggles to find meaning and the solitary movement towards death.

The head of the office in *The Book of Disquiet*, Senhor Vasques, is modelled after Pessoa's real-life boss Carlos Moitinho de Almeida, whom he worked for on Rua da Prata for over a decade. Vasques is described as 'Life – monotonous and necessary, imperious and inscrutable Life. This banal man represents the banality of Life. For me he is everything, externally speaking, because for me Life is whatever is external.'[78] But working in this kind of environment is fruitful for Pessoa's writing, and for Bernardo Soares it is his only lifeline to full-blooded life and the comings and goings of regular people. Other philosophical poets of the twentieth century, such as T. S. Eliot and Wallace Stevens, worked in offices, which gave them focus and appreciation for the time they had to write. In one long entry, dated 1 December 1931, Soares gives various intimations of what the murky sensation of tedium is: 'To think without thinking, but with the weariness of thinking; to feel without feeling, but with the anxiety of feeling; to shun without shunning, but with the disgust that makes one shun.'[79] Are we, in today's world, losing the feeling of tedium? Or at least the kind of tedium that comes from the privilege of being existentially bored, and then after some time passes, whether that be minutes or hours, the imagination starts to take flight, and we think of something creative to do? With the onslaught of social media, mobile phones, gaming and the endless TV series on screens of all shapes and sizes, is there any time left to be bored or experience hours of tedium? Perhaps reading *The Book of Disquiet* is one way to return to tedium: books are portals to dreams, and to wade through a long, disjointed, scrupulous book could allow one to enter a space of slowness, unsettledness, disorientation and transformation.

A year after Campos wrote the poem 'The Tobacco Shop', which begins with the line 'I am nothing', Heidegger, in his inaugural lecture for the chair of professor of philosophy at the University of Freiburg, declared that the human being was 'the place-holder of nothingness'.[80] As Heidegger's life and thought unfolded, he moved more and more into trying to hear and tap into the call of the poet more than that of the philosopher, and reflected deeply on a question posed by Hölderlin: 'What are poets for in a destitute time?' (*wozu Dichter in dürftiger Zeit?*). Later, in an essay titled 'What Are Poets For?', Heidegger wrote: 'In the age of the world's night, the abyss of the world must be experienced and endured. But for this it is necessary that there be those who reach into the abyss.'[81] This is what Pessoa, Guedes and Soares, as Argonauts of modernity, are doing. Heidegger went on to write that to be a poet in a destitute time was 'to attend, singing, to the trace of the fugitive gods', echoing the impulse of Ricardo Reis.[82] To be a poet in a destitute time is also perhaps to articulate this gnawing feeling of tedium of the nothingness that prevails, while at the same time revelling in the glorious activity of creativity that rests on the nothing or void. There is a difference between nothingness and nihilism. Pessoa is not a nihilist, but a creator out of nothingness. For Pessoa, meaning is in the creation out of the void, and his love for the everyday in existence grows as he gets older.

The modern Argonaut is making the voyage to the 'world's void'. That void makes up both the world and what we begin to read and think of as the modern self. Stefan Zweig, in his biography of Ferdinand Magellan, the Portuguese sailor who led the first fleet from Europe to circumnavigate the globe, wrote: 'As so often when a man seems to be at the mercy of the winds, he is in reality being blown back upon his own self.'[83] This is sailing the 'dynamic void' that Campos and Pessoa both wrote of in their poetry. The word 'dynamic' relates to the action of forces, quantum physics, engineering, rupture and mutability. Throughout *The Book of Disquiet*, both Guedes and Soares express nothingness and the tedium of nothingness in a

The last known photograph of Pessoa, taken by Augusto Ferreira Gomes in autumn 1934.

way that connects with dynamism and mathematics. Here are two examples of the dynamic void in literary prose from Soares. First:

> My soul is a black whirlpool, a vast vertigo circling a void, the racing of an infinite ocean around a hole in nothing . . . And amid all this confusion I, what's truly I, am the centre that exists only in the geometry of the abyss: I'm the nothing around which everything spins, existing only so that it can spin, being a centre only because every circle has one. I, what's truly I, am a well without walls but with the walls' viscosity, the centre of everything with nothing around it.[84]

From being a teenager toying with the idea of setting up a Nothingness Club through to the final years of writing *The Book of Disquiet*, the shadow of nothingness always followed Pessoa. In fact, even in his last poem in Portuguese, an untitled poem dated 19 November 1935, his final despairing words are: 'Give me more wine, because life is nothing.'[85] Soares writes: 'I am nothing – just an abstract centre of impersonal sensations, a fallen sentient mirror reflecting the world's diversity.'[86] *The Book of Disquiet*, in its willingness to stay with tedium, is attempting to do the task of 'opening nothings' – a phrase Soares uses in the first dated entry from the second phase of writing the book.[87] The 'I' fits into all three aspects of reality: the impossible, the nothing and the monster.

Eduardo Lourenço brilliantly captures an essential quality of Pessoa's art: 'If S. Kierkegaard was the "spy of God", Pessoa was the "spy of Nothing".'[88] This statement works on different levels. First, it invokes Shakespeare: the 'spy of God' is a reference to King Lear's famous final speech to Cordelia, in Act I, scene 1, before she is taken off to her death. *King Lear* is, in many ways, the great play of 'nothing'. Cordelia sets the whole play in motion when her father asks her what she has to say about her love for him and she answers: 'Nothing, my Lord.' Lear reacts to his daughter with the immortal lines: 'Nothing will come of nothing. Speak again.' Next, the statement takes us to Kierkegaard, who also cherished the final passage from *King Lear*, which he inscribed in his journals after his father died.[89] Kierkegaard often referred to himself as a spy in the streets and parks of Copenhagen, and perhaps all serious writers are spies of a kind – observing, hiding, going undercover, carefully gathering and storing information to communicate it again in some altered form.[90] Almost a hundred years after Kierkegaard, we have Pessoa, 'the spy of nothing', with his heteronym Soares referring to himself as a spy in the office and on the streets of Lisbon.[91] But the world Pessoa was born into was a world where the gods had disappeared, whereas Kierkegaard was one of the last great Christian thinkers of Europe. Kierkegaard was one of the first tortured philosophical poets of existentialism; he created a multitude of perspectives from his pseudonymous authorship. Pessoa, as the poet of nothingness, wandered a landscape without faith, relying on the muses of exiled imagination, othering himself utterly in his heteronymous authorship.

Mastering Language or Mastering the Devil

A final important consideration is Soares's reflections on language itself. He reflects on why he writes prose, on the subtleties, nuances and skill of mastering the grammar and syntax of a language, on the possibility of language being one's only homeland. In a passage from *The Book of Disquiet* published on 18 October 1931 in the magazine *Descobrimento: Revista de Cultura*, Soares explains that he prefers prose to poetry because, first, he is not capable of writing in verse and, second, prose 'encompasses all art' in that it contains 'the whole world' and 'every possibility for saying and thinking'.[92] Thus, prose for Soares is closer to reality. He says that he dreams in prose, and that he writes verses in prose.[93] In another entry, Soares declares: 'There's nothing in life that's less real for having been well described.'[94] This emphasis on prose leads Soares to praise Antonio Vieira's writings – he sees Vieira as the master stylist of Portuguese prose with the 'cold perfection of their synthetical engineering'.[95] Soares explains that he upholds two principles that are the foundations of all good style: first, 'to express what one feels exactly as it is felt'; and second, 'to understand that grammar is an instrument and not a law'.[96]

There is another passage from 1931 that is helpful for understanding Soares's vision: 'It offends my intelligence that a man can master the Devil without being able to master the Portuguese language.'[97] This is the crux of Soares's deliberations and pursuit of exacting sentences. For Soares, the language of human beings is far more extraordinary than the language of gods, and there is no excuse for not being able to write a grammatically correct sentence. Pessoa was obviously irritated by the poor writing in an esoteric book at the time Soares wrote this entry. But the gesture and expression go deeper and reveal something more about the writing and vision of *The Book of Disquiet*. 'In the beginning was the word' is the opening line of the Gospel of St John in the New Testament. 'Word' is a translation of *logos*, which can also mean binding, relation, articulation, language and order. *Logos* is a seductive paradoxical force: an ambiguous tool utilized by both God and the Devil, an arbiter of truth and creator of falsehoods which can both reveal and conceal.

In another section of the text published in *Descobrimento* in 1931, Soares expressed his passion for words: 'Words for me are tangible bodies, visible sirens, incarnate sensualities.'[98] Words and languages are loving, breathing entities, and, for Soares, 'spelling is also a person.'[99] Language and the word create and shape reality, but reality also has to bring language to life through being seen on the written page and heard through the spoken voice. Soares confesses that when reading Vieira's supreme prose, it can make him burst into joyful tears that no joy in life could prompt. There are moments where Soares is seeking to make a work of art in a single, precise sentence. There is an entry dated 27 July 1930 of Soares ruminating on the difficulty of defining a spiral. He defines the word in a sentence three times, refining the definition with each attempt before he is satisfied. This is an example of Pessoa and Soares's joy in working and chiselling language and making sentences as economical as possible. Looking deeper, perhaps Soares chose to define a spiral not just for the challenge of visualizing it in words, but also because it can be linked to the occult via the image of the serpent, non-linear time and eternal recurrence. Hurricanes and tornadoes also take the shape of a spiral as they destroy everything in their path, picking up all things – objects, ideas, even memories – and sweeping them into oblivion. The ouroboros, the serpent eating itself, is a circular shape, and when spoken aloud the word sounds (and feels) like a return, a repetition, the beginning of a mantra. Roberto Calasso, in his book *Ka*, writes: 'What are men in the end if not the dream of a god as he drifts around on a snake's coils?'[100] Soares's final definition of a spiral is 'a snake without a snake, vertically wound around nothing'.[101]

There is a final point on language to be made from the ruins of *The Book of Disquiet*. One of Pessoa's more famous and quoted sentences was written by Soares in the extract published in *Descobrimento* in 1931: 'My native country is the Portuguese language.' Here, the word *pátria* is translated as 'native country', which alludes to both a place of birth and a landscape, but it can also be translated as 'homeland' or 'nation' or, most literally, 'fatherland'. In this sentence, Soares finds peace in knowing where his home is – in the language he thinks, speaks, writes and dreams. This contrasts with what Campos declares in 'Opiary' – his first poem, according to Pessoa, which, of course, is not true, but is real – when he defines *Pátria* (with a capital 'P') as wherever he is not.[102] The condition of seeking a lost homeland runs through Pessoa's work, which takes us back not only to the modern artist but to the modern human who is exiled and adrift in an age of disquiet. We are homeless in a metaphysical and spiritual sense, and are always trying to make our way home, and are never fully reconciled with ourselves and the world but nonetheless can somehow be transformed. This longing for a home without finding that true home is sometimes called *Sehnsucht* in German, 'nostalgia' in English and *saudade* in Portuguese. Soares writes that he had *saudade* only because he was disquieted.[103] Soares and Campos feel *saudade* for Lisbon continually even though they are perambulating its streets daily. Pessoa and his heteronyms travel far and wide all over the world in their imaginations but have great difficulty in finding home where they actually are. Soares articulates the world-weariness, tedium and allure of *saudade*, which perhaps, ultimately, is a longing for eternity.

In what feels and reads like the final entry for *The Book of Disquiet* (and which is inserted as the final passage in the translation by Richard Zenith), Soares captures this *saudade* in reflecting on the transience of existence, the familiar faces and the strangers on the streets, and the names of the downtown streets that he walks along every day. Soares reflects on his own mortality and how one day he too will disappear forever from the urban landscape.[104] But he has found his home in the words he has written, and we find him there today. Blanchot writes: 'Exile, the poem then, makes the poet a wanderer, the one always astray, he to whom the stability of presence is not granted and who is deprived of a true abode.'[105] If Soares achieved a kind of peace in finding his *pátria* in the Portuguese language, it does not seem that Pessoa himself came home fully reconciled to one language. The last line he wrote was not in Portuguese but in English: 'I know not what to-morrow will bring.' His *pátria* was writing.

Epilogue: The Death, Afterlife and Reality of Fernando Pessoa

Having made myself into what I am – at worst a lunatic with grandiose dreams, at best not just a writer but an entire literature.
Fernando Pessoa[1]

In the last week of November 1935, Pessoa was not feeling well. He was vomiting and suffering from severe abdominal pain. His doctor was called, and on 29 November Pessoa was sent to the Hospital St Louis in Bairro Alto in Lisbon. He was given a private room, paid for by his boss Moitinho de Almeida. Pessoa received some visitors that day, and when everyone had gone home, he wrote his last sentence in English on a sheet of paper, 'I know not what to-morrow will bring,' and added the date '29-XI-1935'. The sentence sounds like something Ricardo Reis or Horace would have written. It also evokes the last words Pessoa's father wrote, also on the day before he died, in a letter to his wife: 'I don't know what this might be.'[2] In his last sentence, Pessoa showed himself to be an exile and enigma to the last – these words exemplify his continual meditation on the knowledge of not knowing in the face of the void, and his anxiety about human temporality.

Pessoa died around 8.30 p.m. on 30 November 1935. His doctor, Jaime Neves, was present, as well as a nurse and two businessmen who considered Pessoa as their friend. His brother-in-law Chico had been with him, but left the hospital around 6.30 p.m. thinking Pessoa was stable. The cause of his death was most likely intestinal obstruction, but he also had a damaged liver from alcoholism. Pessoa had probably been drinking daily for most of his adult life, and more heavily in the 1930s. He would drink lots of wine and *aguardente* at lunch or in the evenings at the Café Martinho da Arcada, and still be able to function at work and when writing and conversing. In his forties, he became increasingly aware of his mortality and his waning health. Three years before his death, he had a blackout and had to stay in bed for two weeks unable to do anything. He was shaken by the experience, and Dr Neves concluded that 'general intoxication' was the cause of his deteriorating health. But when Pessoa was back on his feet again, he returned to his usual habit of drinking and smoking heavily. Three years later he would be dead.

On 2 December Pessoa was buried in Prazeres Cemetery, which is a ten-minute walk from his apartment on Rua Coelho da Rocha. Luís de Montalvor, his old friend from the *Orpheu* days, made a speech at the funeral in front of about sixty people, including relatives, journalists, business associates, literary critics, writers, artists and Pessoa's doctor. Some of these mourners have since cemented their names in Portuguese culture in the twentieth century, such as Salazar's propaganda minister António Ferro, the painter José de Almada Negreiros, the poet António Botto and Pessoa's first biographer, João Gaspar Simões. Pessoa's barber, Manassés Seixas, was at the funeral – on the way to the hospital the day before he died, Pessoa requested that he be taken to the barber's to have a shave. There were only two women present at the funeral, one of whom was Pessoa's housekeeper; the other we do not know. A few days after the funeral, Pessoa's journalist friend Augusto Ferreira Gomes, who was also an avid reader of occult works, said to Pessoa's sister Teca: 'Fernando had to die; he knew too much.'[3] Another of Pessoa's friends, Mário Saa, wrote an elegy in which he stated: 'And as absurd as it may sound, he, Fernando, will be born after we have all died and in the same moment that he died. He was born after Our Future Death.'[4]

Pessoa's remains were later moved to the cloister in the enormous Jerónimos Monastery in Belém, so he could be close to other poets and historians, and next door to the large tombs of Vasco da Gama and Luís de Camões, which lie inside the entrance to the church. But he probably should have stayed at Prazeres Cemetery. As a poet of

Pessoa's last written line, 'I know not what to-morrow will bring', 29 November 1935.

modernity, he seems to fit in with the exceptional everyday people. It was in the everyday and in every person that Pessoa ultimately embraced reality and ruminated on his philosophies, esoteric activities and megalomaniac fantasies. Despite his dreams and yearnings to reach for an aristocratic libertarianism, his quotidian life and sudden death occurred among the *lisboetas* of the city that he loved: he lived alongside them as an assistant bookkeeper, an idle naval engineer, a medical doctor, and a female hunchback confined to her room. He conversed with journalists, waiters, barbers, literary critics, poets, translators, copyists, office bosses, tobacco shop owners, astral spirits and bartenders, and fell in love for a moment (or two) with a secretary.

In 1988, a bronze statue was placed in front of the Brazileira Café in Chiado to mark the centenary of Pessoa's birth. The work, by sculptor Lagoa Henriques, shows Pessoa sitting at a table with his right arm in mid-air. To his left is an empty chair that entices passers-by to sit down for a moment. Pessoa did not like to embrace, kiss or touch other people when he was alive, but every day in the twenty-first century this bronze statue receives hugs, kisses and smiles from men, women and children from all over the world.

As the years go by, Pessoa's stature and fame as a poet increase. He has been mythologized in literature since his death by other writers, among them José Saramago. Saramago's novel *The Year of the Death of Ricardo Reis* (1984) begins with the sentence: 'Here the sea ends and the earth begins.' It tells the story of Ricardo Reis returning to Lisbon after many years away in Brazil after receiving a telegram from Campos informing him that Pessoa has died. Reis wanders aimlessly through the city, visited often by his maker, Pessoa, who also turns out to be his grim reaper, as he spends his last year of life in the capital. This philosophical novel is told with compassion and wit against the historical backdrop of the first days of the Estado Novo and the lead-up to the Spanish Civil War. A communist and outspoken critic of Salazar's regime, Saramago, in a mischievous Pessoan gesture, chose the character least like himself and devoted the whole book to the heteronym who was a right-wing monarchist.

Death notice for Fernando Pessoa, 'o poeta intemporal' (the timeless poet), in *Diario de Lisboa* (6 December 1935), with a portrait of Pessoa by José de Almada Negreiros.

There is both subtle humour and dark melancholy in this beautiful novel, as we follow the lonely and disquieted Reis through Lisbon as he tries to read a detective novel called *The God of the Labyrinth* by an Irish author named Herbert Quain. To add fiction to fiction, or invented realities to invented realities, the book and the author are from a short story by Argentine writer Jorge Luis Borges.[5]

The words of Pessoa also found their way into folk and pop music from the 1960s onwards. Notable mentions from Portugal are the iconic singer-songwriter José Afonso, who was the most gifted voice of the resistance in music against the Estado Novo regime, with his musical interpretation of Pessoa's poem 'No Comboio Descendente' (On the Descending Train). There is also the contemporary fado singer Camané, with his rendition of Álvaro de Campos's 'Ai Margarida' (with music composed by Mário Laginha). In Brazil, Caetano Veloso wrote 'Os Argonautas' in prison in 1969 before he was exiled to London during the dictatorship. It is clearly inspired by Pessoa, where in the chorus Veloso sings the mantra for the sailors according to Plutarch that is inserted and transformed in *The Book of Disquiet*.[6] Veloso's sister, Maria Bethânia, also a musical icon, recited many of Pessoa's poems in concerts and recordings. Pessoa was never one to play music, even though he was born in front of Lisbon's opera house and his father was a music critic and music lover, but there is something poignant in being able to hear his words in contemporary songs on both sides of the Atlantic. One of the first written pieces for *The Book of Disquiet*, and which is inserted as the opening text in Jull Costa's English translation and Pizarro's editions of the book, begins with Pessoa comparing his soul to a secret orchestra. There are many instruments inside him, which are tuning up, making noises, playing melodies, fading in and fading out, many of which he does not recognize. He only knows himself as the symphony.[7] Therein lies the magic and mystery of creativity. Pessoa is a swirling assemblage of musical notes for the reader to play. His fragments, loose papers, finished and unfinished poems, plays, short stories, political essays, astrology charts, automatic writings, texts on neopaganism, love letters, epigrams, manifestos and unrealized projects contain a multiplicity of voices, sensations and perspectives – enough tunes to make a dervish whirl.

In the end, considering the multifaceted writing universe of Fernando Pessoa, perhaps one can say that the world is not true, but can be real for a while. And Pessoa, of course, goes further when he writes: 'the only reality that exists is the word "reality" meaning absolutely nothing.'[8] There is no limit to the void. And within that void floats the nothing, the impossible and the monster that makes up reality. All his life Pessoa chiselled away at reality, trying to work out what it must be, what it might mean and how it could be experienced. All three of the aspects of reality interpenetrate, interconnect and intermingle through Pessoa's incessant determination to probe and plummet its depths through his combination of writing, publishing, visions of the Fifth Empire, creation of various '-isms', and of course the invention of the heteronyms and their subsequent voyages as Argonauts of the self, consciousness and sensations. A comment Pessoa made about Charles Dickens can also be read as a reflection on himself: 'He raised caricature to a high art and made unreality a mode of reality.'[9] Soares expressed his own thoughts on reality: 'I prefer reality to truth; I prefer life, yes, to the very God who created it.'[10]

Nietzsche had warned the explorers of consciousness in the nineteenth century that those who fight with monsters must be careful not to become the monster itself.[11] Soares, Campos and Pessoa did not turn into monsters. They carried and contained the monster within, unleashing the various possibilities of the self, simultaneously and in parallel to each other. These are the three voices that are most vocal in Pessoa's life in the 1930s. Each one stares more deeply into the abyss as the abyss stares back at each one of them. Soares never relents from dreaming impossible landscapes, Campos keeps conversing with the void and Pessoa continues to seek answers in the secrets of esoteric explorations. Each one becomes more human rather than more monstrous. Their writing becomes more intimate, compassionate and sensitive and, dare I say, more loving in their observations of the people, streets, buildings and things around them. A year before Pessoa expired,

Campos wrote in a poem: 'And my heart is a little larger than the entire universe.'[12]

This book has been haunted, from the first to the last page, by Lenin's comment to the Romanian poet Valeriu Marcu in 1917, the same year Álvaro de Campos published his manifesto 'Ultimatum'. We come full circle and end with Campos. Perhaps Pessoa's closest friend in his Absolute Reality, he draws a conclusion in another inconclusive poem: 'Like a god, I've put neither truth nor life in order.'[13] Campos lives neither the true life nor the false life that he depicts in the poem at the beginning of this book, but rather he manifests reality by expressing the impossible (dream), the nothing (void) and the monster (self). Unlike the other prominent heteronyms, it feels as if the bisexual naval engineer and sensationist is perhaps still not at rest, bringing his impossible dreams into the humdrum and noise of daily modern living, embodying life rather than truth and chaos rather than order. For he did not die of tuberculosis like Alberto Caeiro, nor was he brought back into the shadows like Ricardo Reis by Pessoa with the help of Saramago; he did not commit suicide like the Baron of Teive, nor did he communicate an aura of finality like the author of *The Book of Disquiet* about leaving that work to Pessoa to publish after he was gone. Nor is he in a tomb like Fernando Pessoa in the Jerónimos Monastery in Belém. No, the real fictional poet Álvaro de Campos may still be out there – gesticulating, writing impulsively and passionately, shouting and crying, being rude and hyperbolic, wandering streets and sailing oceans, or simply sitting smoking at a table in the corner of a café, with a glass of *bagaço* liquor in front of him, amid the pitter-patter sound of footsteps and the rise and fall of voices from the bartender to the passers-by. He claims in 'The Tobacco Shop' to have done more in dreams than Napoleon, held more humanities than Christ and invented more philosophies than Kant ever could, but also admits that it is as if he lived in an attic.[14] But yes, he is also the creation of Fernando Pessoa, who contains multitudes and inhabits countless lives simultaneously, and that is the radicality of his, her, its, their and our reality.

Chronology

1888

13 June   Fernando António Nogueira Pessoa, first son of Maria
Magdalena Pinheiro Nogueira and Joaquim de Seabra Pessoa,
is born at the Largo de São Carlos in the centre of Lisbon

1893

21 January   Pessoa's brother Jorge is born

13 July   Pessoa's father dies of tuberculosis

15 November   Pessoa, his mother and paternal grandmother Dionísia
move to Rua de São Marçal

1894

2 January   Pessoa's brother Jorge dies of tuberculosis
Pessoa's mother meets João Miguel Rosa, a naval officer
Invents his first literary figure, called Chevalier de Pas

1895

26 July   Pessoa recites his first poem, dedicated to his mother,
who writes it down

30 December   Pessoa's mother marries João Miguel Rosa, now a
Portuguese consul in Durban, capital of the British colony
of Natal in South Africa

1896

20 January   Pessoa and his mother move to South Africa to join her
new husband. Pessoa enrols in St John's Convent School
in Durban

27 November	Pessoa's half-sister Henriqueta Madalena, aka Teca, is born

1898

22 October	Madalena Henriqueta, another half-sister, is born

1899

7 April	Pessoa enrolls in Durban High School
October	Beginning of the Boer War

1901

11 January	Pessoa's half-brother Luís Miguel is born
12 May	Pessoa writes his first poem in English, called 'Separated from Thee'
25 June	Madalena Henriqueta dies of meningitis at only two years of age
1 August	The family take a year-long holiday on the island of Ilha Terceira (where his aunt Anica is living) in the Azores Islands and on the mainland of Portugal, visiting Lisbon and Tavira

1903

17 January	Pessoa's half-brother João Maria is born

1904

July	The heteronym Charles Robert Anon publishes a satirical poem in a newspaper in Durban called the *Natal Mercury*

1905

20 August	Pessoa returns to Lisbon alone and lives with his Aunt Anica (who has just moved from Terceira) on Rua de São Bento 98
2 September	Enrols at the University of Lisbon and starts reading philosophy

1906 Alexander Search emerges

July	Moves to Calçada da Estrela to be with his mother and family as they move back from Durban for a while

1907

25 April	His family return to Durban and Pessoa moves in with his paternal great-aunts Rita and Maria and grandmother Dionísia, on Rua Bela Vista à Lapa 17 in the neighbourhood of Estrela in Lisbon
June	Drops out of university
September	Dionísia dies, leaving Pessoa, her only heir, a small inheritance

1908

1 February	Assassination of King Carlos I of Portugal and his son
14 December	First written dated passage of his long unfinished poem *Fausto*

1909

November	Opens the printing and publishing press Ibis with the inheritance from his grandmother Dionísia Pessoa moves into his own apartment for the first time on Rua da Glória 4

1910

June	Ibis goes out of business without having published anything
5 October	End of the monarchy of the House of Bragança after more than five hundred years in Portugal, and the declaration of the Portuguese Republic

1911

June/July	Moves in with his aunt Anica on Rua Passos Manuel 24

1912	Meets his best friend Mário de Sá-Carneiro, who then moves to Paris in October

1913	
August	Publishes his first piece of creative prose, called 'The Forest of Estrangement' (which is also the first text to be associated with *The Book of Disquiet*); writes in English the long sexually explicit poem 'Epithalamium'
1914	Participates in séances for the first time with Aunt Anica and his cousin Maria Freitas and her friend Clara Alves Soares
8 March	Pessoa declares this day to be the 'Triumphal Day' of his life, in which the heteronyms Alberto Caeiro, Ricardo Reis and Álvaro de Campos supposedly emerged and the whole of Caeiro's *The Keeper of Sheep* was written; but in fact, the first dated poem of Caeiro is on 4 March, and Álvaro de Campos actually emerges in June, and the first dated odes by Ricardo Reis are on 12 June
December	The heteronym astrologer Raphael Baldaya emerges
1915	The philosopher of neopaganism António Mora emerges Alberto Caeiro dies of tuberculosis (exact date unknown)
24 March	Publication of *Orpheu 1* (which includes the first two publications of poems by Álvaro de Campos – 'Opiário' (Opiary) and 'Ode Triunfal' (Triumphal Ode), and Pessoa's 'static play' *O Marinheiro* (The Mariner)
June	Publication of *Orpheu 2* (which includes Álvaro de Campos's longest poem 'Ode Marítima' (Maritime Ode) and Pessoa's 'Chuva Obliqua' (Slanted Rain) which comprises six Intersectionist poems
September	Completes the first of six translations of works of various theosophical writers
November	His mother has a stroke
1916	
9 March	Germany declares war on Portugal, which then declares war on Germany the next day
26 April	Mário de Sá-Carneiro commits suicide in Paris

June	Earliest surviving automatic writings by Pessoa

1917

May	Submits a collection of poems called *The Mad Fiddler* to an English publisher, but it is rejected
October	'Ultimatum' by Álvaro de Campos is published in *Portugal Futurista*
December	There is a *coup d'état* in Portugal and Sidónio Pais is established as the dictator

1918

July	Self-publishes a revisited edition of his long homoerotic poem *Antinous* in English, the first version having been written in 1915
14 December	Sidónio Pais is assassinated

1919

	Ricardo Reis emigrates to Brazil after the failure of a monarchist insurrection
7 October	Pessoa's stepfather João Miguel Rosa dies in Pretoria
November	Meets new employee Ophelia Queiroz at the firm Felix, Vallada, & Freitas, Ltd, where Pessoa works

1920

1 March	Writes first love letter to Ophelia
30 March	His mother and her three other children move to Lisbon from South Africa. They all (including Pessoa) move to Rua Coelho da Rocha 16, where Pessoa will live for the rest of his life. His two half-brothers move to England, where they will study at the University of London and settle down
29 November	Ends relationship with Ophelia

1921

December	Publishes *English Poems I–II* and *English Poems III* with his new publishing company and commercial agency called Olisipo

1922	
May	Publishes his short story 'The Anarchist Banker' in the magazine *Contemporânea*
October	Publishes twelve poems (including 'Mar Português') in *Contemporânea*, eleven of which will turn up later in his book *Mensagem* (Message)
November	Olisipo publishes *Canções* (Songs) by António Botto
1923	The poem 'Lisbon Revisited: 1923' by Álvaro de Campos is published in *Contemporânea*
February	Olisipo publishes *Sodoma Divinizado* (Sodom Divinized) by Raul Leal.
1924	
October	Twenty odes by Ricardo Reis are published for the first time, in the magazine *Athena*, in which Pessoa is the literary editor
1925	
January	Twenty-three poems from *The Keeper of Sheep* by Alberto Caeiro are published for the first time in *Athena*
17 March	Pessoa's mother dies
November	Sister Teca gives birth to Manuela Nogueira, Pessoa's only niece
1926	Writes *Lisbon: What the Tourist Should See*, an English-language travel guide for foreigners; it is first published in 1992
28 May	Military dictatorship begins in Portugal
June	'Lisbon Revisited: 1926' by Álvaro de Campos is published in *Contemporânea*
1927	The literary magazine *Presença – Revista de Arte e Crítica* is founded in Coimbra

1928

15 January	Álvaro de Campos writes 'The Tobacco Shop' ('Tabacaria')
March	Pessoa publishes *O Interregno* (The Interregnum)
August	The heteronym the Baron of Teive emerges

1929

22 March	The 'semi-heteronym' Bernardo Soares writes his first dated passage for *The Book of Disquiet*, which begins the second phase of Pessoa's unfinished prose masterwork
September	Rekindles relationship with Ophelia
December	Starts corresponding with Aleister Crowley; publishes 'Tábua Bibliográfia' (Bibliographic Table) in *Presença*, presenting a short literary biography, in which he mentions in publication for the first time the word '*heterónima*' (heteronymy), and describes his project as a '*drama em gente*' (drama in people)
	In 1929 or 1930, Pessoa creates his only female heteronym, called Maria José, who is a hunchback dying of tuberculosis, and who writes a despairing letter of unrequited love

1930

| January | Ends relationship with Ophelia again |
| September | Meets Aleister Crowley and his girlfriend Hanni Jaeger in Lisbon; Crowley stages a fake suicide at the Boca do Inferno (Mouth of Hell) – a cliff off the coast of Portugal – which Pessoa helps to fabricate to the newspapers |

1931

| 1 January | Teca gives birth to Pessoa's only nephew, Luís Miguel Rosa Dias, who will later publish a volume on the correspondence between Crowley and Pessoa called *Encontro Magick – Fernando Pessoa e Aleister Crowley* (2001) Pessoa publishes the eighth poem from Caeiro's *The Keeper of Sheep* in *Presença*, which begins with the line: '*Num meio-dia de fim de Primavera*' (One midday in late Spring) |
| 1 April | Writes 'Autopsicografia' (Autopsychography) |

1932	António de Oliveira Salazar becomes the dictator of Portugal
1933 19 March	The Estado Novo is declared in Portugal and a new constitution is put into action
1934 1 December	Begins writing over 350 Portuguese folk quatrains Publishes *Mensagem*, his only book of Portuguese poetry published in his lifetime. The book is awarded a prize by the National Office of Propaganda
1935 4 February	Publishes an article in the *Diário de Lisboa* against a law to ban Freemasonry
16 March	Writes his first poem against Salazar that is dated, called 'Liberdade' (Freedom)
21 October	Álvaro de Campos writes his last dated poem, which begins with the words: '*Todas as cartas de amor são ridículas'* (All love letters are ridiculous)
13 November	Ricardo Reis writes his last dated poem, which begins with the words: '*Vivem em nós inúmeros*' (Countless lives inhabit us)
19 November	Pessoa writes his last dated poem in Portuguese, which begins with the words '*Há doenças piores que as doenças*' (There are sicknesses worse than any sickness)
22 November	Pessoa writes his last dated poem in English, which begins with the words 'The happy sun is shining'
29 November	Admitted into hospital. Writes his last words, in English: 'I know not what to-morrow will bring'
30 November	Dies in hospital
2 December	Buried in the Prazeres Cemetery in Lisbon

References

Prologue: To Be as Radical as Reality Itself

1 Fernando Pessoa, *The Selected Prose of Fernando Pessoa*, ed. and trans. Richard Zenith (New York, 2022), p. 52.
2 China Miéville, *October* (London, 2017), p. 231.
3 Fernando Pessoa, *Poesia de Álvaro de Campos* (Lisbon, 2002), p. 485 (my translation from the poem 'Dactilografia' (Typewriting)).
4 Alain Badiou, *The Century*, trans. Alberto Toscano (Cambridge and Malden, MA, 2008), p. 54.
5 Fernando Pessoa, *Páginas Íntimas e de Auto-Interpretação*, ed. Georg Rudolf Lind and Jacinto do Prado Coelho (Lisbon, 1966), p. 94.
6 Fernando Pessoa, *The Book of Disquiet*, ed. and trans. Richard Zenith (London, 2015), p. 41.
7 Fernando Pessoa, *Fernando Pessoa and Co.: Selected Poems*, ed. and trans. Richard Zenith (New York, 2003), pp. 178, 113; Fernando Pessoa, *A Little Larger than the Entire Universe: Selected Poems*, ed. and trans. Richard Zenith (London, 2006), p. 77.
8 Pessoa, *The Book of Disquiet*, p. 317.
9 Pessoa, *A Little Larger than the Entire Universe*, p. 407.
10 Clarice Lispector, *Água Viva*, trans. Stefan Tobler (London, 2014), p. 67.
11 'In dreams begins responsibility' was the epigraph to Yeats's collection of poems called *Responsibilities* in 1914. See Yeats, *Collected Poems* (London, 1992), p. 94.
12 Pessoa, *The Book of Disquiet*, p. 108.
13 Pessoa, *Fernando Pessoa and Co.*, p. 173.
14 Pessoa, *The Book of Disquiet*, p. 209.

15 Clarice Lispector, *The Passion According to G.H.*, trans. Idra Novey (London, 2012), p. 12.

16 Pessoa, *The Book of Disquiet*, p. 467.

17 Ibid., p. 463.

18 Pessoa, *Fernando Pessoa and Co.*, p. 176.

19 Pessoa, *A Little Larger than the Entire Universe*, p. 221.

20 Ibid., p. 186.

21 Samuel Beckett, *Molly, Malone Dies, The Unnamable* (London, 1994), p. 418.

22 Pessoa, *Fernando Pessoa and Co.*, p. 176.

23 Ibid., 208.

24 Vilém Flusser, *Language and Reality*, trans. Rodrigo Maltez Novaes (Minneapolis, MN, 2018), p. 118.

25 Johann Wolfgang von Goethe, *Faust: Part One*, trans. David Luke (Oxford, 1987), p. 42 (line 1338: 'Ich bin der Geist der stets verneint!').

26 There is a book by the philosopher José Gil (who has also written philosophical books on Pessoa) called *Monstros* (Monsters), yet to be translated into English, which investigates the presence of monsters in human civilizations – in painting, drawings, cinema, theatre and dance, among other areas, and how this presence reflects on our own humanity. See José Gil, *Monstros* (Lisbon, 1994).

27 T. S. Eliot, *Four Quartets* (London, 1994), p. 4.

28 Pessoa, *The Book of Disquiet*, p. 14.

29 Pessoa, *The Selected Prose of Fernando Pessoa*, p. 90.

30 Pessoa, *The Book of Disquiet*, p. 332.

31 My translation. Original: 'Gott ergreifft man nicht,/ Gott ist ein lauter Nichts,/ ihn rührt kein Nun noch Hier;/ je mehr du nach Ihm greifst/ je mehr entwird Er dir.' See Angelus Silesius, *Cherubinische Wandersmann: Sinnliche Beschreibung der vier letzten Dinge, Sämtliche poetische Werke* (Munich, 1949), vol. III, no. 25.

32 Pessoa, *The Book of Disquiet*, p. 115.

33 Ibid., p. 366.

34 Ibid., p. 115.

35 Pessoa, *A Little Larger than the Entire Universe*, p. 43.

36 Ibid., p. 77.

37 *A biblioteca particular de Fernando Pessoa / Fernando Pessoa's Private Library*, ed. J. Pizarro, P. Ferrari and A. Cardiello (Lisbon, 2010), p. 424.

This is a large bilingual volume with copious images of the covers of many of the books that Pessoa owned. Pessoa's private library collection can be found online on the website of the Casa Fernando Pessoa. See Online Resources in the Select Bibliography for more information.

38 Arthur Schopenhauer, *The World as Will and Representation*, trans. E.F.J. Payne (New York, 1969), vol. I, p. 278.

39 Pessoa, *The Book of Disquiet*, p. 92.

1 The Early Years: Lisbon, Durban and the World

1 Fernando Pessoa, *The Selected Prose of Fernando Pessoa*, ed. and trans. Richard Zenith (New York, 2022), p. 29.

2 Fernando Pessoa, *The Book of Disquiet*, ed. and trans. Richard Zenith (London, 2015), p. 273.

3 Fernando Pessoa, *Teoria da Heteronímia*, ed. F. C. Martins and R. Zenith (Lisbon, 2012), p. 358.

4 Richard Zenith, *Pessoa: A Biography* (New York, 2021), p. 49.

5 See Ramachandra Guha, 'Churchill, the Greatest Briton, Hated Gandhi, the Greatest Indian', *The Atlantic*, www.theatlantic.com, 6 April 2019.

6 Antonio Cardiello, 'Os Orientes de Fernando Pessoa: Adenda', *Pessoa Plural – A Journal of Fernando Pessoa Studies*, 9 (2016), pp. 128–85 (p. 166).

7 Edward Said, *Orientalism* (New York, 1979), p. 1.

8 Pessoa, *The Book of Disquiet*, pp. 60, 150, 353, 424, 472.

9 Fernando Pessoa, *A Little Larger than the Entire Universe: Selected Poems*, ed. and trans. Richard Zenith (London, 2006), p. 149. For further reading on Pessoa's thoughts and links with the philosophies and literatures of India, see Jonardon Ganeri, *Fernando Pessoa: Imagination and the Self* (Oxford, 2024) and 'Pessoa's Imaginary India', in *Fernando Pessoa and Philosophy: Countless Lives Inhabit Us*, ed. B. Ryan, G. Tusa and A. Cardiello (Lanham, MD, 2021), pp. 49–62.

10 Pessoa, *A Little Larger than the Entire Universe*, p. 150.

11 For further reading on the link between Pessoa and Whitman, see Francesca Pasciolla, *Walt Whitman in Fernando Pessoa* (London, 2016); Richard Zenith, 'Pessoa and Walt Whitman Revisited', in *Fernando Pessoa's Modernity without Frontiers*, ed. Mariana Gray de Castro

(Woodbridge, 2013), pp. 1–36; Eduardo Lourenço, 'Walt Whitman and Pessoa', trans. Robert Myers, in *Chaos and Splendour and Other Essays,* ed. Carlos Veloso (Dartmouth, MA, 2002), pp. 55–76.

12 Pessoa, *The Selected Prose of Fernando Pessoa*, p. 229.

13 For Pessoa's first published poem, see http://arquivopessoa.net/ textos/3174, accessed 28 June 2024.

14 Fernando Pessoa, *Fernando Pessoa and Co.: Selected Poems*, ed. and trans. Richard Zenith (New York, 2003), p. 276.

15 Luís Vaz de Camões, *The Lusíads*, trans. and ed. Landeg White (Oxford, 1997), p. 108 (Canto 5, verse 50).

16 Pessoa, *The Selected Prose of Fernando Pessoa*, p. 147; Pessoa, *The Book of Disquiet*, p. 56; Pessoa, *Fernando Pessoa and Co.*, pp. 243, 189.

17 Fernando Pessoa, *Poesia de Álvaro de Campos* (Lisbon, 2002), p. 251 (my translation); Pessoa, *The Book of Disquiet*, p. 353.

18 Fernando Pessoa, *Poesia 1918–1930*, ed. M. P da Silva, A. M. Freitas and M. Dine (Lisbon, 2005), p. 268 (my translation).

19 Pessoa, *The Selected Prose of Fernando Pessoa*, p. 264.

2 I Was a Poet Animated by Philosophy

1 Fernando Pessoa, *The Book of Disquiet,* ed. and trans. Richard Zenith (London, 2015), p. 241.

2 Fernando Pessoa, *The Selected Prose of Fernando Pessoa*, ed. and trans. Richard Zenith (New York, 2022), p. 46.

3 Ibid., p. 12.

4 Fernando Pessoa, *Páginas Íntimas e de Auto-Interpretação*, ed. Georg Rudolf Lind and Jacinto do Prado Coelho (Lisbon, 1966), p. 13.

5 Pessoa, *Textos de Crítica e de Intervenção* (Lisbon, 1980), p. 45. See also http://arquivopessoa.net/textos/3101, accessed 28 June 2024. My thanks to Wanderley Dias da Silva for informing me about this quote.

6 Fernando Pessoa, *Fernando Pessoa and Co.: Selected Poems*, ed. and trans. Richard Zenith (New York, 2003), p. 62.

7 Pessoa, *Páginas Íntimas e de Auto-Interpretação*, pp. 13–14.

8 Fernando Pessoa, *A Little Larger than the Entire Universe: Selected Poems*, ed. and trans. Richard Zenith (London, 2006), p. 58.

9   Søren Kierkegaard, *Papers and Journals: A Selection*, ed. Alastair Hannay (London, 1996), p. 182.

10 Pessoa, *Sobre a arte literária*, ed. Fernando Cabral Martins and Richard Zenith (Lisbon, 2018), p. 31.

11 Alain Badiou, *Handbook of Inaesthetics*, trans. Alberto Toscano (Stanford, CA, 2005), p. 38, emphasis in original.

12 Pessoa, *A Little Larger than the Entire Universe*, p. 247.

13 Ibid., p. 23.

14 Pessoa, *The Book of Disquiet*, p. 178.

15 For an original and penetrating philosophical analysis of the self in the work of Pessoa, and which also makes a deep connection with Indian philosophy, see Jonardon Ganeri's *Virtual Subjects, Fugitive Selves: Fernando Pessoa and His Philosophy* (Oxford, 2021). Ganeri writes in his conclusion: 'Pessoa provides us with a new vocabulary for the self, a new repertoire of conceptual tools for interpreting and analyzing subjectivity' (p. 150).

16 Pessoa, *The Selected Prose of Fernando Pessoa*, pp. 92, 91.

17 Ibid.

18 There are many striking parallels regarding the interests and strategies of Pessoa and Kierkegaard, such as their lifelong fascination with the elusive Faust, the obsession with the interval and interlude, the creative conversation with and reverence for Shakespeare, the strategic othering of oneself in the creation of different voices and masks to show different modes of life, their exploration of tedium and boredom, their reading and appropriation of fairy tales, their deep suspicion and almost utter lack of physical travelling to other places as they confined themselves to their respective cities for most of their adult lives, their brief and only experience of romance with a woman, and their vast unpublished workshop of various passages, fragments and notes. Here are two writers, as a dramatic-poetic philosopher and dramatic-philosophical poet, who are paradoxically pretending and deceiving in an attempt to uncover the riddle of the self, and who leave to posterity some of the most penetrating excavations of the self ever undertaken by a writer. Of course, there are obvious differences in their personalities and in their background. Pessoa, animated by philosophy and spirituality, is more whimsical as the agnostic non-Christian relishing and faltering in pursuing aesthetic perfection; Kierkegaard, meanwhile, is one of the last great Christian ethical thinkers, yearning for the religious realm and emphasizing

spiritual courage. And yet, the powerful aesthetic gesture in Kierkegaard is never completely discarded as the poetic and theatrical element remain central to his philosophical and theological strategies, while the mystical and spiritual quest is always present in Pessoa's oeuvre.

19 Pessoa, *The Selected Prose of Fernando Pessoa*, p. 276; Pessoa, *The Book of Disquiet*, p. xxiii.

20 Pessoa, *The Book of Disquiet*, p. 238.

21 Pessoa, *The Selected Prose of Fernando Pessoa*, p. 16.

22 Fernando Pessoa, *Pessoa Inédito*, ed. Teresa Rita Lopes (Lisbon, 1993), p. 402.

23 Fernando Pessoa, *Da República (1910–1935)*, ed. M. I. Rocheta, M. P. Morão and J. Serrão (Lisbon, 1979), p. 404 (my translation).

24 Pessoa, *The Book of Disquiet*, p. 84; Pessoa, *Fernando Pessoa and Co.*, pp. 178, 31.

25 Pessoa, *The Selected Prose of Fernando Pessoa*, p. 52.

26 Pessoa Archive, Biblioteca Nacional, Lisbon, 133F–5.

27 Pessoa, *Fernando Pessoa and Co.*, p. 81.

28 From the note that Pessoa made beside the text, he was probably citing this passage from a book by the eighteenth-century German historian of philosophy Wilhelm Gottlieb Tennemann, in a French translation by the nineteenth-century philosopher of 'electicism' Victor Cousin. See Fernando Pessoa, *Textos filosóficos*, ed. António Pina Coelho (Lisbon, 1968), vol. II, p. 204.

29 James Joyce, *Ulysses* (Oxford, 2008), p. 186; Jacques Derrida, *Dissemination*, trans. Barbara Johnson (London, 1993), p. 88.

30 My thanks to Richard Zenith regarding this anecdote. See Richard Zenith, *Pessoa: A Biography* (New York, 2021), p. 298, for more information on this episode.

31 See ibid., p. 647.

32 Daniel Defoe, *A Plan of the English Commerce* [1728] (Wilmington, DE, 2013), p. ix.

3 *Orpheu* and the Birth of Modernism

1 Fernando Pessoa, *Páginas Íntimas e de Auto-Interpretação*, ed. Georg Rudolf Lind and Jacinto do Prado Coelho (Lisbon, 1966), p. 119.

2 Harold Bloom, *The Western Canon* (New York, 1994), p. 343.

3 Søren Kierkegaard, *Papers and Journals: A Selection*, ed. Alastair Hannay (London, 1996), p. 350; Karl Marx and Friedrich Engels, *The Communist Manifesto*, in Karl Marx, *The Revolutions of 1848: Political Writings*, ed. David Fernbach (Harmondsworth and New York, 1978), vol. I, pp. 70–71.

4 Friedrich Nietzsche, *The Will to Power*, trans. W. Kaufmann and R. J. Hollingdale (New York, 1968), p. 3 (KSA, 13, 189); Friedrich Engels, 'Preface to the English Edition of 1888' (of *The Communist Manifesto*), in Marx, *The Revolutions of 1848*, vol. I, p. 65.

5 Friedrich Nietzsche, *The Anti-Christ, Ecce Homo, Twilight of the Idols, and Other Writings*, ed. A. Ridley and J. Norman, trans. J. Norman (Cambridge, 2005), pp. 11, 64, 66, 74, 120, 121, 136, 144, 155, 177, 229; Marx and Engels, *The Communist Manifesto*, p. 86.

6 James Joyce, *Ulysses*, ed. Jeri Johnson (Oxford, 2008), p. 198.

7 Fernando Pessoa, *The Book of Disquiet*, ed. and trans. Richard Zenith (London, 2015), p. 11.

8 Fernando Pessoa, *A Little Larger than the Entire Universe: Selected Poems*, ed. and trans. Richard Zenith (London, 2006), p. 213.

9 For more information on comparing *Orpheu* and *Blast*, see Patricia Silva McNeill, 'Orpheu e Blast: Interseções do Modernismo Português e Inglês', in *1915 – O Ano do Orpheu*, ed. Steffen Dix (Lisbon, 2015), pp. 167–83.

10 Pessoa, *The Book of Disquiet*, p. 6.

11 This was a suggestion by Frank Armstrong, editor of the independent magazine *Cassandra Voices*, in a conversation we had after he read about Pessoa, Sensationism and his other '-isms'.

12 On this passage by Pessoa, see note 61 by Zenith in Fernando Pessoa, *The Selected Prose of Fernando Pessoa*, ed. and trans. Richard Zenith (New York, 2022), p. 345.

13 Richard Zenith, *Pessoa: A Biography* (New York, 2021), p. 346.

14 Pessoa, *A Little Larger than the Entire Universe*, p. 279.

15 Pessoa, *The Book of Disquiet*, p. 425.

16 Pessoa, *The Selected Prose of Fernando Pessoa*, p. 69.

17 Ibid., p. 68.

18 Fernando Pessoa, *Fernando Pessoa and Co.: Selected Poems*, ed. and trans. Richard Zenith (New York, 2003), p. 146.

19 Pessoa Archive, Biblioteca Nacional, Lisbon, Notebook 144A–26.

20 Pessoa, *The Selected Prose of Fernando Pessoa*, p. 66.

21 Maurice Blanchot, *The Space of Literature*, trans. Anne Smock (Lincoln, NE, 1989), p. 176.

22 Eduardo Lourenço, 'Pessoa, or Reality as Fiction', in *Here on Douradores Street: Essays on Fernando Pessoa*, ed. and trans. Ronald W. Sousa (Providence, RI, 2010), p. 46.

23 Pessoa wrote this note as late as 1934: 'One can apply the name of "master" to only three poets in Portugal in the nineteenth and twentieth century. They are Antero de Quental, Cesário Verde and Camilo Pessanha' (my translation); see Pessoa, *Sobre a arte literária*, ed. R. Zenith and F. C. Martins (Lisbon, 2018), p. 117.

24 Pessoa, *The Selected Prose of Fernando Pessoa*, p. 67.

4 Heteronymy and the Plurality of the Subject

1 Fernando Pessoa, *The Selected Prose of Fernando Pessoa*, ed. and trans. Richard Zenith (New York, 2003), p. 274.

2 Maurice Blanchot, *The Space of Literature*, trans. Anne Smock (Lincoln, NE, 1989), p. 227.

3 See Paul Muldoon, '*Autopsychography* by Fernando Pessoa', in *The End of the Poem* (London, 2006), pp. 222–44 (p. 225); and Richard Zenith, *Pessoa: A Biography* (New York, 2021), p. 777.

4 Henrik Ibsen, *Peer Gynt*, trans. Peter Watts (London, 1970), p. 94 (III.3).

5 Fernando Pessoa, *The Book of Disquiet*, ed. and trans. Richard Zenith (London, 2015), p. 295.

6 Søren Kierkegaard, *Either/Or*, trans. H. V. Hong and E. H. Hong (Princeton, NJ, 1987), p. 19.

7 Fernando Pessoa, *Poesia 1931–1935 e Não Datada*, ed. M. P. da Silva, A. M. Freitas and M. Dine (Lisbon, 2005), p. 45 (my translation).

8 Friedrich Nietzsche, 'On Truth and Lie in an Extra-Moral Sense', in *The Portable Nietzsche*, trans. Walter Kaufmann (New York, 1982), pp. 42–6 (p. 46).

9 Friedrich Nietzsche, *Beyond Good and Evil*, trans. R. J. Hollingdale (London, 1987), p. 51 (para. 40).

10 Ibid., p. 197 (para. 289), emphasis in original.

11 Jacques Derrida, *Dissemination*, trans. Barbara Johnson (London, 1993), p. 93, emphasis in original.

12 Fernando Pessoa, *The Selected Prose of Fernando Pessoa*, ed. and trans. Richard Zenith (New York, 2022), p. 209.

13 Alessandro de Francesco, 'Propositions on the Philosophical Nature of Poetry', *Crisis and Critique*, IX/1 (2022), pp. 143–63 (p. 151).

14 Fernando Pessoa, *Fernando Pessoa and Co.: Selected Poems*, trans. Richard Zenith (New York, 2003), p. 174.

15 Pessoa, *The Book of Disquiet*, p. 332.

16 Pessoa, *Poesia 1931–1935 e Não Datada*, p. 117.

17 Pessoa, *Fernando Pessoa and Co.*, p. 137.

18 Pessoa, *The Selected Prose of Fernando Pessoa*, p. 274.

19 My translation. See 'Tábua Bibliográfica', where the text is located, on the online Pessoa Archive: http://arquivopessoa.net/textos/2700, accessed 1 July 2024.

20 Pessoa, *The Selected Prose of Fernando Pessoa*, p. 264.

21 John Keats, *Selected Letters* (Oxford, 2009), pp. 148–9.

22 Pessoa, *The Selected Prose of Fernando Pessoa*, pp. 2, 5.

23 Søren Kierkegaard, *Concluding Unscientific Postscript*, trans. H. V. Hong and E. H. Hong (Princeton, NJ, 1992), p. 626.

24 Ibid., p. 625.

25 Fernando Pessoa, *Páginas Íntimas e de Auto-Interpretação*, ed. Georg Rudolf Lind and Jacinto do Prado Coelho (Lisbon, 1966), p. 133.

26 Pessoa, *The Selected Prose of Fernando Pessoa*, p. 271.

27 Pessoa, *Fernando Pessoa and Co.*, p. 45.

28 Plato, *Timaeus and Critias*, trans. Desmond Less (London, 1977), p. 132.

29 Martin Heidegger, 'Letter on Humanism', trans. Frank A. Capuzzi, in *Pathmarks*, ed. William McNeill (Cambridge, 1998), p. 252.

30 *Holzwege*, translated as 'Off the Beaten Track', is the title of a collection of texts that Heidegger published in 1950, his first publication after the Second World War. See Martin Heidegger, *Off the Beaten Track*, ed. and trans. Julian Young and Kenneth Haynes (Cambridge, 2002).

31 Fernando Pessoa, *A Little Larger than the Entire Universe: Selected Poems*, ed. and trans. Richard Zenith (London, 2006), p. 23.

32 For more discussion on the source of this sentence, see George Monteiro, *Fernando Pessoa and Nineteenth-Century Anglo-American*

Literature (Lexington, KY, 2000), p. 57. Here is the original Greek from Menander: 'ὃν οἱ θεοὶ φιλοῦσιν, ἀποθνῄσκει νέος', which Leopardi uses as the epigraph for his poem 'Love and Death' (*Amore e Morte*) (Giacomo Leopardi, *Canti*, trans. Jonathan Galassi (London, 2010), p. 224). Byron quotes the line in his poem *Don Juan*: 'Who the gods love die young was said of yore' (Lord Byron, *Don Juan* (London, 1996), p. 192 (Canto IV, stanza 12)); and Pessoa also quotes it in Portuguese: 'Morre jovem o que os Deuses amam, é um preceito da sabedoria antiga' (Fernando Pessoa, *Textos de Crítica e de Intervenção* (Lisbon, 1980), p. 149).

33 Pessoa, *A Little Larger than the Entire Universe*, pp. 43, 61, 7.

34 Pessoa, *The Selected Prose of Fernando Pessoa*, p. 57.

35 Immanuel Kant, *Critique of the Power of Judgment*, trans. P. Guyer and E. Matthews (Cambridge, 2008), p. 211 (para. 54). See also Eduardo Lourenço, '"Master" Caeiro's Curious Singularity', in *Here on Douradores Street: Essays on Fernando Pessoa*, ed. and trans. Ronald W. Sousa (Providence, RI, 2010), pp. 49–62 (p. 49).

36 Pessoa, *A Little Larger than the Entire Universe*, p. 15.

37 Ibid., p. 77.

38 Ibid., p. 58.

39 Pessoa, *Fernando Pessoa and Co.*, p. 76.

40 Baruch Spinoza, *Ethics*, trans. G.H.R. Parkinson (Oxford, 2000), p. 114 (Part 2, def. 6).

41 Ibid., p. 304 (Part 5, prop. 24).

42 Pessoa, *The Selected Prose of Fernando Pessoa*, p. 47.

43 Ibid., p. 45.

44 Pessoa, *A Little Larger than the Entire Universe*, p. 7.

45 Pessoa, *The Selected Prose of Fernando Pessoa*, p. 59.

46 Ibid., p. 51.

47 Pessoa, *Fernando Pessoa and Co.*, p. 117.

48 Pessoa, *The Selected Prose of Fernando Pessoa*, p. 276.

49 Ibid., pp. 51–2.

50 Pessoa, *Fernando Pessoa and Co.*, p. 110.

51 Ibid., p. 113.

52 Pessoa, *The Selected Prose of Fernando Pessoa*, p. 276.

53 Yuri Slezkine, *The Jewish Century* (Princeton, NJ, and Oxford, 2004), p. 1.

54 See Zenith, *Pessoa: A Biography*, pp. 801, 1009 (note 7).

55   In one of his first poems, called 'Three Sonnets' (made up of three poems), Campos could be alluding to being a pederast, as he writes in the third sonnet: 'Listen Daisy . . ./ To tell that poor young lad/ who gave me so many happy hours, of which you know nothing, that I died.' See Fernando Pessoa, *The Complete Works of Álvaro de Campos*, ed. J. Pizarro and A. Cardiello, trans. Margaret Jull Costa and Patricio Ferrari (New York, 2023), p. 5.

56   Friedrich Nietzsche, *Ecce Homo*, trans. R. J. Hollingdale (London, 1992), p. 35.

57   These words were written in a letter to Johann Heinrich Köselitz (whom Nietzsche called Peter Gast) on 14 August 1881 (KSB 6, in Friedrich Nietzsche, *Sämtliche Briefe: Kritische Studienausgabe*, ed. G. Colli and M. Montinari (New York, Munich and Berlin, 1986), p. 112).

58   Pessoa, *The Complete Works of Álvaro de Campos*, p. 129.

59   Ibid., p. 127. Here is the original Portuguese (in Fernando Pessoa, *Poesia de Álvaro de Campos* (Lisbon, 2002), p. 251): '. . . *toda a realidade é um excesso, uma violência,/ Uma alucinação extraordinariamente nítida/ Que vivemos todos em comum com a fúria das almas,/ O centro para onde tendem as estranhas forças centrífugas/ Que são as psiques humanas no seu acordo de sentidos./ Quanto mais eu sinta, quanto mais eu sinta como várias pessoas,/ Quanto mais personalidades eu tiver,/ Quanto mais intensamente, estridentemente as tiver,/ Quanto mais simultaneamente sentir com todas elas,/ Quanto mais unificadamente diverso, dispersadamente atento,/ Estiver, sentir, viver, for,/ Mais possuirei a existência total do universo,/ Mais completo serei pelo espaço inteiro fora . . .*'

60   Zenith translates the sentence as 'Where we are is who we are' in Pessoa, *The Selected Prose of Fernando Pessoa*, p. 207 (see also note on the translation, p. 358); and M. J. Costa and P. Ferrari translate the sentence as 'To be is to exist' in Pessoa, *The Complete Works of Álvaro de Campos*, p. 333.

61   Pessoa, *Fernando Pessoa and Co.*, p. 146.

62   Walt Whitman, 'Song of Myself', in *Complete Poetry and Prose* (New York, 1982), p. 246 (verse 51).

63   Pessoa, *A Little Larger than the Entire Universe*, p. 153.

64   Ibid., p. 154.

65   Ibid., p. 160.

66 Eduardo Lourenço, 'Álvaro de Campos II, or the Erostratus–Pessoa Agony', in *Here on Douradores Street*, pp. 139–68 (p. 146).

67 Fernando Pessoa, *Teatro Estático*, ed. F. de Freitas and P. Ferrari (Lisbon, 2017), p. 276 (my translation).

68 Pessoa, *The Selected Prose of Fernando Pessoa*, p. 31.

69 Jorge Luis Borges, 'The Circular Ruins', trans. J. E. Irby, in *Labyrinths*, ed. D. A. Yates and J. E. Irby (London, 1985), p. 76.

70 Pessoa, *The Selected Prose of Fernando Pessoa*, p. 36.

71 Ibid., p. 4.

5 Radical Politics and the Fifth Empire

1 Fernando Pessoa, *The Selected Prose of Fernando Pessoa*, ed. and trans. Richard Zenith (New York, 2022), p. 270.

2 For the theory of an aristocratic republic, see Fernando Pessoa, *Ultimatum e páginas de sociologia política*, ed. M. I. Rocheta and M. P. Morão (Lisbon, 1980), pp. 335, 159, 197, 343, 233.

3 Pessoa, *The Selected Prose of Fernando Pessoa*, p. 73.

4 Ibid., p. 75.

5 Fernando Pessoa, *Da República (1910–1935)*, ed. M. I. Rocheta, M. P. Morão and J. Serrão (Lisbon, 1979), pp. 331–2, emphasis in original.

6 This is a term coined by Edward Clarke. See Edward Clarke, *The Vagabond Spirit of Poetry* (Winchester, 2014), p. 12.

7 Fernando Pessoa, *Pessoa Inédito*, ed. Teresa Rita Lopes (Lisbon, 1993), p. 298.

8 Pessoa, *The Selected Prose of Fernando Pessoa*, p. 81.

9 See the essay by Richard Zenith that also takes this point of view: 'Nietzsche and the Super-Pessoa', in *Pessoa in an Intertextual Web: Influence and Innovation*, ed. D. Frier (London, 2012), pp. 10–31 (p. 20).

10 Pessoa, *The Selected Prose of Fernando Pessoa*, p. 92.

11 Pessoa, *Da República*, pp. 231–8.

12 Ibid., p. 236 (my translation).

13 The journal had been founded in 1915 by José Pacheco, who had also designed the cover of *Orpheu 1*.

14 Arpad Kadarkay, *Georg Lukács: Life, Thought, and Politics* (Oxford, 1991), p. 274.

15 Fernando Pessoa, *Obra essencial de Fernando Pessoa*, vol. VII: *Cartas*, ed. Richard Zenith (Lisbon, 2007), p. 235.

16 Other readers have made this connection between 'The Anarchist Banker' and Max Stirner. See, for example, Richard Zenith, *Pessoa: A Biography* (New York, 2021), p. 620; Fernando Luso Soares, in the preface to an anthology of Pessoa called *O banqueiro anarquista e outros contos de raciocínio* (Lisbon, 1964); Maria do Carmo Castelo Branco, 'O caso policial: Classificações e argumentos', in *Revista da Faculdade de Ciências Humanas e Sociais* (Lisbon, 2006), p. 16; Patricio Ferrari and Bernd Kast, 'Nichts und Mittelpunkt der Welt: Der Einfluss Max Stirners auf Fernando Pessoa', in *Der Einzige: Jahrbuch der Max-Stirner-Gesellschaft*, ed. Maurice Schuhmann (Leipzig, 2010), pp. 212–44.

17 Pessoa, *The Selected Prose of Fernando Pessoa*, p. 198.

18 Ibid., p. 202.

19 Fernando Pessoa, *Sobre o Fascismo, a ditadura militar e Salazar*, ed. José Barreto (Lisbon, 2015), pp. 312, 358.

20 Ibid., pp. 143 and 213.

21 Ibid., p. 143.

22 Pessoa, *The Selected Prose of Fernando Pessoa*, p. 339.

23 Ibid.

24 Zenith, *Pessoa: A Biography*, p. 915.

25 Fernando Pessoa, *A Little Larger than the Entire Universe: Selected Poems*, ed. and trans. Richard Zenith (London, 2006), p. 348.

26 Ibid., p. 373.

27 Pessoa, *Pessoa Inédito*, p. 235.

28 Fernando Pessoa, *Mensagem* (Lisbon, 2006), p. 96 (my translation).

29 Pessoa Archive, Biblioteca Nacional, Lisbon, Docs 17/51v. 905/83v. These words are found in the lines: '. . . *mens agitat molem et magno se corpore miscet/ inde hominum pecudumque genus vitaeque volantum*' in Virgil's *The Aeneid*, Book VI, line 727. Cecil Day Lewis translates the lines as: '. . . for immanent Mind, flowing/ Through all its parts and leaving its mass, makes the universe work' (Virgil, *The Aeneid*, trans. C. D. Lewis (Oxford, 1986), p. 181).

30 Fernando Pessoa, *The Book of Disquiet*, ed. and trans. Richard Zenith (London, 2015), p. 366.

31 Walt Whitman, *Complete Poetry and Prose* (New York, 1982), p. 24.

32 Ibid., p. 25.
33 Pessoa, *The Selected Prose of Fernando Pessoa*, p. 168.
34 Ibid., p. 172.
35 Pessoa, *A Little Larger than the Entire Universe*, p. 231.
36 Alain Badiou, *The Century*, trans. Alberto Toscano (Cambridge and Malden, MA, 2008), pp. 111–30.
37 Ibid., p. 24.
38 Pessoa, *A Little Larger than the Entire Universe*, p. 382.

6 The Esoteric Journeys of the Soul

1 Fernando Pessoa, *The Selected Prose of Fernando Pessoa*, ed. and trans. Richard Zenith (New York, 2022), p. 277.
2 Fernando Pessoa, *The Complete Works of Álvaro de Campos*, ed. Jerónimo Pizarro and Antonio Cardiello, trans. Margaret Jull Costa and Patricio Ferrari (New York, 2023), p. 127.
3 The passage (BD 218) is included in Richard Zenith's edition (in both Portuguese and English) of *The Book of Disquiet*: Fernando Pessoa, *The Book of Disquiet*, ed. and trans. Richard Zenith (London, 2015). See his explanation on p. 503.
4 See Fernando Pessoa, *Cartas Astrológicas*, ed. P. Cardoso, and in collaboration with J. Pizarro (Lisbon, 2011); Pessoa's private library collection can be found online on the website of Casa Fernando Pessoa: https://bibliotecaparticular.casafernandopessoa.pt. It is also available in published form in a large bilingual volume, with copious images of the covers of many of the books Pessoa owned: J. Pizzaro, P. Ferrari and A. Cardiello, eds, *A biblioteca particular de Fernando Pessoa / Fernando Pessoa's Private Library* (Lisbon, 2010).
5 Richard Zenith, *Pessoa: A Biography* (New York, 2021), p. 786.
6 Pessoa, *The Book of Disquiet*, p. 132.
7 Roberto Calasso, *Ka*, trans. Tim Parks (London, 2001), p. 202.
8 Fernando Pessoa, *Fernando Pessoa and Co.: Selected Poems*, trans. Richard Zenith (New York, 2003), p. 200.
9 Maurice Blanchot, 'Literature and the Right to Death', in *The Work of Fire*, trans. Charlotte Mandell (Stanford, CA, 1995), pp. 300–344 (p. 330).

10 W. B. Yeats, 'Magic', in *Essays and Introductions* (New York, 1972),
    p. 28. Yeats is mocked in Álvaro de Campos's manifesto 'Ultimatum':
    'Get out, Yeats of the Celtic brume wafting around a sign pointing
    nowhere, sackful of flotsam that washed up on the shore of
    shipwrecked English symbolism!' (Pessoa, *The Selected Prose of
    Fernando Pessoa*, p. 80). For a study on Pessoa and Yeats, see Patricia
    Silva McNeill, *Yeats and Pessoa: Parallel Poetic Styles* (London, 2010).

11 Pessoa, *The Selected Prose of Fernando Pessoa*, p. 114.

12 Ibid., p. 131.

13 Pessoa, *Fernando Pessoa and Co.*, p. 209.

14 Jean-Jacques Rousseau, *Reveries of the Solitary Walker*, trans. Peter
    France (London, 2004), p. 54.

15 Pessoa, *Fernando Pessoa and Co.*, p. 265. Interestingly, the date of the
    poem is also the birthday of Kierkegaard, a writer who probed deeply into
    the problem of doubt, faith, belief and despair. It is also the birthday of
    Karl Marx, the other formidable critic and inheritor of Hegelian thought,
    and philosopher of dialectical materialism and collective transformation.
    This poem is explicitly grappling with the problem of faith and belief,
    so is Pessoa having fun here in inserting this date that makes a link
    to the existential Christian and the revolutionary atheist? Is there
    someone communicating to Pessoa? Most probably the date is mere
    coincidence and Pessoa never actually noticed its significance. We will
    never rationally know, but remember that Pessoa attached great worth
    and paid much attention to numerology and applying dates to texts.

16 Pessoa, *The Book of Disquiet*, p. 221.

17 Pessoa, *The Selected Prose of Fernando Pessoa*, p. 339.

18 Ibid., p. 49.

19 Antonio Cardiello, 'Fernando Pessoa's Vision of Neopaganism as Life's
    Supreme Art', in *Fernando Pessoa and Philosophy: Countless Lives Inhabit
    Us*, ed. B. Ryan, G. Tusa and A. Cardiello (Lanham, MD, 2021), p. 5.

20 Pessoa, *Fernando Pessoa and Co.*, p. 65.

21 Pessoa, *The Selected Prose of Fernando Pessoa*, p. 159.

22 Ibid., p. 156.

23 Fernando Pessoa, *O regresso dos deuses*, ed. M. P. da Silva (Lisbon,
    2013), p. 185.

24 Pessoa, *The Selected Prose of Fernando Pessoa*, p. 163.

25 Pessoa, *O regresso dos deuses*, p. 42.

26 Fernando Pessoa, *A Little Larger than the Entire Universe: Selected Poems*, ed. and trans. Richard Zenith (London, 2006), p. 17.

27 Søren Kierkegaard, *The Concept of Anxiety*, trans. Reidar Thomte (Princeton, NJ, 1980), p. 89.

28 Pessoa, *A Little Larger than the Entire Universe*, p. 86.

29 Pessoa, *O regresso dos deuses*, p. 97.

30 Pessoa, *The Selected Prose of Fernando Pessoa*, p. 129.

31 Ibid., p. 277.

32 On the 'metabolic process' (*Stoffwechsel*), see Karl Marx, *Capital*, vol. I, trans. Ben Fowkes (London, 1982), pp. 200, 217, 228, 290, 512, 637.

33 Karl Marx and Friedrich Engels, 'The Communist Manifesto', trans. Samuel Moore, in *Karl Marx: Selected Writings*, ed. David McLellan (Oxford, 1977), p. 224.

34 Fernando Pessoa, *Páginas Íntimas e de Auto-Interpretação*, ed. Georg Rudolf Lind and Jacinto do Prado Coelho (Lisbon, 1966), p. 185.

35 Hargrave Jennings, *The Rosicrucians: Their Rites and Mysteries* (New York, 1907), p. vi.

36 Ibid., p. viii.

37 Eduardo Lourenço, 'Álvaro de Campos II, or the Erostratus–Pessoa Agony', in *Here on Douradores Street: Essays on Fernando Pessoa*, ed. and trans. Ronald W. Sousa (Providence, RI, 2010), pp. 139–68 (p. 142).

38 Pessoa, *A Little Larger than the Entire Universe*, p. 363.

39 Ibid., p. 399.

40 Ibid., p. 364.

41 F. C. Martins and R. Zenith, 'Prefácio', in *Poemas Esotéricos*, ed. F. C. Martins and R. Zenith (Lisbon, 2014), p. 11.

42 See the weekly magazine called *John Bull*, 24 March 1923.

43 Somerset Maugham, *The Magician* [1908] (London, 2007), p. 4.

44 Zenith, *Pessoa: A Biography*, p. 871.

45 F. Pessoa and A. Crowley, *Encontro Magick*, ed. Miguel Roza (Lisbon, 2001), p. 78.

46 Ibid.

47 Zenith, *Pessoa: A Biography*, p. 763.

48 Fernando Pessoa, *Poesia, 1918–1930*, ed. M. P da Silva, A. M. Freitas and M. Dine (Lisbon, 2005), p. 399 (my translation).

7 Love, Sex, Friendship and Self-Fecundation

1 Fernando Pessoa, *The Book of Disquiet*, ed. and trans. Richard Zenith (London, 2015), p. 204.

2 Ibid., p. 231.

3 Fernando Pessoa, *The Selected Prose of Fernando Pessoa*, ed. and trans. Richard Zenith (New York, 2022), p. 126.

4 Friedrich Nietzsche, *On the Genealogy of Morals*, trans. Douglas Smith (Oxford, 1996), p. 86 (3.7).

5 Fernando Pessoa, *A Little Larger than the Entire Universe: Selected Poems*, ed. and trans. Richard Zenith (London, 2006), p. 309.

6 Pessoa, *The Selected Prose of Fernando Pessoa*, p. 112.

7 Ibid., pp. 116–17.

8 Pessoa Archive, Biblioteca Nacional, Lisbon, Doc. 54A–56.

9 Pessoa, *A Little Larger than the Entire Universe*, p. 351.

10 Richard Zenith, *Pessoa: A Biography* (New York, 2021), p. 587.

11 Pessoa, *The Selected Prose of Fernando Pessoa*, p. 138.

12 Ibid., p. 143.

13 Ibid., p. 146.

14 Ibid., p. 147.

15 Ibid., p. 150.

16 Fernando Pessoa, *Fernando Pessoa and Co.: Selected Poems*, ed. and trans. Richard Zenith (New York, 2003), p. 211.

17 Ofélia Queiroz and Maria da Graça Queiroz, 'O mistério duma pessoa', *Jornal de Letras* (12 November 1985), p. 4.

18 Pessoa, *The Selected Prose of Fernando Pessoa*, p. 50.

19 Pessoa, *A Little Larger than the Entire Universe*, p. 51.

20 Ibid., p. 50.

21 Ibid., p. 51.

22 Pessoa, *Fernando Pessoa and Co.*, p. 70.

23 Pessoa, *The Selected Prose of Fernando Pessoa*, pp. 52, 11.

24 Ibid., p. 40.

25 Pessoa, *Fernando Pessoa and Co.*, p. 71.

26 Ibid., p. 70.

27 Pessoa, *A Little Larger than the Entire Universe*, pp. 177, 181, 182.

28 Ibid., pp. 187, 186.

29 Ibid., p. 197.

30 Ibid., p. 198.

31 Pessoa, *The Selected Prose of Fernando Pessoa*, p. 209.

32 Ibid., pp. 51, 275, 160; Pessoa, *The Book of Disquiet*, p. 84.

33 Pessoa, *The Selected Prose of Fernando Pessoa*, p. 261.

34 James Joyce, *Ulysses* (Oxford, 2008), p. 465; Declan Kiberd, *Ulysses and Us: The Art of Everyday Living* (London, 2009), p. 229.

35 Pessoa, *The Selected Prose of Fernando Pessoa*, p. 209.

36 Teresa Rita Lopes, *Pessoa por Conhecer: Textos para um Novo Mapa* (Lisbon, 1990), p. 215.

37 Fernando Pessoa, *Poemas ingleses*, ed. Jorge de Sena (Lisbon, 1994), p. 90.

38 Ibid., p. 140.

39 Jack Kerouac, *On the Road* (London, 1976), p. 11.

40 Eliezer Kamenezky was a wandering Russian Jew, born in Ukraine, who preached vegetarianism, naturism and detachment from worldly goods. As a young man he set off to travel through the Middle East, Europe, India, the USA, Argentina and Brazil, where he learnt Portuguese. He was born in the same year as Pessoa and in 1920 arrived in Lisbon, where he lived and began to write poetry. He looked like some kind of prophet with his long black beard and long hair, and wearing a white robe. Pessoa and Kamenezky became friends, and Pessoa translated some of his prose poems and was asked to write a foreword to his book of poems called *Alma errante* (Wandering Soul), which was published in 1932. However, Pessoa's foreword was no ordinary one, as he began it with a controversial discussion on the idea of Jewishness before going on to give a negative assessment of Kamenezky's poetry. See Zenith, *Pessoa: A Biography*, pp. 800–802.

41 For an analysis on the life and work of Botto, see Anna Klobucka, *O mundo gay de Antonio Botto* (Lisbon, 2018).

42 Fernando Pessoa, *Páginas Íntimas e de Auto-Interpretação*, ed. Georg Rudolf Lind and Jacinto do Prado Coelho (Lisbon, 1966), p. 99 (my translation).

8 The Ruin of Disquiet

1 Fernando Pessoa, *The Book of Disquiet*, ed. and trans. Richard Zenith (London, 2015), p. 368.

2 Ibid., p. 139.
3 Fernando Pessoa, *The Complete Works of Alberto Caeiro*, ed. J. Pizarro and P. Ferrari, trans. M. J. Costa and P. Ferrari (New York, 2020), p. 5.
4 Ibid., p. xxii.
5 Eduardo Lourenço, 'The Book of Disquietude, Suicidal Text', in *Here on Douradores Street: Essays on Fernando Pessoa*, ed. and trans. Ronald W. Sousa (Providence, RI, 2010), pp. 197–215 (p. 208).
6 Ibid., p. 197.
7 Richard Zenith, 'Introdução', in *Livro do Desassossego* (Lisbon, 2007), p. 13; Jerónimo Pizarro, *Ler Pessoa* (Lisbon, 2018), p. 141 (my translation).
8 Pessoa, *The Book of Disquiet*, p. 478.
9 Ibid., pp. 477–8.
10 Ibid., p. 466.
11 Fernando Pessoa, *Páginas Íntimas e de Auto-Interpretação*, ed. Georg Rudolf Lind and Jacinto do Prado Coelho (Lisbon, 1966), p. 202.
12 Pessoa, *The Book of Disquiet*, p. 25.
13 See the essay by José Gil on landscape in *The Book of Disquiet*: José Gil, 'Bernardo Soares's Becoming Landscape', trans. Jethro Soutar, in *Fernando Pessoa and Philosophy: Countless Lives Inhabit Us*, ed. B. Ryan, G. Tusa and A. Cardiello (Lanham, MD, 2021), pp. 167–78.
14 Pessoa, *The Book of Disquiet*, p. 11.
15 Ibid., p. 21.
16 Fernando Pessoa, *The Selected Prose of Fernando Pessoa*, ed. and trans. Richard Zenith (New York, 2022), p. 276.
17 Ronald W. Sousa, 'Introduction: Here on Douradores Street', in *Here on Douradores Street*, pp. 11–38 (p. 32).
18 Pessoa, *The Book of Disquiet*, p. 150.
19 Ibid., p. 57.
20 Ibid., p. 232. Thomas J. Cousineau wrote a book on *The Book of Disquiet* with a title using these words. See Thomas J. Cousineau, *An Unwritten Novel: Fernando Pessoa's 'The Book of Disquiet'* (Champaign, IL, London and Dublin, 2013).
21 Pessoa, *The Book of Disquiet*, p. 12.
22 Ibid., pp. 32 and 33.
23 Ibid., p. 201.
24 Ibid., p. 107.

25 Ibid., p. 14.

26 Ibid., p. 32.

27 Fernando Pessoa, *Mensagem* (Lisbon, 2006), p. 94 (my translation).

28 Pessoa, *The Book of Disquiet*, p. 346.

29 Ibid., p. 228.

30 Ibid., pp. 46–7.

31 Ibid., p. 216.

32 Ibid., p. 28.

33 Ibid., p. 424.

34 Ibid., p. 120.

35 Ludwig Wittgenstein, *Philosophical Investigations*, trans. G.E.M. Anscombe (Oxford, 1968), p. vii.

36 Theodor W. Adorno, 'The Late Style (I)', in *Beethoven: The Philosophy of Music*, trans. Edmund Jephcott (Cambridge and Malden, MA, 2002), pp. 123–37 (p. 126).

37 Robert B. Pippin, *Modernism as a Philosophical Problem* (Oxford, 1999), p. 29.

38 In 1927, Joyce asked fellow Irish writer James Stephens to finish *Finnegans Wake* for him. But Stephens, though saying that he would help Joyce in any way he could, encouraged him to keep going and finish it himself. Given the name of 'James Stephens', his whimsical and witty style and Irish fairytale interests, and that Stephens and Joyce were born on the same day and in the same year, Joyce was convinced for a while that he was the man for the task. See Richard Ellmann, *James Joyce* (Oxford, 1982), p. 591.

39 Pessoa, *The Book of Disquiet*, p. 62.

40 Ibid., p. 217, emphasis in original.

41 Fernando Pessoa, *A Little Larger than the Entire Universe: Selected Poems*, ed. and trans. Richard Zenith (London, 2006), p. 382.

42 Thomas Carlyle, *On Heroes, Hero-Worship and the Heroic in History* (London, 1842), p. 173 (Lecture III).

43 T. S. Eliot, *Selected Poems* (London, 1961), p. 67.

44 Pessoa, *The Book of Disquiet*, p. 252.

45 Pessoa, *The Selected Prose of Fernando Pessoa*, p. 230.

46 See, for example, Harold Bloom, *Shakespeare: The Invention of the Human* (New York, 1998).

47 Fernando Pessoa, *Sobre a arte literária* (Lisbon, 2018), p. 161.

48   Pessoa, *The Book of Disquiet*, p. 115.
49   Ibid., p. 473.
50   Ibid., p. 282.
51   Epistle of Paul the Apostle to the Corinthians I, 15:52, King James Holy
     Bible; Søren Kierkegaard, *The Concept of Anxiety*, trans. Reidar Thomte
     (Princeton, NJ, 1980), pp. 82–90; Martin Heidegger, *Being and Time*,
     trans. J. Macquarrie and E. Robinson (Oxford, 1962), pp. 376, 388, 437,
     444.
52   Pessoa, *Páginas Íntimas e de Auto-Interpretação*, p. 17.
53   G.W.F. Hegel, *Phenomenology of Spirit*, trans. A. V. Miller (Oxford,
     1977), p. 19.
54   Søren Kierkegaard, *Concluding Unscientific Postscript* (Princeton, NJ,
     1992), p. 85.
55   John Keats, *Selected Letters* (Oxford, 2009), p. 40.
56   Dante Alighieri, *The Divine Comedy. 1: Inferno*, trans. John D. Sinclair
     (New York, 1939), Canto I, lines 1–3, pp. 22–3.
57   Pessoa, *A Little Larger than the Entire Universe*; Fernando Pessoa, *Poemas
     ingleses*, ed. Jorge de Sena (Lisbon, 1994), pp. 202–3.
58   Fernando Pessoa, *English Poetry*, ed. Richard Zenith (Lisbon, 2016),
     p. 161.
59   Fernando Pessoa, *Poesia de Álvaro de Campos* (Lisbon, 2002), p. 265.
60   Pessoa, *A Little Larger than the Entire Universe*, p. 218.
61   Fernando Pessoa, *Fernando Pessoa and Co.: Selected Poems*, ed. and
     trans. Richard Zenith (New York, 2003), p. 200.
62   Mário de Sá-Carneiro, *Obras Completas de Mário de Sá-Carneiro II:
     Poesias*, ed. João Gaspar Simões (Lisbon, 1978), p. 57 (my translation).
63   Pessoa, *The Book of Disquiet*, pp. 39, 62, 78, 194, 255, 345.
64   Ibid., p. 182.
65   João Guimarães Rosa, *Grande sertão: Veredas* (São Paulo, 2019), p. 53
     (my translation).
66   Claudio Magris, *Danube*, trans. Patrick Creagh (London, 2001), p. 311.
67   Pessoa, *The Book of Disquiet*, p. 88.
68   Ibid., p. 156.
69   Ibid., p. 422.
70   Ibid., p. 423.
71   Ibid., p. 6.
72   Ibid., pp. 451, 33, 15.

73 My thanks to Brendan O'Donoghue for bringing up this idea of the 'nightbook' in the modern age.

74 Cesário Verde, *The Feeling of a Westerner: A Bilingual Edition*, trans. R. Zenith (Dartmouth, MA, 2011), p. 24 (my translation).

75 Pessoa, *Fernando Pessoa and Co.*, p. 189.

76 See, for example: Søren Kierkegaard, 'Crop Rotation', in *Either/Or*, trans. H. V. Hong and E. H. Hong (Princeton, NJ, 1987), pp. 281–300; Kierkegaard, *The Concept of Anxiety*, pp. 132–3; and Martin Heidegger, *The Fundamental Concepts of Metaphysics: World, Finitude, Solitude*, trans. W. McNeill and N. Walker (Bloomington and Indianapolis, IN, 1995), pp. 78–167.

77 Pessoa, *The Book of Disquiet*, p. 234.

78 Ibid., p. 19.

79 Ibid., p. 233.

80 Wolfram Eilenberger, *Time of Magicians: The Great Decade of Philosophy, 1919–1929*, trans. Shaun Whiteside (London, 2020), p. 363. Heidegger also wrote elsewhere that 'a shepherd who has so little to do with bucolic idylls and nature mysticism that he can become the shepherd of being only if he remains the place-holder for the Nothing' (Martin Heidegger, 'Anaximander's Saying', in *Off the Beaten Track*, trans. J. Young and K. Haynes (Cambridge, 2002), pp. 242–81 (p. 262)).

81 Martin Heidegger, *Poetry, Language, Thought*, trans. Albert Hofstadter (New York, 1975), p. 92.

82 Ibid., p. 94.

83 Stefan Zweig, *Conqueror of the Seas: The Story of Magellan*, trans. E. and C. Paul (New York, 1938), p. 66.

84 Pessoa, *The Book of Disquiet*, p. 232.

85 Pessoa, *A Little Larger than the Entire Universe*, p. 367.

86 Pessoa, *The Book of Disquiet*, p. 186.

87 Ibid., p. 26.

88 Eduardo Lourenço, 'Kierkegaard and Pessoa or the Indirect Communication', in *Obras Completas IX: Pessoa Revisitado Crítica Pessoana I (1949–1982)*, ed. Pedro Sepúlveda (Lisbon, 2020), p. 143.

89 Søren Kierkegaard, *Papers and Journals: A Selection*, ed. Alastair Hannay (London, 1996), p. 117.

90 Søren Kierkegaard, *The Point of View*, trans. H. V. Hong and E. H. Hong (Princeton, NJ, 1998), p. 89; Kierkegaard, *Papers and Journals*, p. 322.

91 Pessoa, *The Book of Disquiet*, p. 361.

92 Ibid., p. 200.

93 Ibid., pp. 140, 182.

94 Ibid., p. 30.

95 Ibid., p. 228.

96 Ibid., p. 82.

97 Ibid., p. 227.

98 Ibid., p. 229.

199 Ibid.

100 Roberto Calasso, *Ka*, trans. Tim Parks (London, 2001), p. 312.

101 Pessoa, *The Book of Disquiet*, p. 108.

102 Pessoa, *A Little Larger than the Entire Universe*, p. 148.

103 Pessoa, *The Book of Disquiet*, p. 319.

104 Ibid., p. 397.

105 Maurice Blanchot, *The Space of Literature*, trans. Anne Smock (Lincoln, NE, 1989), p. 237.

Epilogue: The Death, Afterlife and Reality of Fernando Pessoa

1 Pessoa, *The Selected Prose of Fernando Pessoa*, ed. and trans. Richard Zenith (New York, 2022), p. 3

2 Richard Zenith, *Pessoa: A Biography* (New York, 2021), pp. 24, 926.

3 Ibid., p. 934.

4 Ibid., p. 935.

5 The title and author are to be found in Borges's short story 'A Survey of the Works of Herbert Quain', originally published in 1941. See Jorge Luis Borges, *Complete Fictions*, trans. Andrew Hurley (London and New York, 1999), pp. 107–11.

6 Fernando Pessoa, *The Book of Disquiet*, ed. and trans. Richard Zenith (London, 2015), p. 125.

7 Ibid., p. 266.

8 Pessoa, *The Selected Prose of Fernando Pessoa*, p. 253 (Pessoa Archive, Biblioteca Nacional, Lisbon, E3-88-11). This line is from a brief text about Sensationism, probably written in 1916.

9 Ibid., p. 235.

10 Pessoa, *The Book of Disquiet*, p. 178.

11 Friedrich Nietzsche, *Beyond Good and Evil*, trans. R. J. Hollingdale (London, 1987), p. 84 (para. 146).

12 Fernando Pessoa, *A Little Larger than the Entire Universe: Selected Poems*, ed. and trans. Richard Zenith (London, 2006), p. 254.

13 Ibid., p. 237.

14 Fernando Pessoa, *Fernando Pessoa and Co.: Selected Poems*, ed. and trans. Richard Zenith (New York, 2003), p. 175.

Select Bibliography

A Selection of Writings by Fernando Pessoa Published in English
(with a Few Exceptions in Portuguese), in Chronological Order

Páginas Íntimas e de Auto-Interpretação, ed. G. R. Lind and Jacinto do Prado
    Coelho (Lisbon, 1966)
Textos Filosoficos, vols I and II, ed. António de Pina Coelho (Lisbon, 1968)
Da República (1910–1935), ed. M. I. Rocheta, M. P. Morão and J. Serrão
    (Lisbon, 1979)
Textos de Crítica e de Intervenção (Lisbon, 1980)
Ultimatum e páginas de sociologia política, ed. M. I. Rocheta and M. P. Morão
    (Lisbon, 1980)
Pessoa Inédito, ed. Teresa Rita Lopes (Lisbon, 1993)
A Centenary Pessoa, ed. Eugénio Lisboa (Manchester, 1995)
(and A. Crowley), *Encontro Magick*, ed. Miguel Roza (Lisbon, 2001)
Fernando Pessoa and Co: Selected Poems, ed. and trans. R. Zenith (New York,
    2003)
The Education of the Stoic, trans. R. Zenith (Cambridge, MA, 2005)
A Little Larger than the Entire Universe: Selected Poems, ed. and trans.
    R. Zenith (London, 2006)
Obra essencial de Fernando Pessoa, vol. VII: *Cartas*, ed. Richard Zenith
    (Lisbon, 2007)
Lisbon: What the Tourist Should See (Swindon, 2008)
Message, trans. R. Zenith, illustrations P. S. Pereira (Alfragide, 2008)
Sensacionismo e outros ismos, ed. J. Pizarro (Lisbon, 2009)
Cartas astrológicas, ed. P. Cardoso, and in collaboration with J. Pizarro
    (Lisbon, 2011)
Sebastianismo e Quinto Império, ed. J. Uribe and P. Sepúlveda (Lisbon, 2011)
Philosophical Essays: A Critical Edition, ed. N. Ribeiro (New York, 2012)
Teoria da Heteronímia, ed. F. C. Martins and E. Zenith (Lisbon, 2012)

Eu sou uma antologia: 136 autores fictícios, ed. J. Pizarro (Lisbon, 2013)
Forever Someone Else, ed. and trans. R. Zenith (Lisbon, 2013)
Livro do Desassossego, ed. J. Pizarro (Lisbon, 2013)
Livro do Desassossego, ed. R. Zenith (Lisbon, 2013)
The Transformation Book, ed. N. Ribeiro and C. Souza (New York, 2014)
The Book of Disquiet, ed. and trans. R. Zenith (London, 2015)
Sobre o Fascismo, a ditadura militar e Salazar, ed. J. Barreto (Lisbon, 2015)
English Poetry, ed. R. Zenith (Lisbon, 2016)
The Book of Disquiet: The Complete Edition, ed. J. Pizarro, trans. M. J. Costa
    (New York, 2017)
Teatro Estático, ed. F. de Freitas and P. Ferrari (Lisbon, 2017)
Fausto, ed. C. Pittella (Lisbon, 2018)
The Complete Works of Alberto Caeiro, ed. J. Pizarro and P. Ferrari, trans.
    M. J. Costa and P. Ferrari (New York, 2020)
Orpheu Literary Quarterly, vols I and II, trans. D. Swartz (Philadelphia,
    PA, 2021)
The Selected Prose of Fernando Pessoa, ed. and trans. R. Zenith (New York,
    2022)
The Complete Works of Álvaro de Campos, ed. J. Pizarro and A. Cardiello,
    trans. M. J. Costa and P. Ferrari (New York, 2023)

A Selection of Secondary Reading on Fernando Pessoa in English (with a Few Exceptions in Portuguese)

Badiou, Alain, 'A Philosophical Task: To Be Contemporaries of Pessoa', in
    Handbook of Inaesthetics, trans. Alberto Toscano (Stanford, CA, 2005),
    pp. 36–45
—, 'What Does the Poem Think?', in *The Age of the Poets*, trans. Bruno
    Bosteels (London and New York, 2014), pp. 23–35
Balso, Judith, *Pessoa, the Metaphysical Courier*, trans. Drew S. Burk (New
    York and Dresden, 2011)
Borges, Paulo, *The Apocalypse According to Fernando Pessoa and Ofélia
    Queirós*, trans. N. P. Castanheira, and F. Pasciolla (London, 2019)
Boscaglia, Fabrizio, 'Fernando Pessoa and Islam: An Introductory
    Overview with a Critical Edition of Twelve Documents', *Pessoa Plural –
    A Journal of Fernando Pessoa Studies*, 9 (Spring 2016), pp. 37–107
Brown, Susan M., 'Pessoa and Whitman: Brothers in the Universe', in *The
    Continuing Presence of Walt Whitman: The Life after the Life*, ed. Robert
    K. Martin (Iowa City, IA, 1992), pp. 167–81

Cardiello, Antonio, and Pietro Gori, 'Nietzsche's and Pessoa's Psychological Fictionalism', *Pessoa Plural – A Journal of Fernando Pessoa Studies*, 10 (Fall 2016), pp. 578–605

Castro, Mariana Gray de, *Fernando Pessoa's Shakespeare: The Invention of the Heteronyms* (London, 2016)

—, ed., *Fernando Pessoa's Modernity without Frontiers* (Woodbridge, 2013)

Coelho, António de Pina, *Os fundamentos filosóficos da obra de Fernando Pessoa*, 2 vols (Lisbon, 1971)

Cousineau, Thomas J., *The Unwritten Novel: Fernando Pessoa's 'The Book of Disquiet'* (Champaign, IL, London and Dublin, 2013)

De Francesco, Alessandro, 'Propositions on the Philosophical Nature of Poetry', *Crisis and Critique*, VII/1 (2022), pp. 142–63

Dix, Steffen, 'The Plurality of Gods and Man, or *The Aesthetic Attitude in All Its Pagan Splendor* in Fernando Pessoa', *Pluralist*, V/1 (Spring 2010), pp. 73–93

—, 'Democratization and the Aristocracy of the Occult: Fernando Pessoa between Theosophy and Rosacrucianism', *Pessoa Plural – A Journal of Fernando Pessoa Studies*, 6 (Fall 2014), pp. 1–19

—, ed. *1915 – O Ano do Orpheu* (Lisbon, 2015), pp. 167–83

Feijó, António M., *Uma admiração pastoril pelo diabo (Pessoa e Pascoaes)* (Lisbon, 2015)

Ferrari, Patricio, and Jerónimo Pizarro, eds, *Fernando Pessoa as English Reader and Writer*, Portuguese Literary and Cultural Studies, vol. XXVIII (Dartmouth MA, 2015)

Ganeri, Jonardon, *Virtual Subjects, Fugitive Selves: Fernando Pessoa and His Philosophy* (Oxford, 2021)

—, *Fernando Pessoa: Imagination and the Self* (Oxford, 2024)

Gil, José, *Fernando Pessoa ou a metafísica das Sensações* (Lisbon, 1986)

—, *O Espaço Interior* (Lisbon, 1993)

—, *Diferença e negação na poesia de Fernando Pessoa* (Lisbon, 1999)

Gusmão, Manuel, *O poema impossível: O 'Fausto' de Pessoa* (Lisbon, 1986)

Jackson, K. David, 'The Adventure of the Anarchist Banker: "Reductio ad absurdum" of a Neo-Liberal', *Portuguese Studies*, XXII/2 (2006), pp. 209–18

—, *Adverse Genres in Fernando Pessoa* (Oxford, 2010)

Jennings, Hubert Dudley, *Fernando Pessoa: The Poet with Many Faces*, ed. C. Pittella (Lisbon, 2019)

Klobucka, Anna M., and Mark Sabine, eds, *Embodying Pessoa: Corporality, Gender, Sexuality* (Toronto, 2007)

Kotowicz, Zbigniew, *Fernando Pessoa: Voices of a Nomadic Soul* (London, 2008)

Krabbenhoft, Ken, 'Fernando Pessoa's Metaphysics and Alberto Caeiro e
    Companhia', Pessoa's Alberto Caeiro, *Portuguese Literary and Cultural
    Studies 3* (Fall 1999), pp. 73–85
Losa, Margarida L., 'A Modernist's Nature: Fernando Pessoa/Bernardo
    Soares's *The Book of Disquietude*', *Review of National Literatures and
    World Report*, I (1998), pp. 87–97
Lourenço, Eduardo, *Fernando Pessoa revistando* (Porto, 1973)
—, *Chaos and Splendour and Other Essays*, ed. C. Veloso (Dartmouth, MA,
    2002)
—, *Here on Douradores Street: Essays on Fernando Pessoa*, ed. and trans.
    Ronald W. Sousa (Providence, RI, 2010)
McGuirk, Bernard, *Erasing Fernando Pessoa* (London, 2017)
McNeill, Patricia Silva, *Yeats and Pessoa: Parallel Poetic Styles* (London,
    2010)
Martins, Fernando Cabral, ed., *Dicionário de Fernando Pessoa e do
    modernismo português* (Lisbon, 2008)
Medeiros, Paulo de, *Pessoa's Geometry of the Abyss: Modernity and the Book of
    Disquiet* (London, 2013)
Miranda, Rui Gonçalves, *Personal Infinitive: Inflecting Fernando Pessoa*
    (London, 2017)
Monteiro, George, ed., *The Man Who Never Was: Essays on Fernando Pessoa*
    (Providence, RI, 1982)
—, *The Presence of Pessoa: English, American and South African Literary
    Responses* (Lexington, KY, 1998)
Muldoon, Paul, '*Autopsychography* by Fernando Pessoa', in *The End of the
    Poem* (London, 2006), pp. 222–44
Pasciolla, Francesca, *Walt Whitman in Fernando Pessoa* (London, 2016)
Pizarro, Jerónimo, *Fernando Pessoa: Entre génio e loucura* (Lisbon, 2007)
—, 'Not One but Many Isms', in *Portuguese Modernisms: Multiple
    Perspectives on Literature and the Visual Arts*, ed. S. Dix and J. Pizarro
    (Oxford, 2011), pp. 24–41
—, *Ler Pessoa* (Lisbon, 2018)
—, P. Ferrari and A. Cardiello, eds, *A biblioteca particular de Fernando Pessoa
    / Fernando Pessoa's Private Library* (Lisbon, 2010)
Queiroz, Ofélia, *Cartas de amor de Ofélia e Fernando Pessoa*, ed. M. Nogueira
    and Maria de Conceição Azevedo (Lisbon, 1996)
Ramalho-Santos, Irene, *Atlantic Poets: Fernando Pessoa's Turn in Anglo-
    American Modernism* (Hanover, NH, 2003)
—, *Fernando Pessoa and the Lyric: Disquietude, Rumination, Interruption,
    Inspiration, Constellation* (Lanham, MD, 2022)

Riccardi, Mattia, 'António Mora and German Philosophy: Between Kant and Nietzsche', in *Pessoa in an Intertextual Web: Influence and Innovation*, ed. D. Frier (Oxford, 2012), pp. 32–45

Ryan, B., 'Mythologising the Exiled Self in James Joyce and Fernando Pessoa', *Pessoa Plural Plural – A Journal of Fernando Pessoa Studies*, 4 (Fall 2013), pp. 75–103

—, 'A Voyage in Immanence: Alberto Caeiro as an Expression of Spinoza's Ethics', in *Literature and the Encounter with Immanence*, ed. B. Swenson (Leiden and Boston, MA, 2017), pp. 153–77

—, 'Navegar é Preciso; Viver não é Preciso: The Impossible Journeys of Kierkegaard and Pessoa', in *Philosophy in the Condition of Modernism*, ed. A. Falcato and A. Cardiello (London, 2018), pp. 385–414

—, 'The Children of Nietzsche: Chaos, Plurality and Cosmopolitanism in James Joyce and Fernando Pessoa', in *European/Supra-European: Cultural Encounters in Nietzsche's Philosophy*, *Nietzsche Studies*, ed. M. Brusotti et al. (Berlin and Boston, MA, 2020), pp. 363–77

—, M. Faustino and A. Cardiello, eds, *Nietzsche e Pessoa: Ensaios* (Lisbon, 2015)

—, G. Tusa and A. Cardiello, eds, *Fernando Pessoa and Philosophy: Countless Lives Inhabit Us* (Lanham, MD, 2021)

Sadlier, Darlene, *An Introduction to Fernando Pessoa: Modernism and the Paradoxes of Authorship* (Gainesville, FL, 1998)

Sepúlveda, Pedro, and Jorge Uribe, eds, colab. Pablo Javier Pérez López, *O Planeamento Editorial de Fernando Pessoa* (Lisbon, 2016)

Sena, Jorge de, *Fernando Pessoa e cia: Heterónima* (Lisbon, 1984)

Simões, João Gaspar, *Vida e obra de Fernando Pessoa* (Lisbon, 1950)

Visser, Rehan P., 'Fernando Pessoa's Art of Living: Ironic Multiples, Multiple Ironies', *Philosophical Forum*, L/4 (2019), pp. 435–54

Zenith, Richard, 'Alberto Caeiro as Zen Heteronym', *Portuguese Literary and Cultural Studies*, III (1999), pp. 101–9

—, *Pessoa: A Biography* (New York, 2021)

Online Resources

Casa Fernando Pessoa (private library of Pessoa):
https://bibliotecaparticular.casafernandopessoa.pt/index/index.htm

Livro do Desassossego Archive:
https://ldod.uc.pt

Pessoa Archive:
http://arquivopessoa.net

Pessoa Plural – A Journal of Fernando Pessoa Studies, founded in 2012
    at Brown University, published biannually, ed. O. Almeida, P. de
    Medeiros and J. Pizarro (Providence, RI): www.brown.edu

Acknowledgements

I would like to thank the Association KURS and the Ministry of Culture and Media of the Republic of Croatia for awarding me a writing residency in Split in 2023 to write a large part of this book. I would also like to express my gratitude for the support of national funds through FCT – Fundação para a Ciência e a Tecnologia – under the project UIDP/00183/2020. I also wish to thank CultureLab, the Nova Institute of Philosophy (IFILNOVA) and the Faculty of Social Sciences and Humanities (FCSH)/Universidade Nova de Lisboa (UL) for their continual support. Particular heartfelt thanks to Richard Zenith for his friendship, generosity and patience in answering my various questions and ongoing queries regarding Pessoa's life and work, and for the use of many of his translations. I am indebted to Zenith's monumental biography of Pessoa, published in 2021, for the many years of research gone into that book and for providing such a wealth of information for the rest of us on the poet's life, thoughts and times. I am also very grateful to various friends for their support and encouragement during the writing, especially Željka Somun, Jonardon Ganeri and Anisa Shaikh. I would like to thank Melaina Barnes for her impeccable editing work. Thank you also to my friend Jethro Soutar for his sharp skills in helping me out with some of the verses in translating Pessoa. A special thank you to Antonio Cardiello for helping me find some of the images included in this book from the National Library of Portugal. Particular thanks to my mother Eilis, my sisters Lisa and Karin, my brothers-in-law Laurent and Mark, and my niece Lena and nephews Barra, Niko, Killian and Dylan, for their love and support. Finally, I would like to thank the team at Reaktion Books, such as Amy Salter and Alex Ciobanu for all their work and attention, and especially Michael Leaman for commissioning this book on the mercurial Fernando Pessoa.

Photo Acknowledgements

The author and publishers wish to express their thanks to the below sources of illustrative material and/or permission to reproduce it. Some locations of works are also given below, in the interest of brevity:

© Catarina and Rita Almada Negreiros: pp. 66 (photo João Dordio, courtesy Casa Fernando Pessoa, Lisbon), 72, 77, 181; Arquivo Histórico da Fundação António Quadros (PT/FAQ/AFC/06/00173): p. 109; Arquivo Municipal de Lisboa: p. 59; Biblioteca Nacional de Portugal, Lisbon: pp. 9, 12, 40, 52, 65, 67, 68, 79, 84, 85, 88, 91, 131; Casa Fernando Pessoa, Lisbon: pp. 17, 27, 32, 33, 34, 45, 51, 103, 106, 108, 111, 119, 130, 148, 180; Centro de Arte Moderna Gulbenkian, Lisbon: pp. 69, 101; courtesy Maria da Graça Queiroz: pp. 141, 172; Hardijzer Photographic Research Collection, The Heritage Portal: p. 29; Harry Price Library of Magical Literature, University of London/Mary Evans Picture Library: p. 129; iStock.com: pp. 16 (johncopland), 22 (bauhaus1000); Library of Congress, Prints and Photographs Division, Washington, DC: p. 169; courtesy Manuela Nogueira: pp. 6, 23, 24, 25; Sächsische Landesbibliothek – Staats- und Universitätsbibliothek Dresden: p. 127; Universal Images Group North America LLC/Alamy Stock Photo: p. 139.